In Movement There Is Peace

In Movement There Is Peace

Stumbling 500 Miles Along the Way to the Spirit

Elaine Orabona Foster, Ph.D.
Joseph Wilbred Foster III

PsyConOps

All maps are from Gronze.com with their kind permission
Poems are graciously provided by Rochelle Arellano
Dessert recipes provided by:
Carina Alves, Centro De Turismo Rural, Hospital de Órbigo
Cover design by Cornelia G. Murariu

PsyConOps Website: http://www.BanxietyFree.com

Library of Congress Cataloging – in – publication data
Foster, Elaine Orabona & Foster, Joseph Wilbred, III
ISBN: 098950770X
ISBN-13: 978-09895077-0-7
Published by PsyConOps
Copyright © 2013 E. O. Foster/J. W. Foster
All rights reserved.

DEDICATION

We dedicate this book to our parents. The older and wiser we get the more amazed we are at the sheer magnitude of responsibility you took on by raising us. We're grateful for the sacrifices, the love and the faith you've always had in us, even when we didn't have it ourselves. Con mucho cariño.

Table of Contents

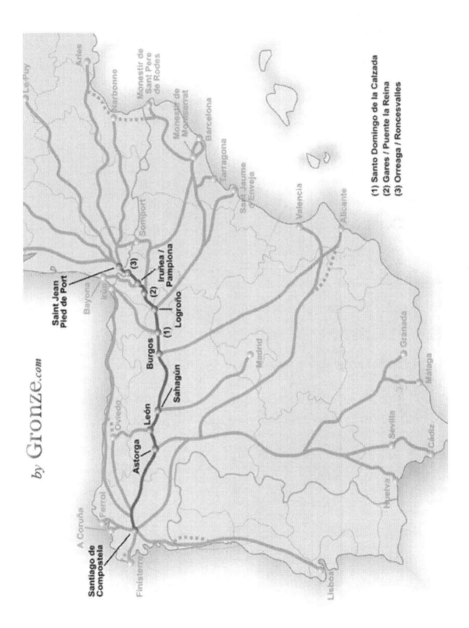

ACKNOWLEDGMENTS

There are so many people that supported and helped us in writing this book, even before we knew ourselves that we'd be writing it. We'd like to offer our sincerest appreciation to Dan for his unending faith in our journey, to Pat and Lynn for so freely opening their lives up to us, to Bret for acting as our guide in Santiago, and to Rochelle for her poetic contributions.

Introduction

The decision to write a book about a life changer like the Camino de Santiago was a real struggle for us. Do we publish and take the risk of turning this sacred experience into a cliché? The lessons we derived from the pilgrimage are good enough to stand alone in our memories. So why write them all out and go through the extra work of publishing? It came down to our discussion in the book about service beyond self. We knew our lives had improved, but we wanted more. We wanted to pass on the inspiration we received from our pilgrimage to others. In that way, we could leave something behind to motivate anyone who cared to use it. As Joe noted in one of the final chapters, on our deathbeds, it would help us to know we made a difference because we opened a treasure box for others. Not through our meager words, but by revealing the deeper meaning The Way has for its pilgrims.

The Camino is a very personal journey. Each individual has different lessons to learn and so the events that happen for each will be unique and specially tailored to his or her life. The most important thing is to stay open to the people and places you come across with the expectation that they are there to teach you something valuable. Once that openness, that receptivity, is in place, the insights will flow in their own time, not yours. A pilgrimage is an act of surrender, through faith, of one's own comfort and desires. If it's exercise you seek, it will certainly harden your muscles, but it is capable of so much more. A pilgrimage is seeking in its purest form. The sacrifice is a small one considering the abundant gifts that flow naturally from it. Even if you begin your journey with doubt, as we did, the act of staying curious and compassionate may open the door just a crack, but wide enough to allow your world to change through your capacity to understand it.

Admittedly, we saw many people who walked the Camino as if it were a race or a marathon. Was it to achieve self-confidence by proving their speed and endurance? A worthy goal. But an even worthier goal, that Joe and I accidentally stumbled upon through the unfolding events on the path, was finding *peace* through our movement.

Despite our good intentions, we still fell into the trap of trying to reach our destination with time to spare. When we did, there was always a reminder to slow down and relinquish these worldly goals in favor of deeper awareness. There is nothing wrong with doing the hike to improve physical fitness, or as an escape from work or from agonizing grief. But that would be the equivalent of seeing only one color in a rainbow. We hope everyone who reads this book finds his or her own path to peace. The Camino is just one spoke leading to a spiritual hub. Whatever you choose for your life, no matter the path you take, we wish you the same, "Buen Camino."

Chapter 1: Breaking Away from Security

Be careful going in search of adventure - it's ridiculously easy to find.
- William Least Heat Moon

Trail Day 1: Mid-September, Saint-Jean-Pied-de-Port, France

Elaine: I awake to total darkness in the strangeness of this new place. Joe isn't lying here beside me but I can at least hear his soft breathing from a cot on the other side of our small attic room. I fumble for my cell phone on the bedside table; it's 5:10 a.m. This is our first night in an *albergue*, Spanish for a low-cost hostel for pilgrims. We're in a small town in southern France called, *Saint-Jean-Pied-de-Port* at the foot of the Pyrenees Mountains separating Spain from France. Even though I'm feeling lonely and nervous in my solitary bed, I tell myself to do what I say to all my patients when they are feeling panicky: "First exhale, then take a long, slow inhale before you even try to think about what to do next." An exhale can trick your mind into relaxing because we usually do it unconsciously when we've just finished something challenging like going to the dentist: "Ahhhh, I'm glad that's over." I follow my own advice. *Slow exhale, even slower inhale.* Why am I still feeling scared?

I know I'm not ready for this…this…I don't even know what to call it. A hike? A pilgrimage? A vacation? None of these words capture what's going on in my head or what I'm trying to do here. I'm not particularly religious, so I feel phony calling myself a *peregrina* (Spanish for female pilgrim). It's not a vacation; those are supposed to be relaxing, with built-in itineraries, swimming pools, tropical drinks and cabanas. We have no idea where we'll be

3

sleeping any night for at least the next month. We don't even know how many days it will take us to complete this trek and I suspect the cabanas are going to be few and far between. I guess I can live with the word "trek," because those can be long and the accommodations primitive.

Is it wrong to want short and luxurious?

If I have the stamina to finish what I start today, it will be the longest journey of my lifetime. In fact, if I took *every* hike I've ever done and strung them end-to-end, I would still have to multiply by ten to reach the 800 kilometers standing between me and Santiago de Compostela.

Why the heck did I agree to do this? Has anyone ever stopped on the first day?

Joe: The path that brought us to this small room in St-Jean, France started two months ago, in early July. Tuesday night was poker night. Six of us were sitting around a table in the back room of an ancient brick auto repair garage. It was a bit surreal, the smell of cigars and engine grease, the sound of a compressor occasionally starting to replenish the slowly leaking air tank, a dog barking outside in the fenced storage lot. I was sitting across the table from my younger brother, Steve, and some childhood friends, all of them now with graying hair and mid-life paunches. We'd all grown up in or around Holyoke, a blue-collar town in western Massachusetts. I'd been gone for over twenty-five years. My need to explore the world had led me to leave this comfortable community of family and friends. I was afraid that if I'd remained I'd have stagnated. That fear kept me away for a very long time. After Elaine's decision to quit her job, we returned back home to be closer to our family and friends. Here they were sitting in front of me; bluffing at poker, laughing at crude jokes, and making fun of me as if I'd never left.

I walked away from the poker table several hours later, down eighty-five dollars. It was just shy of midnight. I was tired so I decided to spend the night at Steve's house instead of making the hour-long trip back home.

I woke up the next morning with a hangover, not from drinking too much, but from smoking too many cigars. My lifestyle had diverged from theirs a long time ago and now my body couldn't keep up with the abuse. Needing some aspirin and a strong cup of coffee, I climbed out of bed and headed for the kitchen. Steve had beaten me to the coffee maker and the smell of fresh brewed coffee filled the kitchen.

I greeted Steve with a grunt, poured my coffee and sat down at the kitchen table. We'd talked the day before about where and when Elaine and I might take our next big trip. I told him we really didn't have a clue yet. We talked some more about my past journeys to Croatia, Israel, Cuba and Panama and how they've altered my perspective of the world. After a few minutes we moved on to more immediate concerns like our plans for the day. While we sat with the morning sun streaming through the window, I heard a large, lumbering aircraft passing overhead. Glancing out, I saw a low-flying C5 transport. Steve reminded me that Westover Air Force Base was just a few minutes away and there were several flights a week taking off for parts unknown. That simple comment is what started the journey that brought me here to the base of these mountains in southern France, to the beginning of my Camino.

Elaine: I stuffed all my belongings into my backpack. This bag is now my dresser, my medicine cabinet, my closet and my pantry for the next couple of months. None of my friends would believe this is really me, the person who travels with carry-on and checked luggage and still mails a few boxes ahead.

Hold on – gotta exhale and breathe again.

I'm supposed to be carrying this pack on my back for the next 500 miles. Why? Because this is one step stuck inside a series of huge steps I've recently taken. Joe and I talked a lot about it and we both decided; it's time.

I'd decided to do something I was always too scared to do. I quit my job. I gave up the instant credibility of being Doctor and Lieutenant Colonel Foster. I left the security of a good salary. More importantly, I made a decision to stop being an impostor: to stop telling other people how to overcome anxiety, even prescribing medicines for it, while I continued to hide behind my desk, paralyzed by the very thing I was helping them to battle. During one of my more rational moments, I decided, "I'm going to live before I die."

It's the hardest decision I've had to make in my life, and I'm still struggling. I'm at the peak of my earning capacity and my roles are comfortable because I've played them for over twenty-five years: doctor, military officer, professor, examiner. I'd worked long and hard, sacrificing many things, including my first marriage, to build my reputation. Now I'm walking, *no, hiking*, away from all of it and trying not to look back. But none of that matters this morning. What matters is whether I can make it up, over and down the other side of the damn Pyrenees before nightfall.

I'm scared. I don't know what to expect from the mountains or myself. Geez! I knew I should have trained for this. Why was I just laying in bed back home reading books about the Camino when I should have been backpacking in the Berkshires, or at least practicing on some hills behind the house? Face it: avoiding scary stuff is part of anxiety, and now it's time to pay for putting it off; it's too late to change the past. I just need to lace up these hiking shoes I bought last week and get moving.

Joe: As Steve and I sat at his kitchen table back in July; I explained that one of the perks of retiring from the military is what's called "Space-A Travel." It's a program where military and their families can fly for free if there are empty seats available.

He asked, "You mean you can fly for free anyplace in the world?"

I felt myself relaxing into a decision as I answered him,
"Any place the military flies."

Elaine and I had heard about this benefit but had never delved any deeper into it. I'd decided that as soon as I finished my coffee I was driving over to Westover to investigate.

Steve taunted me, "Here we go again, off to prove that your career isn't going to run your life."

I said, "Anybody can travel the world if they're willing to make the right choices, even a homebody like you...and you don't have to take a military hop to get there either."

I walked into the Space-A Terminal less than thirty minutes later. It was your typical military aircraft hanger with cinder block offices painted that pale blue color I'd come to expect from the interiors of old Air Force buildings. It seemed completely empty until I walked down a long hall and into another room with benches, tables, a TV and a kitchenette. There were three men in casual clothes just picking up their carry-on luggage. They were being escorted out the door by a female, uniformed master sergeant.

"This must be the place," I said as a greeting.

A sixtyish, white-haired, goateed civilian walked up to me and said, "Hi, I'm Pete, do you need some help?"

I told him, "I want to learn everything there is to know about Space-A travel."

Pete looked back at the departing passengers. He apparently had time on his hands so he snapped into action and led me to his office. This man seemed to have more energy than someone half his age and he appeared to relish the challenge of taking on a novice.

Over the next hour, Pete covered it all: how to sign up for a flight, when to arrive, where flights went, and who had priority. I learned that most of the Westover C5 flights went to Rota, Spain. Elaine's family is from the Canary Islands and she's always wanted to visit Spain. *Hmmm...might be a nice way to entice her to travel.* As Pete explained all the cool things we could do while relaxing in the Mediterranean, I mentioned to him that I was looking for something a little more active, something that would expose us to the real people and culture of Spain, someplace away from the typical tourist destinations.

Pete's professorial manner dissolved as a warm smile grew on his face. "Oh, then you need to walk the Camino de Santiago."

I looked at him quizzically and he added, "I did it myself last year!"

Pete described his journey eagerly. As his words flowed I noticed in him a strength of presence, an ability to appreciate the here and now. He talked like a man who relished life. In no time, we were like old friends sharing stories after a long absence. For the rest of the morning, Pete inspired me with his tales of adventure on the Camino. He told me about the terrain, what he brought in his backpack, the memorable places he stopped. Then his demeanor and his voice shifted into a sort of reverence. As if he were about to share a secret.

"Joe, I've gotta tell ya, the Camino changed my life."

Pete's words had power and meaning. I would soon hear those words repeated in scores of blogs, books, and movies about "The Way of Saint James."

I left Pete with an urgency to learn more about a journey that had changed a retired military, no-nonsense, crew chief into an irrepressible philosopher. Before I even drove back home I was on my iPhone typing in a quick Google search: c-a-m-i-n-o d-e s-a-n-t-i-a-g-o:

The Way of Saint James (the Camino de Santiago) is a 500-mile spiritual pilgrimage across the Pyrenees, through the provinces of northern Spain, ending at the Saint James Cathedral in Santiago de Compostela. The route has existed for over a thousand years. It was one of the most important Christian pilgrimages during medieval times, together with the pilgrimage to Rome and Jerusalem.

I then searched for another definition, p-i-l-g-r-i-m:

Pilgrim, "peregrino" in Spanish, stemming from the Latin word peregrinus, which literally means 'one who has come from afar on a journey to a holy place.'

I learned that, according to the Catholic faith, a plenary indulgence (forgiveness on Earth) could be earned upon completion of the Camino. Neither Elaine nor I were practicing Catholics. In fact, I was raised Lutheran, with the teachings that forgiveness can only be received through God's grace and not through some good deed recognized by the Pope of the Roman Catholic Church. But, for some reason, the plenary indulgence still appealed to me. Also, the idea of being pardoned for our sins might entice Elaine to join me on another adventure.

Elaine was raised Catholic, attending twelve years of Catholic school before moving on to college. It seemed the perfect journey; it appealed to my desire to push my limits and to Elaine's desire to find a new path. I knew, though, that it would take more than a plenary indulgence for Elaine to sign up for a 500-mile walk.

There was also a deeper meaning that called me to the Camino. Several years ago, I'd made a promise to my dad, John, to hike the Appalachian Trail with him. Not the whole 2000 miles at once, just parts of the trail each year. Dad died on the trail. It would've been our third year backpacking together. He'd called me the week before his death. He was excited and had our latest trip planned out. I'd told him I couldn't make it. I'd blown off the trip at the last minute because of work and my budding relationship with Elaine after a very painful divorce.

Dad and I had decided to embark on this annual event after he'd undergone triple-bypass surgery. During his recovery, he'd committed to living a healthier lifestyle. I'd committed to accompanying him on these yearly hikes as "insurance" for his safe return.

Dad was alone that day when he stepped onto the trail and his death has left a permanent scar on me. After his funeral, I was cleaning out his Ford camping van and found my old, well-worn hiking stick. He had brought it with him on the trip hoping that I would be there for our yearly journey. I wasn't and I've suffered the guilt ever since.

To this day I use John's backpack for all my travels and that walking stick hangs on my office wall waiting, reminding me of my responsibility to make my steps meaningful. I decided I was walking the Camino and Dad's backpack would be with me for every step; maybe that plenary indulgence really could earn me a pardon for past sins.

Elaine: After learning about the Camino, Joe watched a movie called, *The Way*. Three times. He was determined. He said, "Elaine, I want to walk The Way of St. James, and I want you to walk with me."

The movie is about a man who lost his son to the Camino but found himself when he flew to Spain to recover the body. The main character is a doctor who resisted the idea of his son's pilgrimage, bluntly declaring it a waste of time. Once he arrives in Spain though, the pull of the Camino begins. His life takes a course he never expected, or ever thought he wanted.

The Way spoke to Joe because he lost his father on the Appalachian Trail. He lives every day with the regret of not being there for him. It spoke to me because the main character was a doctor living a comfortable life; one he had purposely chosen for himself. But there was a big difference between that character and me. He had never doubted the correctness of his comfortable life until his son died. I knew I could no longer stay in the military without getting sucked into a vortex of permanent anger, anxiety and regret.

As a military psychologist, I was treating war-fighters who had deployed to Iraq and Afghanistan as part of Operations Iraqi Freedom and Enduring Freedom. The stories that led them to my office were getting more gruesome and harder to listen to. The deployments, known as "time in the sandbox," were layered one on top of the other. It wasn't just one or two years in the desert; it was four, five and six deployments over the span of several years with more losses, more injuries, more tragedies.

How many times can a person leave his family for almost two years at a clip, watch close friends die, and still keep a healthy bond with loved ones back home? How many times can you go to funerals for the people you love, people you might even owe your life to, before becoming angry and mistrusting?

As the stories became more gut wrenching, I started to feel like the service members I was treating. I was taking their stuff home with me and into my personal life. The act of showering and imagining I was washing off all the turmoil, grief, anger, anxiety and hopelessness wasn't working anymore. I was the person putting the oxygen mask on everyone else, and had forgotten to put it on myself. I turned in my notice at the hospital and left the life I had known for twenty-five years.

For me, the Camino represents the start of my new life, the one where I face my own anxiety and take the time to develop an unquantifiable treatment plan. This is considered heresy in the field of mental health, where all of our treatment goals must be measureable in order to receive insurance and hospital approval. Mine starts with an outrageously broad intention taken from a quote by Sheldon Kopp:

> *And remember, too, you can stay at home, safe in the familiar illusion of certainty. Do not set out without realizing that the way is*

not without danger. Everything good is costly and the development of the personality is one of the most costly of all things.

Joe: I can hear Elaine packing up her backpack on the other side of the room. I'm already awake. I'm excited for this journey to begin, but also worried about our readiness. Are we in good enough shape? We'll be going straight up into these mountains for twenty-seven kilometers.

Elaine notices that I'm awake. "Joe, are we going to make it to the other side by nightfall?" She's searching for me to provide assurance.

Then she asks, "How about we just get an early start?"

I'm not completely sure we'll make it myself, so I agree, "Yeah, we're already awake, let's do it! Besides, what's the worst thing that can happen? We get stuck in the mountains, huddling in our sleeping bags, drinking spring water and eating granola bars?"

Elaine gives me a look. "That doesn't help; you know I hate granola."

She's already lacing up her hiking shoes as I roll out of my cot and start getting dressed.

Dressing and packing is a slow process. On the old wooden box serving as a bedside table there's one small lamp with a light bulb the size of a Christmas tree ornament. It lights the angled ceilings of our attic room with barely enough light to see by.

I zip up the last zipper on my pack.

"I'm ready," I announce.

While shouldering my backpack, I notice Elaine is still slathering on sunblock. I want to say, "C'mon, let's do this!" but I don't want to push. I have to remind myself to give her the opportunity to mentally prepare for these first few steps. They are huge for someone who has never hiked up mountains before. I've stepped into these journeys many times; this is her first.

I try to make my way quietly down the narrow rear staircase, feeling awkward with my bulky backpack. The old age of the steps causes the boards to creak and groan as I work my way to the ground floor. I worry that the noise is waking the others, but before reaching the bottom, I hear the soft whispers of other pilgrims in their rooms. They are also preparing to leave. I wait for Elaine by the front door.

Selling Elaine on walking the Camino was a struggle initially. She expressed every worry she could imagine, and then some more after reading about the different terrains and the possibility of crowded sleeping quarters.

In a moment of inspiration, I offered, "We can stop at any time. I won't ask any questions. We'll come right back to the States if you want or go relax on the Med. It'll be totally your call."

Secretly, I knew enough about Elaine to know that once she started, it would become a personal challenge and she would probably surpass me in our commitment to complete it. But even more importantly, I knew she consistently underestimates her abilities. Most of the time, I just start the new exploration and then step back and watch as she weaves her way through it, step by step, turning our journey into a hard-core adventure.

Because of this long-distance trek, it was critical for us to minimize the weight of our backpacks, to reduce our possessions down to the absolute minimum. This was a very individual task, each of us having different ideas as to what's the most important, what's the most desired. Elaine and I had a few heated arguments over what the other should or shouldn't be bringing. It was a real conflict; the fear of carrying too much weight against the fear of not having what we needed. When doing our research, I found that the standard recommendation was no more than sixteen pounds for women and twenty-two pounds for men. That's exactly what Elaine and I shot for and exactly what we stepped out with on our first day of this pilgrimage.

Several minutes later, Elaine comes down the stairs and stands next to me by the front door.

"I'm ready!" she says and I open the door for her.

It's 6 a.m. as we step onto the cobbled streets of Saint-Jean-Pied-de-port. We're the first pilgrims to head out.

Elaine's Backpack

1) Backpack, REI, Lightweight, 52 liter	19) Thermal Underwear, polyester
2) Trekking Poles, Aluminum	20) Pants, L.L. Bean, Hiking
3) Sleeping Bag, down, 45+F	21) Underwear, nylon/lycra, 2 ea.
4) Sleeping Bag Liner, silk	22) Sun Block, 45
5) Rain Jacket	23) Cream, moisturizing
6) Rain Pants	24) Shampoo/Conditioner
7) Crocs, Lightweight Footwear	25) Towel, camping, fast drying
8) Socks, 2 pair, SmartWool	26) Toothbrush/Toothpaste/Floss
9) Sock Liners, Injinji (with toes)	27) EmergenC, powdered drink
10) Gloves	**Wearing**
11) Band Aids, Moleskin	Hiking Pants
12) Carmex Lip Balm	Trail Shoes, Keen
13) Benadryl, Naproxen	Wool Socks, SmartWool
14) Vaseline (for feet)	Long Sleeve Shirt, Columbia
15) Head Lamp, LED	Underwear, Nylon/Lycra
16) Toilet Paper	Wool Socks & Hat
17) iPad	Passport, ID, Cash, Debit Card
18) Sarong	Sunglasses

Joe's Backpack

1) Backpack, Kelty, 82 liter	18) Pocketknife, Leatherman
2) Trekking Poles, carbon fiber	19) Head Lamp, LED
3) Pants, Hiking, North Face	20) Whistle
4) Shirt, Hiking, SilverBack	21) iPhone w/ Adapter & Cords
5) Underwear, polypro, 2 ea.	22) Knee Brace, Elastic
6) Socks, SmartWool, 2 ea.	23) Vaseline (for feet)
7) Sock Liners, Injinji	24) Toothbrush/Toothpaste/Floss
8) Bush Hat	25) Razor
9) Down Jacket , North Face	**Wearing**
10) Shirt, Short Sleeve, polypro	Hiking Pants, North Face
11) Crocs, Lightweight Footwear	Trail Shoes
12) Rain Jacket, Patagonia	Wool Socks, Smart Wool
13) Rain Pants, North Face	Hiking Shirt, Fox
14) Rain Cover for Backpack	T-Shirt, polypro
15) Sleeping Bag, REI, 20+F, down	Underwear, polypro
16) Gloves	Passport, ID, Cash, Debit Card
18) Towel, Camp, Fast Drying	Sunglasses, Reading Glasses

Chapter 2: Now That's a Big Plane

4 Days Ago, Westover AFB, MA

A wonderful gift may not be wrapped as you expect.
- Jonathan Lockwood Huie

Joe: It was four days ago when we arrived at the Space-A Terminal at Westover. It occurred to me just then that we'd unwittingly started our travel on September 11th, now infamously known as 9/11. It just happened to work out that way. I hadn't even noticed, but I couldn't ignore the symbolism. Legend holds that St. James rose from the dead to battle the Moors (Muslims) who had conquered the Iberian Peninsula. Ironically, the Muslims had introduced a very peaceful period of democracy, tolerance and religious freedom to the area. The historic battles between the Christians and the Moors eventually led to the re-establishment of the Catholic Church, which to this day has been the dominant religion in both Spain and Portugal. Our September 11th departure reminded me of these religious conflicts, not only within Spain, but between Christians and Muslims throughout the world.

What a perfect time and occasion to celebrate my belief in an all-loving God; one that does not hate or reject those of different creeds. I'm not particularly devout, but boarding the plane that day was my own step toward redemption. It did not revolve around fears of religious or political conflict but rather on a completely unrelated desire to explore. I hadn't planned to travel on such an infamous date, but then again, how much in life turns out as we envisioned. It's like the old joke: "How do you make God laugh? Make plans."

15

Elaine: We walked into the terminal at Westover with all of our belongings loaded on our backs. It was 8 o'clock in the morning and we were early. The terminal was completely empty except for a master sergeant standing behind the counter. My nerves were already rattled as she checked us in; it was 9/11.

I was startled when Joe said, "I need to go move the car to the long-term parking lot. I'll be right back."

As I sat waiting and worrying about flying on such an infamous day, I noticed a man walking straight toward me. He behaved as if he already knew me, and I immediately wondered if he might be a former patient. I wracked my mind for any traces of pleasant or aversive memories. We often get a good or bad feeling from our primitive, reptilian brain milliseconds before our frontal lobe determines the name or identity of a specific individual. In this case nothing was registering.

"Hi, I'm Pete."

It was Joe's Space A-Camino tutor. *Now I get a pleasant association.* Joe had already described Pete in detail during the days I was still obsessing about this trip.

Pete had retired from the Air Force several years ago, and had already walked the Camino. He'd made a special trip to the terminal just to see us off and to answer any last minute questions. He probably regretted it because I bombarded him with every one I could think of.

"Do you think I should bring these walking sticks, or are they just extra weight?

Pete didn't even have to think about this one. "I brought walking sticks with me and they were really useful, especially on the goat trails where it gets pretty rocky and unstable."

I asked, "Are blister-free socks really any better or is it just hype?"

He said, "I used socks made of merino wool because they dry fast. But for blisters, I stuck with roll-on Compeed. You'll see Compeed products everywhere you go over there."

I wasn't sure how to ask the next question without sounding like I had a problem with crowds, so I made it generic, "What are the albergues really like? Is it hard to sleep with so many people around you?"

He thought longer about this one and then said, "All the albergues are different. Some of 'em sleep eighty people in a room and then others have private rooms...and there's everything in between. So I guess there's no single answer. I'll tell ya, I personally had no trouble sleeping when I was there. I *prefer* the albergues. You get to meet some really great people."

I thought about another question, but I didn't have the nerve to ask it: *When people say I'm crazy for doing this, how do I stop myself from agreeing with them?*

Pete talked about his Camino, and from his patient, nostalgic responses, it was easy to see he was happy for the chance to relive some of the wonder and excitement he'd experienced as part of his own pilgrimage. His speech grew more animated as it became more personal for him.

"The Camino is like nothing else I've ever done in my entire life. It was incredible. Even after I thought I was done, it still had more lessons to teach me."

He looked straight into my eyes in a way he hadn't up until that moment. "You can't understand it now, Elaine, but there's nothing random on the Camino. The pilgrims you're going to meet are *supposed* to be there. It's all *on purpose*...to teach you something you still have to learn for your life. And *you're* there on purpose, to teach someone else. It's so amazing how it works."

I wondered if Pete had been a child of the 60's – maybe a little pot, some acid? Or maybe he was just one of those people who believed in mystical experiences. In psychology, there's a character style called Schizotypal personality. People who have it see hidden meaning in simple events. They receive messages in their dreams and even during the day when they're awake. Many of them believe they have powers of extra-sensory perception, or that they can see the future. They're the people you might describe as "odd" or "bizarre." When these character traits interfere with their relationships and ability to hold down a job, it's diagnosed as a personality *disorder*.

Pete seemed pretty well adjusted, pretty grounded in reality as far as his other answers to my questions. Another possible explanation was that there could be some truth to his words. After all, this pilgrimage has been traveled for about a thousand years by hundreds of thousands of people. There must be some reason it endures.

Pete also explained how the Camino helped him to heal after he lost his wife to cancer. They were just starting to enjoy their retirement: traveling without schedules, answering to no one but each other. The two of them had just started living when they heard the prognosis: "terminal." She died just a few short months later.

He said, "I thought my life was over after my wife died, but the Camino changed all that."

He quoted from a book by John Updike in which a character says something like, "I had no idea this experience would hold the key to the rest of my life." For Pete, the Camino held the key to a second chance in his life.

He described how he was angry at the beginning. He was so angry he wanted nothing to do with God or spirituality of any kind. He had walked the Camino not entirely sure of his purpose but knowing he needed to continue healing. Or die. He walked away from his home, refusing to be crippled by his loss. He became a reluctant pilgrim carrying his grief and pain with him through every step. The physical act of walking, the movement itself, allowed the mountains, the rain and the sunshine to clean his spirit. He made new friends along the way and they helped him to hold and carry his loss. At the end, he walked away a wiser man.

Pete also met someone special along the way, a woman who revived his passions. "We never planned to be in a relationship, in fact, she avoided it until almost the very end," he said.

Pete joked about how this fellow pilgrim even accused him of stalking her about midway through the Camino. "It really looked like it because I would end up everywhere she was." He smiled at the memory and said, "I promised her I wasn't a stalker but even when I tried to avoid her, we'd still end up in the same place. Then one time, I ran into her and she was in real trouble. She was anaphylactic and I was the one who got her to the hospital. After that, we both knew why I kept running into her. I was meant to help her. She even said the doctor told her I had saved her life."

The two of them spoke often, even after the Camino was over and they had both returned to their separate lives, he in the States and she in Germany. Their communication became more intimate, and a seed of romance grew.

"She made me feel like getting up and working on the house again. I had let it all go, even basic repairs, the lawn... Hell! I wasn't even bothering to check the mail before I left for the Camino. Things were really starting to fall apart."

Pete's motivation wasn't the only thing that the Camino revived. "It made me realize I can still love a woman, even though she's not my wife. I mean, my wife is gone, and I understand she's not coming back. Before the pilgrimage, I thought there's no way I could love anyone else, that's just totally impossible."

I could tell there was more to the story by the way he hesitated and then he quickly concluded, "But it happened."

Pete's transformation made me wonder how the Camino would affect Joe and me as a couple. Alone, I'm a walking science experiment: "Look class, you're in luck! What are the chances of seeing the Great Northern Anxiety-Speckled Psychologist out here in the wild like this? Take a good look, boys and girls, but don't get too close, or you might frighten her away. It's rare to see them this far from their natural habitat." With Joe it's different; he's my fear buffer. I don't want to disappoint him. No. It's more than that; I don't want to lose him. A divorce is the emotional equivalent of a stroke: it paralyzes trust, and attacks the belief that a relationship can be permanent. I'm still building back up from mine.

I had rejected the church and pulled away from anything that smacked of religion after twelve years of Catholic school and a heart-crushing divorce. I only attended Mass for Christmas or major holidays and I mostly did that for my children's sake.

I've always felt more of a connection to the Holy Spirit, preferring to think of God as an energy inside every creature regardless of faith. It's there just because we're all alive and we struggle. I wanted to think of this Camino as a spiritual journey that would draw me closer to God because sometimes I have trouble even believing there is a God. When I see young people die, or hear about faithful army soldiers getting their skulls blown off, or parents whose children die early deaths, I question how God could let that happen. I know He won't stop physical death, and that we supposedly have free will, but why not offer more mercy?

My list of reasons to doubt has no end. Regardless, I've already made the decision to attend church as part of this pilgrimage. One thing I do know for sure is I'm a sinner. For all my doubt, I still want to earn a plenary indulgence. Even if it's only psychological, I want to believe that there's a way for me to wash my spirit clean of all the wrongs I've done in my life. I know I will still sin after it's over, but I expect my sins to spill forth from a wiser spirit. Also, I'm carrying the weight of so many offences right now, I'd be grateful to strip down clean for a "do over."

Pete's story replayed in my head. For now, I'm only going to focus on his words; his courage to change his routine, to walk away from the sadness in his life. That's what made all the difference. By the end of his Camino, his willingness to take action despite his loss had allowed him to release his sorrow and despair. It reminded me of a plaque I had received as a gift from a coworker inscribed with a quote by Kahlil Gibran:

Your living is determined not so much by what life brings to you as by the attitude you bring to life; not so much by what happens to you as by the way your mind looks at what happens.

When Joe got back from the parking lot, he wasn't surprised by Pete's visit and called out, "I suspected you might drop by to wish us a *Buen Camino*." We all talked together for a while. Then we said our goodbyes to Pete and sat down to wait for our flight.

Joe: The strangest thing happened while we were waiting for our departure. As Pete was leaving, the Space-A terminal was slowly filling with passengers. Elaine and I watched the newly arriving passengers and noticed two men enter through the terminal doors. Their rugged appearance stood out from the rest of the travelers. They were dressed in cargo pants, hiking shirts and high-tech trail shoes. They weren't pulling luggage behind them; they carried backpacks on their shoulders. *They were dressed like us.* We casually watched them from across the terminal for several minutes before Elaine said, "I'm going to talk to them."

I was shocked; Elaine rarely approaches strangers.

Elaine: I pushed past my shyness long enough to experiment with Pete's philosophy about the Camino. "Hi. How's it going? I'm Elaine and that's my husband, Joe, over there. Are you guys heading to Rota?"

"Oh, we're doing fine! I'm Jim and this guy over here's my buddy, Earl."

Jim was thirty-nine years old and recently retired from the Army. He'd been an Army scout and sported a strong muscular build compressed into a lithe physique that made him look as solid as a rock but remarkably agile. He had a full, auburn beard, penetrating blue eyes, and a broad, confident smile.

I wasted no time, "Are you guys going hiking?"

His words were assured, "Oh, yeah, we're most definitely going on a hike." Jim spoke with a classic West Virginian accent.

"It's called the 'Cah-mee-noh day San-tee-ah-go.' I did some research on it after I walked the Appalachian Trail last year, and I hear this one's got more history and more chances to meet new people."

I stopped myself from laughing reflexively when he said his purpose was to meet new people. It took me a second to realize he wasn't joking. I still had a hard time believing there are people in this world who actually look forward to meeting strangers — something I dread so instinctively. Joe is one of these people, the kind without social anxiety. Maybe this is *their* natural habitat, an airport terminal.

Jim was still talking. He had no idea about all the thoughts that were flashing through my mind,

"...come from all over the world to do this pilgrimage, and I'm ready to make some friends outside of the U.S and definitely outside of the Army."

This time I did laugh, but in agreement. It was time to learn more about the world belonging to civilians. All three of us expressed our astonishment about our coincidental destination.

"What are the chances of meeting two other people who are walking the Cah-mee-noh?" Jim marveled.

I said, "Joe and I are going to be starting in St. Jean Pied-de-Port. How about you?"

Jim laughed openly, "That's rich!"

He turned to Earl and prodded, "Hey Earl, tell them where we're starting our hike from."

Earl, Jim's co-traveler, pulled out his guidebook and pointed, "We're leaving from right here in France."

Then he winked. He was like a cat playing with a mouse; his finger was pointing directly to St. Jean Pied de Port.

Earl was seventy-six years old. He'd retired in 1976 but still looked tough and athletic, only with a more weathered appearance; picture Robert Redford. Jim and Earl had just met each other at the airport the previous day. Earl planned to tour the French countryside alone, but when Jim told him about his plans to walk the Camino, Earl changed his mind. Just like that. The two had found a sporting goods store and within an hour, Earl was stocked up on hiking gear, each of them ready and willing to accompany the other on a 500-mile pilgrimage across northern Spain.

After a while, Joe came over to investigate what all the laughing was about. He was just as surprised by their story, and Jim seemed happy for the larger audience.

He described his life after the Army with pride. "I sold my house and most of my belongings, and I don't miss a single stitch of it. When I'm home in Virginia I live in an RV parked at my sister's house, and it's perfect." He paused, "I don't want nothing to tie me down because I plan to travel until the day I die."

Jim made a no-frills lifestyle sound like the only satisfying way to live. "I don't need a big refrigerator because I only eat fresh food. Do you know that most of the stuff you put in your refrigerator is processed and's got mostly preservatives? I found out since I left the Army that I don't need to keep all that much stuff cold and I need even less to be happy."

I had already heard about the minimalist movement before we left on the Camino. It's based on the idea of living a simple life with only vital possessions and being open to the freedom it affords. Our decision to rent out our house and put all our furniture into storage was our first step toward minimalist living. Traveling to Spain with a backpack containing only eighteen pounds of essentials was the next step toward freedom. I don't think Jim had studied much about minimalism, but he was the real thing. He wasn't reading about it; he was living it.

Earl enjoyed his senior years with a more serious, no-nonsense attitude. "I say what I mean and mean what I say. I'm seventy-five and I've earned that right," he told us.

No sugarcoating for this guy. It was clear he was accustomed to being in charge, and it was no surprise when he explained he could take off as often as he liked because he owned his own company and made sure his employees were able to carry on without him. Earl said he takes trips every year using Space-A flights to get him out of the country and back. He'd traveled all around the world but had never taken an extended trek like the Camino.

The four of us shared our plans and our reasons for doing the pilgrimage and often repeated how odd it was that all four of us were on the same path starting on the very same day. I hoped we could keep track of one another as we moved into the next phase of our trip.

Joe: Our departure time was delayed several times and I could feel myself growing impatient. I also became introspective, blocking out the world. We'd moved into that zone where we were still anxious but getting tired of the waiting. I wanted to just get on the plane and lay back for an uninterrupted nine-hour nap.

An hour later before the Master Sergeant announced that the plane was ready to board. With a collective sigh of relief, we all grabbed our belongings and headed out of the terminal. There were about twenty of us slowly loading into a large van with a young airman sitting behind the wheel. As I stepped up into the van, I could just make out the tail of an aircraft sticking up from behind the roof of the hangar next to us. My perspective must have been off. That looked like quite a large hangar. How could the tail of an airplane be that high? Isn't it supposed to fit *inside* the hangar?

The Master Sergeant sat down in the front seat of the van and radioed to the flight crew that we were in transit. With all of us loaded and anxious to go, she nodded to our driver, who put the van in gear and headed first toward and then around the adjacent hangar.

Elaine: Have I mentioned that I have a fear of flying? This has always been a sore spot for me considering that I was a psychologist in the U.S. Air Force, a branch of service whose mission is to "fly and fight." It's even more ironic that I had to sign off on "fear of flying" separation paperwork discharging service members from the Air Force because they couldn't board an airplane.

My flying phobia hasn't stopped me from traveling, but I still feel nervous during liftoffs, air turbulence and landings. It's not just the fear of dying, but the image that plays in my mind. When I'm flying, I literally picture the plane free-falling with all of the passengers panicking around me in a mass of tangled chaos, fighting for survival. I can feel my stomach leap into my throat struggling for the same limited space and choking me. I always regret boarding within the first few seconds of clicking my seat belt. In order to calm myself, I start every flight by looking at the flight attendants and telling myself, *They do this every day, multiple times a day, for year after year without crashing. They even make it through to retirement. That's a lot of flying without dying. Statistically the odds of walking off this airplane alive are on my side.*

As our transit van turned the corner around the hangar, my heart did a terrified somersault. The airplane was the size of a Costco warehouse! My immediate reaction was, "How the heck does something that massive get off the ground, let alone stay airborne?" Not only did I have my regular fear of flying, it was now compounded by my ignorance, or maybe my complete disbelief, in the physics behind such a thing.

Joe grinned and nodded like he had just been handed the keys to Air Force 1. Then he broke out with an, "Oh yeah!"

Damn it! He was enjoying the idea of climbing into this flying freak of science. I immediately turned to the Master Sergeant and asked, "Is there any other plane flying to Spain today?"

I knew the answer before I even asked. But it didn't matter. My heart was begging my mind, *Quick! Do something. Get me out of here!*

But my mind answered, *You already know what to do. You don't have to stop being scared; you just have to stare at one step at a time and start climbing. Don't look up – or down.*

And I did it.

Joe: The C5 Galaxy is one of the largest military aircraft in the world. It has the largest airlift capacity, in excess of 100 tons, of any aircraft in the Air Force. As our van approached, the relative size between our van and the plane was difficult to fathom. Passing by the outer engine, I felt like we could have driven right through it. We approached the rear-left quarter and parked next to a set of boarding stairs. I turned to Elaine and noticed that she looked a little pale. We stared at each other for a couple of seconds and then back at the C5, both of us were awestruck. I knew she was a bit nervous, but I hoped her excitement might be winning the battle.

Looking up the stairway, I saw a small hatch in the otherwise smooth and windowless exterior of the aircraft. It looked about the size of a manhole cover and I wondered how we were going to get through it while carrying our backpacks. Then the C5's rather large crew chief stepped easily out of the hatchway and onto the top landing of the stairs. That's when I realized the hatch was much larger than it looked, but since it was about three stories up, it looked tiny from where we were. Anyone falling from that hatchway onto the hard pavement below would surely die from their injuries. As we stepped out of the van and approached the stairway, I felt like we were starting our Camino right then and there.

Elaine: We climbed the three flights of stairs and boarded that monster even though every nerve in my body was screaming *Run!* I don't think Joe realized the kind of mental lockdown I had to use on my nervous system in order to keep moving forward. Actually, I should say moving *vertically*, since the steps went directly north. There was Joe, smiling like a school kid, as if this was some great start to a dream come true. All I could think was, *If I have to die, at least I'll be with Joe.* I think the idea came to me because I like to tell him, "If you live to be 100, I hope I live to be 100 minus one day, so I never have to live without you." It's from *Winnie the Pooh*, and I've said this to him since the day we got married. I never thought it would be useful for a flying phobia.

I was shocked when I entered through the narrow hatchway. There were eighty wide, comfortable seats just waiting for the twenty of us. Once inside, the C5 was a traveler's dream. There was so much empty space, every one of us could have stretched out completely. Joe and I were the last to board. As soon as we made it inside, Joe went in the complete opposite direction as everyone else. He asked the loadmaster if we were allowed to sit up front where the crew sits and he was told this was perfectly acceptable. So there we were with five seats all to ourselves. I would've never had the nerve to expect I could sit up there with the crew, or to even ask them. Apparently, no one else did either.

After we took our seats, I immediately put on my headphones and turned on some calming, meditative music; it kept me from bolting when the engines started spinning. Imagine a noisy subway ride in New York City, and then multiply by a hundred. When we were undeniably airborne and floating like any other plane, my coiled muscles relaxed. I even felt like smiling. I was sitting in an empty row of seats, with a pillow and blanket, listening to soothing music and holding hands with the man who convinced me to confront my fears.

I had quit my job only half-believing that the decision would eventually bring me some peace, and my fear had almost stopped me from boarding. Now we were riding on "free tickets" in a military aircraft with the world's finest flight crew. I'm glad I didn't run away because even though the plane was gargantuan, it came with an equally massive life lesson.

Lesson for the Day: Remain open to your dreams but don't be too quick to decide by what means they'll come true.

Chapter 3: Charting a New Course

If a man walks in the woods for love of them half of each day, he is in danger of being regarded as a loafer. But if he spends his days as a speculator, shearing off those woods and making the earth bald before her time, he is deemed an industrious and enterprising citizen.
- Henry David Thoreau

Joe: Elaine and I arrived in Rota, Spain. The flight was uneventful and we enjoyed a relaxing evening in a small hotel close to the beach. In the morning, we walked through the door of a small storefront travel agency located just off the main street in town. It was a hot, sunny Mediterranean day and the cool, conditioned air of the office brought a welcome chill. Jose, of the Pacos Travel Agency, greeted us as we walked in.

Feeling confident, I spoke first, "We're here to hike the Camino de Santiago. We just need some help routing our way to Saint-Jean-Pied-de-Port, France."

Since he was Spanish, I assumed Jose would be quite familiar with the Camino and most certainly had a preplanned route he could just print from his desktop. My confidence quickly deflated when I saw the questioning expression on his face.

Then I realized *Oh, he probably doesn't speak English.*

I started turning to Elaine for help when Jose said, in perfect English, "I'm not really sure where that is, but if we can find it on a map, I'll get you there."

I was surprised but explained that we needed to get to Saint-Jean as directly as possible. We all sat down at his desk. Jose pulled out a map and started searching for Saint-Jean-Pied-de-Port. After several minutes of watching him struggle, I politely wrestled the road atlas from his hands. We searched together for several more minutes before I spotted it.

"There it is!"

I put my finger on a little dot on the border of southern France. Once we had identified the location, Jose became much more animated about our options.

Jose was very thorough as we investigated our options using planes, trains and automobiles, searching for the fastest and cheapest route. We monopolized his time for almost two hours, keeping the only other travel agent hopping with a steady steam of other customers. Three hundred and fifty euros later, we'd settled on the best approach. It went like this: Walk to the bus station and catch a bus to Sevilla (pronounced "Sayveeyah"), find a hotel and spend the night. Walk back to the bus station the next day, catch a bus to the airport and take a night flight on Ryan Air to Bilbao, Spain. Catch another bus to the center of town and find another hotel for the night. Next morning, walk to the bus station and catch a bus to San Sebastián, Spain, then catch a second bus to Bayonne, France. In Bayonne, take a city bus to the train station. Once there, buy tickets and board the train to Saint-Jean. Well, that was the plan.

Elaine: I think we should have rented a car.

Joe: We would've rented a car if we could have. Renting a car one-way for 1000 kilometers and dropping it off in a different country is next to impossible, hence the "enhanced" travel option.

Saying goodbye to Jose, we hoisted our backpacks and walked out of the travel agency. We were happy to be on the move as we headed out to catch a bus to Sevilla.

Lesson for Today: When traveling, flexibility and the ability to solve problems creatively are just as important as carrying the right gear.

Chapter 4: Security Alert

2 Days Ago, Sevilla to Bilbao

Only those who will risk going too far can possibly find out how far it
is possible to go.
- T.S. Eliot

Elaine: We thought today would be pretty uneventful, just a quick jaunt from Sevilla to Bilbao on the North Atlantic coast of Spain. Jose, the travel agent, had purchased us a flight on Ryan Air, a no-frills airline that offers cheap direct flights throughout Europe. We expected that the most stressful challenge today was going to be compressing our backpacks down to carry-on size. We were wrong. We'd been told back at the Rota Naval Air Station that we would have to get our passports stamped at a police station so we'd have an official record of entering the country. Military planes don't have to follow the same procedures as civilian airports, so we'd left Rota with no record of our arrival in Spain. In order to get our passports stamped for commercial travel, we shouldered our backpacks and walked under the blistering hot sun through the city streets of Sevilla searching for a police station. It was Saturday and the city was packed. It was still Africa-hot here even in the middle of September. We were soon soaked with perspiration.

Joe: It was a nice day, a lot like New Mexico in the summer. It was a dry heat.

Elaine: After finding the police station closed, we worked our way back to the center of the city to the tourist office. The line moved quickly, and the woman behind the counter politely directed us to the police headquarters, about three kilometers away. "They're open twenty-four hours a day," she assured us. We headed that way, strolling through the fashion district and then into a "gypsy" neighborhood with a large central courtyard. There were some locals carousing, laughing, smoking cigarettes and drinking beer in the street. I spotted the police building on the other side of the plaza and headed straight for it without even waiting for Joe. I found the entrance and walked up to an officer sitting just inside the door. He looked tired, but still listened intently as I explained our problem. He even seemed apologetic when he shook his head and declared, "You were supposed to do that in Rota."

We'd unwittingly traveled to Sevilla thinking we could get our passports stamped at any police station in Spain. It turns out that the passports had to be stamped at any police station *in Rota*. The alarms went off in my head: *We're fugitives!*

Maybe it was the sweat streaming down both our faces, or our pathetically wilted expressions (and clothing) that prompted him to offer up a simple solution: "Why don't you just go to the airport to get them stamped?"

What...go to the airport to get our passports stamped? Will they allow us to do that? We're already headed there!

Joe: By now Elaine was starting to wear down and the stress was starting to get to me as well. We had several potential issues coming up at the airport. We were in a foreign country without proper documentation. We had carry-on baggage that was slightly over-sized. Ryan Air charges as much for checked baggage as for passengers, and they're very strict on size. We had potential "weapons" consisting of aluminum and carbon-fiber trekking poles, a Leatherman utility knife and a titanium spoon and fork that I wanted to try to get through security.

We thanked the officer for his assistance, stepped outside the building and flagged down a cab. Off we went to the airport for the next few hurdles.

Elaine: First the passport stamps. We entered the airport and headed straight for the official sitting behind a desk at an open window. I asked her where to go to get our passports stamped. She instructed us to enter through the arrivals door to the security office. We both glanced over at the sliding arrivals door labeled in bright red letters **"Security Zone: Do Not Enter"** and then back to the attendant. "Are you sure we should go in there?" She assured us, that's exactly what she meant and then quickly dismissed us by turning back to her paperwork.

We hesitantly headed in that direction. There was a crowd standing back from a set of large sliding glass panel doors. They were all eagerly waiting for their loved ones to come walking through as *arrivals*. Each stared in disbelief as we pushed our way through the crowd, practically moon walking our way toward the doors. I tried my best to pass unnoticed. We reached the glass and I tried pushing, pulling and sliding at the sleek frosted panels. They refused to budge. There were no handles, and no matter how much force I used, they stayed shut. Once I got over the immediate desire to run, it didn't take much mental agility to figure out that automatic doors won't open automatically from the wrong side of a security zone!

We self-consciously stood there alone with a couple of dozen people staring at the backs of our heads and waited. After what seemed like hours but was just seconds, an arriving passenger triggered the doors. She was shocked for a second at seeing us standing before her but then casually walked past, unwittingly colluding with our break-in. I was fully prepared for a take-down by the security agents as we brazenly took our first step through the doorway. We instantly received attention by an Uzi-toting airport security officer, but instead of attacking, he greeted us warmly. "May I help you?"

After we explained our dilemma, he pointed us to the international police office on the other side of the expansive terminal. Incredibly, we were allowed to walk freely within the secure area while carrying two large, fully stuffed, uninspected backpacks.

We made our way to the police lieutenant's office and explained how we got there. He asked where we were heading. I nervously stuttered, "Balboa."

I think he sensed how close I was to becoming incontinent and said, "Oh, you mean Bilbao? You must be thinking of the movie with Rocky Balboa." He said it with such a warm smile that it brought a wave of relief to my petrified heart. After that gentle ribbing, he graciously stamped our passports without a second thought. I thought we'd gotten through the worst of it, but I was wrong again.

Joe: Elaine and I exited the arrivals area while bowing our heads and thanking every official we walked past, including the janitor. We then made our way to the airport departures with confidence on the outside and trepidation on the inside. Approaching the x-ray machine at security, we did the typical drill: emptied our pockets, removed our shoes, and threw all of our paraphernalia on the conveyor belt. I had Elaine go through first so she could distract them with her beauty. I followed quickly behind with a smile on my face and a simpatico "Buenos dias!" I cleared the metal detector, walked over and quickly reached for my backpack lying on the conveyor belt.

Before I could even make contact with the straps, I heard a booming voice cry, "Alto! Alto!"

They had nailed me! I didn't have to understand a single word of Spanish to know the security guard sitting at the x-ray monitor was saying, "This guy's got a knife and a titanium spoon and fork in his bag!"

The guard called over to his supervisor, a senior uniformed officer who was just arriving on site. They hunched over the monitor as the security guard pointed out the articles on the screen. I was done for. *Midnight Express*, here I come.

I started stuttering, "Minuto knife, minuto knife," and "Camino de Santiago," several times but they just looked at me strangely.

Elaine laughingly told me later that "minuto" doesn't mean "miniature"; it means "minute" in Spanish.

The chief of security walked over to me while taking off his jacket, as if preparing for a long *physical* interview with this foreigner.

He said sternly, "Collect up your belongings and follow me," as he headed for a closed door next to the security area.

I grabbed all the stuff I'd emptied out of my pockets, my shoes, my backpack and shuffled behind him in my stockinged feet to the private office while envisioning the cavity search and jail time. Elaine followed right behind me talking in non-stop staccato

Spanish while waving her Lt. Col. military ID card with fire in her eyes.

The next thing I know they are laughing (at me?) and I'm hearing the words "Camino" and "Frances" repeated several times. The chief then starts drawing an imaginary map of Spain on the wall with his finger, indicating several different starting points for our route. He doesn't even open my backpack.

He politely tells Elaine (in Spanish), "Could you please tell him not to pull out his knife while he's in the terminal?"

We then hear our first authentic "Buen Camino" and he sends us on our way with a smile.

Elaine: Did you really say "fire" in my eyes? If f-i-r-e is the new spelling for *fear*, then you would be right. I was so scared I didn't even remember I had a military ID, so it wasn't my idea to wave it around. It was the chief who asked me to produce identification and I didn't even stop to look down when 50 euros and several credit cards tumbled onto the floor while I searched my pockets for ID. I don't even remember what I was babbling in Spanish. I just recall how relaxed he seemed for a man who was about to penetrate Joe right in front of his own wife. Thank God he turned out to be pro-military. We were now in the airport on the correct side of the security zone waiting for our plane to Bilbao. *Please let the boarding be boring.*

Lesson for Today: Even if there's no time for a run, you can still get a good cardiac workout at the local airport security station.

Chapter 5: Every Stranger Has a Message

1 Day Ago, Bilbao to Saint-Jean-Pied-de-Port, France

Treat everyone you meet as if they were going to be dead by midnight. Extend to them all the care, kindness and understanding you can muster, and do it with no thought of any reward. Your life will never be the same again.
- Og Mandino

Joe: We arrived by train to the medieval French village of Saint-Jean-Pied-de-Port. There were about a dozen other pilgrims, unsure of which direction to go. We eventually found the all-volunteer pilgrim's office operating out of a small room in the center of town. It was a strange feeling as we stood in the crowd of potential pilgrims waiting to receive our Camino passports (*credenciales*). I could feel the excitement, see the curiosity. I even sensed some fear. People from all over the world, young and old, all speaking different languages, were standing in line, all preparing for an amazing journey. Elaine's fluency in Spanish jumped us ahead in line to the one attendant who spoke only Spanish. The two of them discussed details of the Camino as well as local restaurants and lodging for the night. The attendant even made some phone calls to find out if there were any rooms available. We'd purposely refrained from making reservations based on a travel philosophy I had formulated before leaving for the Camino: "The plan is not to have a plan." Elaine had tentatively agreed to try this approach, I think mostly to humor me until she could scope out all the accommodations.

After receiving our credenciales, we headed off in search of the local albergue the attendant recommended. Most pilgrims use the lower cost, barracks-style rooms, but Elaine wanted a private room in order to be well rested for our first day. St. Jean is a popular starting point and there would be a lot of people here preparing for the pilgrimage. We were tired and mentally numb from all this traveling in a foreign land. We'd had to adapt at every turn, but the stress was invigorating. A good meal and a restorative night's rest would do us good.

Elaine: When we stepped off the train in Saint-Jean, I was surprised. I'm not sure what I was expecting, but I pictured people mingling, reaching out to one another and immediately bonding as an assembly of newly minted pilgrims. Instead, I saw passengers boisterously disembarking and heading into town in already-formed groups. There were a few couples and many stray but quiet singles. Mostly they looked self-contained. I understood that the customary greeting is "Buen Camino!" but I felt awkward saying it, wondering if it was the right time. No one else seemed to be using the phrase yet and I didn't want to be the first to break some unspoken protocol.

We went to the local Camino office to get our credentials. It was in a cramped little room with three civilians who divvied up the eager pilgrims by language. I got the "Spanish-only" woman. She was very friendly. She held up a topographical chart of our first day's walk showing 25 kilometers going essentially straight up.

I was shocked. Of course I had read books on the Camino before I left and I knew that the first day was going to be exceptionally difficult, but now it was real. It would all start as soon as I woke the next day. I could see the mountains as a right triangle on the map. I thought, *This walk is about 200 city blocks, and the climb is the equivalent of 400 flights of stairs!*

That's when I said it out loud for the first time: "I don't think I'm ready for this."

Our attentive helper practically shouted her response, "*Sí, seguro que puedes!*" (Yes, of course you can!).

I could feel the heat of stares suddenly turning in our direction, probably wondering why the need for a pep talk so soon. Or maybe I just imagined it.

We left the credenciales office and wended our way through town, which can be described as "all things pilgrim." Pilgrim signs, pilgrim pictures, life-sized pilgrim dolls, water gourds, staffs and picnic lunches. If you'd forgotten to pack anything, it was there.

We immediately started the ritual of washing our clothes by hand and line drying. We were sharing a bathroom with others at our albergue and I was feeling self-conscious about the etiquette. Was it okay if I walked back to our room wrapped in a towel? Why didn't I think ahead about all the things I needed to carry in with me to the bathroom? Why were Joe and I sleeping in separate beds like two characters out of some 1950's sitcom? The excitement I had had when I came into town was slowly transforming into full-blown worry.

As with most worries, the intensity grew with inactivity, so I decided to set aside my thoughts about tomorrow and focus on the evening. It's the old "pink elephant" theory. If I try to stop thinking about a pink elephant, it stays right there in my mind's eye. But if, instead of denying the pink elephant, I decide to remember the most beautiful sunset I've ever seen: the deep rich colors, the position of the sun, the way I felt when I saw it, *poof*! No more pink elephant. What better way to forget my worries than to get out into the fresh air and find a beautiful sunset, or some comfort food? Perhaps a little wine?

Joe found a secluded restaurant about the size of a studio apartment just a few meters off the main street. This is Basque country even though almost all the vendors speak Spanish. The Basque language—Euskara—is much older than the Latin-based languages that developed after the Roman occupation of the region. It's very different from Spanish, which was confusing at first.

We sat at a small table for two and noticed most of the other diners sitting quietly. We decided to break the ice by talking to the man at the table next to us. He was a redheaded, twenty-something guy with an easygoing expression. He seemed happy to have some company. His name was "Sean-from-Ireland," or at least that's how he introduced himself. He was walking the Camino during his two-week vacation from work as a cartoonist.

He described his personal life as "non-existent," eager to lament his days as a workaholic.

"I spend most of my time at work, and when I'm home, I'm too exhausted to do anything but watch television."

Sean revealed he had no time for a relationship and no time for exercise. He purposely chose to walk the Camino for his only two weeks of vacation to boost his mental and physical health.

"Who knows, I might even meet someone to start a romance with here. I heard that happens on the Camino, you know."

This started a discussion about our individual goals for walking. I wanted to say that my decision was based on a desire to prove my faith and devotion to God. But I didn't, because that would be a lie. I didn't even want to walk the Camino after Joe told me it was 500 miles from Saint-Jean to Santiago. So instead I answered, "Exercise."

Joe was more optimistic. "We're finally taking as much time as we need to enjoy ourselves."

"I wish I could do what you two are doing, but I just can't afford to lose the income and my boss would fire me if I tried to take off to walk the entire Camino," Sean said dolefully.

Sean had barely gotten the last word out when Joe exclaimed, "If they fire you for taking care of yourself, then let 'em!"

Both Sean and I were taken aback. Joe is usually soft-spoken and prides himself on living and letting others live. His authoritative position with a guy he'd just met seemed completely out of character. Stunned, I said nothing, and Sean just listened. That's when Joe disclosed how he had left his forty-hour-a-week job with only the promise of his ability to be creative and to solve problems.

"I knew I didn't need much to survive. I could live on my sailboat, catch fish, eat fruit from trees and drink water—and I'd be perfectly happy," he noted with absolute certainty.

He continued passionately, "But it never came to that. Without the job bogging me down, I was free to find my dream job. Now I can work on my computer from anywhere in the world. I'm actually more productive because when I work I'm refreshed and I see solutions instead of problems."

I'm not sure how Sean understood it all, but before we knew it, our desserts were finished and it was time to rest up for the next day's big challenge. A simple meal had transformed from simply delicious to emotionally nourishing for all of us. Sean and Joe were excited about the next day and I was swept up by their enthusiasm.

Lesson for Today: Reaching out to strangers requires an active effort. The payoff: connecting with another soul walking this Earth in human form who is searching for the same bond.

Chapter 6: Why Is Everyone Passing Us?

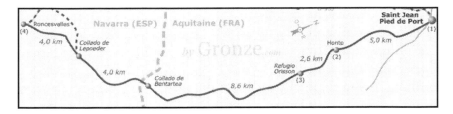

Trail Day 1, Saint-Jean-Pied-de-Port to Roncesvalles, 25.1 km

March on. Do not tarry. To go forward is to move toward perfection.
March on, and fear not the thorns, or the sharp stones on life's path.
- Kahlil Gibran

Joe: It's cold and a fog is drifting through the dark, cobbled streets. We can barely see the signs or the soon to be familiar yellow blazes pointing us in the direction of Santiago. Elaine lights the trail in front of us with her headlamp. We walk through the empty streets and start our ascent out of the village. The multi-storied homes quickly transition to farmhouses, barns and fenced pastures. We continue to climb into the mountains. After an hour, the sun lights the eastern sky and we hear voices gaining on us from behind. The young and old alike steadily approach and walk past us in the morning mist.

I start wondering whether we're in over our heads, but it doesn't take us long to adapt to being left behind so effortlessly.

I say to Elaine, "These people are pushing themselves way too hard. This isn't a race. We're going to just take our time and enjoy the journey."

The sun burns off the surrounding mist and formerly hidden vistas open up before us. I then realize…this isn't fog.

"Elaine, we've been climbing through clouds!"

As the sun and the temperature climb, so do our heart rates and exhaustion. Still, the young and the old pass us by.

"Buen camino!" is all we can say between labored breaths.

How are they doing this? We search for answers…anything to help maintain a shred of dignity, something we can grasp onto in the face of our snail's pace.

"It must be the altitude; we just haven't had time to acclimate," I reason.

My ultimate embarrassment was when a white-haired lady, appearing to be in her mid-seventies passed us.

Elaine: I love competition. But the best part of competing for me has always been winning. I admit my preferred contests were rarely physical, and today I understand why. The day started out with us as early birds. We were first out the door and onto the cobbled streets. Ironically, a half-hour later, as we walked up the dark mountain road, the first person to gain on us was Sean-from-Ireland. He asked if he could walk with us and we were delighted to have a familiar face to accompany us. It was instructive to see the things that made him stop to take pictures. I was too busy absorbing it all and trying to keep up with "giraffe-legs" Joe to remember to pull out my camera.

Sean walked with us at a natural pace. We climbed and shared our awe of the great beauty around us. It seemed we would go on spending the day like this, just the three of us laughing, telling stories and me catching my breath. But that was before the others started outpacing us.

One pilgrim in particular, a young woman in her early twenties with jet-black, curly hair and long, lean legs in safari shorts, slowed down to introduce herself rather than pass us. Her name was Inanna and she was proud to declare she planned to walk the entire Camino solo. I asked if she was anxious about trekking such a long distance alone. She cocked her head and looked at me curiously, "Why should I be any more afraid here than anywhere else?"

She asked the question so candidly, I could only agree. "I guess you're right...and this is so much more beautiful than anywhere else," I added.

A curious thing happened as we walked. Sean, who had moved ahead with Joe, abruptly turned back toward us. "Can I borrow some sun block?" he asked. Inanna happened to have some hanging off her belt within easy reach. She handed it to him before I could even think of which pocket I had dedicated to sun block. The two started talking as she waited for him to hand it back. They volleyed questions back and forth about themselves with mounting enthusiasm. Within twenty minutes, a natural separation occurred. Sean and Inanna were several meters in front of us, and not long after they were just dots on the horizon. Joe and I looked at one another with wry, knowing smiles, thinking, *Could Sean have found romance on the very first day of the Camino?*

Joe: Reaching Orrison, a mountainside town of about three buildings, we took a much needed midmorning break. Breakfast consisted of *café con leche* and a tortilla, a potato omelet that looks a lot like quiche, but with mostly potatoes, served at room temperature. By now there were a number of pilgrims on the trail, many crowding in at the bar. This is a popular point of convergence simply because it's the only show in town. The next stop was Roncesvalles, 16 kilometers and several mountaintops away. It was our first taste of Camino camaraderie. Pilgrims dropped their backpacks to the ground and walked into the bar without a worry about losing their possessions. We all seemed more relaxed than the day before, spontaneous conversations between strangers lit up like torches all around us. After replenishing our water supply at a roadside fountain made of stone, we continued our climb up into a sky so blue it could have come straight out of a Degas.

The march up the steep slopes of the mountains was grueling. We ascended above the tree line where there was little shade or shelter. Herds of cattle and sheep grazed on the hillsides undaunted by the steady stream of strangers coursing through their home. We'd become part of *their* scenery but the grass proved far more attractive. They paused only for brief seconds to acknowledge our passing. Elaine and I stopped often to readjust our gear, drink some water, tighten our shoes, loosen them, tighten them and then, still later, loosen them again. Sometimes we sat down and just took them off altogether, just to let our constricted toes breathe for a while. When we sat, it often served as a signal to others that they, too, could stop and take a break. Funny how one or two people can start a chain reaction.

We reached the top of the mountains around lunchtime and walked along the ridges and peaks. It was beautiful with the bright blue sky above us, the billowy clouds below, and a hundred shades of green spreading out to the horizon. The trail wasn't as steep up here and the temperature was milder. I found ancient fountains built into the sides of the hills to replenish my constantly dwindling water supply. The Spaniards had simply routed the spring water to bronze taps mounted in elaborate granite headstones. I must have drunk a gallon of water, and yet I felt constantly thirsty. I worried that Elaine would become dehydrated. She was pushing hard and I rarely saw her reaching back for her water bottle.

"Elaine, remember to drink," I reminded her.

After several more meters of watching her abstain I'd pull her water bottle out of it's holder and implore her once again.

"Will you please drink something? I don't want you to get heat stroke and have to carry you to Roncesvalles."

This was all very new for her.

Reaching the southern side of the Pyrenees, I soon remembered that I'm much better at climbing up. Elaine labored much more than me on the ascent, but when we finally started to descend, it was my turn to lag behind. The terrain turned steep and gravely, and my knees rebelled with pain from the constant impact. Elaine took to the down slope like an Olympic skier, appearing to glide rather than walk. It took all my will and the fear of being left behind to force my knees into submission.

Hours later, we completed our first day of the Camino, walking through lush highland forests and open meadows, crossing cold mountain streams and finally stepping into the courtyard of the Roncesvalles Royal Collegiate Church of Saint Mary. We made it, and it was still daylight.

Since the 12th century, this church has been receiving all manner of pilgrims: the healthy and the sick, Catholic, Jew, pagan and heretic, the rich, the poor and the wandering. I wasn't sure which category Elaine and I best fit into, but after what we'd endured on this first day, we were certainly open to any category that would get us through the front door and onto a bed.

From the outside, St. Mary's looked like an ancient addition to a centuries-old church. On the inside it was a fully modernized albergue capable of supporting up to 183 tired pilgrims. This albergue is operated completely by volunteer *hospitaleros*. Our hiking shoes were checked at the door and placed in the "mud room." Next, we got in line for a bunk bed assignment to one of the many four-person "quad" cubicles filling the three floors of the sanctuary. Most of the arriving pilgrims were walking around in a daze, but some still had enough energy to laugh and sport with the hospitaleros.

As we were settling into our assigned quad, I noticed a guy wander into the girl's showers. A minute later the confused soul was gently guided out by a half-dressed woman and led over to the men's side. Sometimes the lost and confused men were just left alone to have their shower and walked out without a clue as to where they'd been.

Our bunkmates were two beautiful women from Berlin in their late twenties, Jen and Glinde. We'd met them earlier on the trail after Glinde took a spill over a bed of rocks. She was wearing shorts and got pretty scraped up, but she refused to let it slow her down. As we prepared our beds, I knew I was out of my element when, instead of enjoying this man's slice of "quad-heaven," I said, "I bet all of you I'll be the first to fall asleep."

We'd walked 25 kilometers (15 miles), and we'd climbed a total of 4000 feet and descended another 1400 feet. I'd read that the first day is always the worst, and I sure won't argue, but it might also have been the most magnificent. Only time will tell. While my three bunkmates talked excitedly about their first day on the Camino, I rolled over and fell asleep.

Elaine: As a medical officer in the Air Force, I'd never hiked more than two hours. The non-medical, or line officers, consider themselves "real Air Force" and like to make fun of us, saying we're *prima donnas*. Well, this prima donna reached the Promised Land, today, baby! HOOAH! I could have easily ended my pilgrimage right here and felt completely victorious...maybe.

Crawling into bed, I got the answer to my question about whether I could sleep with a bunch of strangers around me. The answer was yes, but not immediately. Every muscle in my body was exhausted in a way I had never felt. My mind, on the other hand, was racing through the images of the day. I had seen such beauty. The skies were so blue, the cows and sheep walked freely right in front of me with no fear. Then more memories flashed by: our birds-eye view above the clouds, the rustic and simple homes, the people passing us...it was already like a dream. My mind played the scenes of the day like a projector with no option for pause.

I learned about my endurance that day and it made me proud. I also learned how intolerant I am of being left behind. Then again, the more people that passed me, the more opportunities I had to question why I needed to be first, always ahead of the pack. Is it ever okay to be last? The thought reminded me of a joke I used to tell myself while I was going to medical school: "What do you call the medical student who graduates at the bottom of his class?"

"Doctor."

I learned something else. I'm claustrophobic! I didn't realize the bathrooms here had lights (and shower faucets) on timers. I hadn't made a mental note of where the light switch was when I walked in, and I didn't have my phone to use as a flashlight. I was in a tiny room just large enough to hold a toilet and a small sink. As I was washing my hands, the light suddenly went out and I instinctively searched for the light switch. When I couldn't find it, the nervousness started bubbling inside me. I gave up on the switch and went straight for the door. The doorknob was nowhere to be found! I started hyperventilating and alarming thoughts started jabbing at me: *I can't get out...I'll never get out of here!* Now my heart is pounding and I'm starting to feel dizzy. I know exactly what's happening: I'm having a panic attack!

I start my ritual. First a full, slow exhale. Next, I focus on slowing my breathing. Then I tell myself, "You're in a bathroom. If you can't get out, somebody is going to want to use it so it's just a question of seconds before you're out of here... it's okay."

I start to feel less faint. But my heart is still pounding fast. I prefer not to start yelling for somebody to let me out of a garden-variety bathroom. It's just the darkness that's causing my distress.

At least the breathing is helping me to slow everything down in my mind. I tell myself, "Think about it, every door has a knob or something to open it. *Feel* for it." I do, but this time more slowly.

That's when my fingers land in the groove. It's a pocket door! It slides; it doesn't pull open. Less then a second later, I'm walking out the door overjoyed and smoothing my hair, pretending nothing happened.

I started the day worrying that I couldn't hike this far or climb the tall mountains. I ended it with panic over being locked in a cubicle-sized bathroom. I learned that I could walk as far as necessary and eventually find my way out of a lavatory. In both cases, the thing that saved me was stopping long enough to catch my breath, and giving myself the time I needed. It also helped to loosen my expectations about where I should be and when.

Lesson for Today: Looking up at clouds in the sky while lying in the grass will nourish the body. But reaching out to clouds so close you can touch them is soothing to the spirit. Maybe it's because we feel closer to heaven.

Chapter 7: With Risk There Is Reward

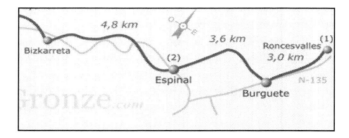

Trail Day 2, Roncesvalles to Bizkarreta, 12 km

Previous journeys in search of treasure have taught me that a zigzag strategy is the best way to get ahead.
- Tahir Shah

Joe: The women were already up by the time I opened my eyes. I stretched the stiffness out of my sore muscles and climbed down from the top bunk. I had a smile on my face; I bent over and gave Elaine a good morning kiss while she packed.

"What are you so happy about?" she asked.

"I just feel good! This is exciting!" I said.

She smiled and continued stuffing her sleeping bag back into her backpack.

There were about fifty pilgrims on our floor alone. Everyone was busy washing, dressing or packing for the new day's challenge. The anticipation, or maybe the anxiety, kept the conversations to a minimum. A simple "Excuse me" or "Good morning" spoken in a dozen different languages were the extent of the words exchanged as we maneuvered around each other in the cramped quarters. Most everyone was focused on themselves and their preparedness. I was kneeling down, pulling clothes from my backpack, when Jen came walking out of the bathroom across the hall and into our small cubicle. She was wearing only panties and a bra while drying her wet hair with a small camp towel. I was shocked for a moment until I remembered, "We're in Europe." I shrugged it off and went back to my packing.

As we all maneuvered in the enclosed space to get dressed and pack, Glinde complained about her shoulders aching. Glinde is almost as tall as I am (6 feet, 2 inches) and I noticed her brand new backpack lying on the floor. It was obviously a female version judging by its size and I suspected the likely problem.

"Glinde, when you're all finished packing, why don't you let me help you adjust it?"

"Thank you!" was her reply. "It just didn't feel right yesterday."

After we finished packing, Glinde stepped into the hallway and hoisted the pack to her shoulders. The problem was immediately apparent; the hip belt was sitting way too high.

Large backpacks are not designed to be carried on your shoulders. The majority of the weight must be carried on your hips or you will soon be suffering from back and shoulder pain. Glinde was new at this so I spent several minutes adjusting straps and buckles while explaining to her the philosophy of carrying a heavy load. Her problem was that she'd mistakenly purchased a women's backpack. She wasn't a large woman, but she was tall and it just didn't fit right.

The spacing between the shoulder straps and the waist belt of all good backpacks can be adjusted to match an individual person's torso. We kneeled down on the floor and I dismantled and readjusted the shoulder strap anchor points to their maximum spacing, an exercise that should have taken place at the backpacking store when she purchased it. Glinde then hoisted the pack to her shoulders again. It was still a little too short, but it made a world of difference; the hip belt was now on her hips. Here's how to adjust a backpack for a great fit (after insuring that your backpack is matched to the length of your torso):

Four Steps to a Great Pack Fit

Load your backpack and loosen all of the straps and hip belt first.

Step 1: Hip Belt
- Put the pack on your back so that the hip belt is resting <u>over</u> your hipbones.
- Close the hip belt buckle and tighten it.
- Check the padded sections of the hip belt to make sure they wrap around your hips comfortably. Keep at least 1" of clearance on either side of the center buckle.
- If the hip belt is too loose or tight, try repositioning the hip belt buckle. If this doesn't solve the problem, you may need a different pack (or hip belt).

Step 2: Shoulder Straps
- Pull down and back on the ends of the shoulder straps to tighten them.
- Shoulder straps should fit closely to hold the pack body against your back and thus keeping the load forward. They should NOT be carrying the weight.
- Have a helper check to see that the shoulder strap anchor points are 1" to 2" inches below the top of your shoulders.

Step 3: Load Lifters
- Load-lifter straps are located just below the tops of your shoulders (near your collarbones) and should angle back toward the pack body at a 45° angle.
- Gently snug the load-lifter straps to pull weight off your shoulders. (Over tightening the load lifters will cause a gap to form between your shoulders and the shoulder straps.)

Step 4: Sternum Strap
- Adjust the sternum strap as needed to a comfortable height across your chest.
- Buckle the sternum strap and tighten until the shoulder straps are pulled inwards comfortably from your shoulders, allowing your arms to move freely.
- Pull the stabilizer straps located on either side of the hip belt to snug the pack body toward the hip belt and stabilize the load.
- Go back to the shoulder straps and carefully take a bit of tension off of them. This ensures your hips carry the majority of the weight.

After helping Glinde, Elaine and I were soon hoisting our own packs to our shoulders and saying "Buen Camino" to our bunkmates. We walked away from our cubicle, down the stairs and out the Roncesvalles monastery. The trail transitioned from yesterday's steep terrain to mostly flat, wooded farmland as we walked through an early morning rain. There were about 100 or so pilgrims starting out on the trail. Since everyone walks at different speeds, we quickly spread out. After the first hour, we rarely saw more than a half dozen at any one time. We walked under the overcast skies, through pastures bordered by dense groves of trees, up and over mountains and through two small villages. It was lunchtime as we entered the small, picturesque village of Bizkarreta. Other than the 13th century Church of St. Peter, there's not much to see in this quiet little town. The next village was 7 kilometers away and required a 1000-foot descent down the side of a steep mountain. Our muscles were sore and my knees were stiff from the previous day so we decided to call it quits and take the challenge in the morning.

Elaine entered a small grocery store just to browse before starting our search for a bed. I sat and waited outside with negative thoughts going through my head about women and their need to go shopping at the most inopportune moments. The next thing I knew, Elaine was walking out of the store with her newest friend, Maria.

Elaine had booked us into a restored *casa rural*. Maria unlocked a door next to the grocery store and we climbed up to the top floor of this beautiful home. As Maria turned to leave us, Elaine negotiated for an evening meal to be cooked by the "Mama" of the *casa*. We had the whole top floor of this home to ourselves including a living room with a fireplace, a kitchen and several empty bedrooms. The total cost was 44 euros, and that included a full breakfast, Internet access and all the espressos we cared to drink.

I laid back on the couch in front of the fireplace, sipping red Rioja wine, and listening to classical Spanish guitar music. Elaine has offered to massage my worn out feet, and I can't think of any gift that would be more satisfying. It's funny how my desires have shifted over the course of only a few days.

Elaine: What a find! I had no idea that these casas rurales even existed until I stumbled upon this one. The way it works, especially in the high season, is a group of pilgrims book the whole house. This allows them the run of the entire place, including the kitchen. If others had come by to rent a room today, we would have been sharing the place, but on this occasion, we were completely alone. It seems Bizkarreta is too small or too early of a stop for most pilgrims. After the packed crowds at last night's albergue, this was like hitting all three cherries on a slot machine. Imagine: a three-course homemade dinner for two, a bottle of wine and all the coffee you can drink, served in a private kitchen with soft lighting and mood music, all for just an extra 10 euros ($13).

Lesson for Today: Invest some time getting to know the local people. There are many perspectives and hidden treasures that will never show up in a guidebook.

Chapter 8: Would Anyone Do This Again?

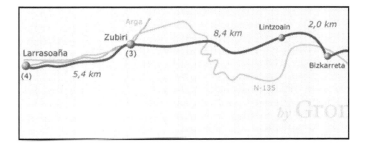

Trail Day 3, Bizkarreta to Akerreta, 15 km

Now shall I walk or shall I ride?
'Ride,' Pleasure said;
'Walk,' Joy replied.
- William Henry Davies

Elaine: Just a few kilometers into our morning hike we met a couple from Madrid; Carmen and Miguel. They were both in their early thirties. We struck up a conversation and became instant travel buddies. I asked them what they did when not walking the Camino. Miguel said, "Yo trabajo de sanitario pero no quiero hablar de eso," which I understood as, "I'm a sanitation worker, but I prefer not to talk about it."

I thought he might be embarrassed about his job handling trash so I tried to respond in the most supportive way I knew, using my Americanized Spanish: "Well, if you make the kind of money our waste management people do in the States, you have nothing to feel bad about!" Upon hearing this comment, Miguel and Carmen looked at one another for a moment and then both broke out into sidesplitting, and in my case ear-splitting, laughter.

She was the first to break through their roaring, long enough to say, "My husband works in radiology; *sanitario* means he is a health worker, not a sanitation worker." From then on, there was nowhere for me to go but up.

We walked alongside each other with Joe trailing behind, which is pretty incredible since he's about a foot taller than all three of us. We talked about their metropolitan life in Madrid, but what really grabbed my attention was Miguel's casual comment about how they had already walked the Camino nine times. Carmen said, "The Camino is an anniversary present we started ten years ago. We loved it so much, it became a tradition." They have continued the trek faithfully every year. This couple's infectious energy kept us animated for miles. They seemed happy in a way that surprised me. Had I become jaded working with couples in marital therapy for so long?

The couples I saw in treatment were usually bitter over too much or too little sex, too little money and time, or even worse, the stain of infidelity. By the time they sought out therapy, the love and passion that flourished at the beginning of their relationship had often eroded into a stump of dependence or mistrust. They each expected to be hurt or rejected by the other. Most of the time, asking for help was more of an exit strategy than a true hope for healing. Still, there were some moments of unexpected happiness and humor. Like when one patient proudly introduced her new husband to me, saying, "I'm clingy and he has a fear of abandonment, so I think it's going to work out."

Some couples worked hard and learned new ways to communicate, others raged and eventually divorced. Miguel and Carmen were far removed from my clinical experience. They communicated almost effortlessly. They were both passionate about each other and their mutual love of nature. Their commitment to walking the Camino each year was only one facet, one example of their capacity for devotion. It felt good to see them on the path. It reminded me of Pete's words about there being no random events on the Camino and how people would be put there purposely to teach me something. This lesson I could feel in my heart instead of my head.

I wonder how long I can keep that kind of vitality alive with Joe. I've always thought that passion just mellows with time and transforms into agape, or what is called "I, Thou" love. After years of marriage, Miguel and Carmen's romance still sparkled. Here was a couple that regularly exercised their bodies *and* spirits together.

Before we knew it, Miguel was pointing out the *Puente de la Rabia*, a medieval bridge over the Río Arga. He explained how the bridge is believed to cure rabies. We each used the occasion to share colorful images of how the bridge might have cured those who traveled on it. Miguel won the unofficial contest with the most believable reason: "Maybe since the patient has to cross the bridge three times, the real cure is the walking."

We all liked that one.

We parted ways with them at the bridge, opting for lunch before pressing on to Larrasoaña. Lured into the first modern-looking bar we'd seen since Sevilla, we found a table and sat down. It had Wi-Fi and a large selection of fresh food. The menus are divided into a pincho (*"pintxos"* in Basque country), a *ración*, and a *plato*. It's like the Goldilocks fairytale: A pincho is a skewered "pinch" of food, a racion is a snack (medium size), and a plato is a full plate (entree size). We tried a wide assortment and realized we could satisfy multiple cravings all at once by eating the pinchos. Oh, and don't make the mistake of calling them *tapas* in Basque country.

I'm consuming more calories than ever before in my life. The difference is in the guilt. I'm eating a Mediterranean diet and I know I'm burning calories and building muscle with every kilometer. The pleasure of eating without remorse makes me wonder why I spend so much time worrying about calories back home. This life of eating more and exercising for the greater part of the day puts more emphasis on the physical: moving, doing, climbing—even trudging seems healthier than sitting behind a desk counting calories and sizing portions as I think up excuses for why I can't work out: "I have to work late today...I'm too exhausted...I don't feel like going to the gym." Every day is a workout here, but with one big difference: after one or two hours of activity, I'm in a whole new town instead of standing in the same place at the gym.

It's easier for me to talk to complete strangers while moving along this path. Why is that? Is it just a way to kill time, to make the walking easier? It feels like more. Our range of conversations has expanded to include more meaningful discussions than you might have at a dinner party.

Is it the Camino, or is it the people who choose to walk the Camino that allow us to explore our personal lives as we watch the scenery flow by?

Joe: It was late afternoon and we were tired and ready to quit for the day. We sat down on a rock wall next to a farmhouse. I studied the map one more time, trying to figure out where we were and where we might find some lodging. After a few minutes, we stood up again and took a few more steps down the trail. Something was nagging at me, as if I'd missed something. I stopped in mid-stride, looking at the map again.

Elaine asked, "What's wrong?"

"I don't know. Something just doesn't look right."

I abruptly turned around and started heading back the way we'd come.

"Where are you going?" Elaine called after me.

After about twenty paces, I spotted the sign; it was on another rock wall right next to where we'd been sitting. It read "Hotel Akerreta" in large bold letters.

I turned back to Elaine and said with a smile, "Hey darling, we're here. We're finished!"

We checked into a beautifully restored Basque farmhouse. The clerk told us the home had been built in 1723 and they had just spent the last four years restoring it to its original charm.

I'd wondered if we'd recognize any places out of *The Way*, the movie we'd seen about the Camino. Here it was, the Hotel Akerreta. This was the place where Tom (Martin Sheen) met the woman from Canada, stumbled upon the French guy in his underwear hanging out laundry, and watched the proprietor fighting an imaginary bull.

Elaine: The Hotel Akerreta was nice, but it didn't speak to me. Or maybe it did. It said, "I'm not an albergue. I'm a hotel." I felt guilty staying here because we were separated for yet another night from the more ascetic pilgrim's journey. This was our second night staying in private accommodations. I felt like we were missing the challenges and treasures of nighttime fellowship. Joe completely agreed.

Lesson for Today: Walking may be the best approach to life's challenges, whether it's managing weight, stress or even relationships. The simple motion of stepping together with fellow pilgrims through changing terrain builds more than muscles.

Chapter 9: Pilgrim! You Are In the Basque Country!

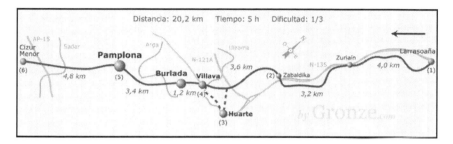

Trail Day 4, Akerreta to Cizur Menor, 19 km

Tell me what you pay attention to and I will tell you who you are.
- José Ortega y Gasset

Joe: After a restful night in a comfortable bed, we ate a simple breakfast of chocolate croissants and coffee. We then said goodbye to the proprietor and headed for Pamplona. These last few days have been hard on my feet and shoulders, but I'm slowly starting to enjoy the physical exertion. My muscles and joints are adapting.

We walked 15 kilometers through beautiful forests, small farms, and ancient towns before entering the huge, modern city of Pamplona. It's in the heart of the Basque country and is most widely known for its annual festival, the Running of the Bulls. It took us half the day just to walk from one end of the city to the other; through concrete neighborhoods, both rich and poor, through the 2000-year-old center and then through Pamplona's modern university where it seemed like every other student would smile at us and say "Buen Camino." We then departed the city, heading toward another hill and the hot afternoon sun.

Cizur Menor sits atop a hill on the western side of Pamplona. Looking east we have a sprawling view of the city. To the west is a long line of mountains topped with huge, modern-day windmills. We'll be crossing over those mountains tomorrow and I couldn't help but think about Don Quixote's battle with windmills and how our world and the people in it haven't really changed that much.

An hour later, we entered Cizur and quickly found our albergue. Walking through an arched doorway into a courtyard, we met a lovely volunteer hospitalera; she must have descended from Florence Nightingale.

A hospitalero (or hospitalera) is a person who manages one of the many albergues along the Camino. The word *hospital* originally meant "place of hospitality" and comes from the Latin *hospes*, signifying a stranger or foreigner, who is also a "guest." Our hospitalera that night sure met the bill. She made a special effort to treat anybody whose feet needed attention, no matter how noxious the conditions. She had an extensive medical kit and worked for several hours on the battered pilgrims as they entered her oasis. The experience is a far cry from that of our modern-day hotel clerk, who often remains locked behind a registration desk, never making physical contact with the weary traveler.

From the amount of limping and bandages I saw, it seemed the first days were rife with foot injuries. Our own feet were abused and had yet to fully toughen to the rigors of the trail. That said – we were still in comparatively good shape compared to those around us. After I received some excellent foot care of my own, we just relaxed for a while. We talked with our bunkmates and later attended evening Mass at the local church. We finished the night at a restaurant where they served us a three-course "pilgrim's meal," including a bottle of wine, all for 10 euros apiece. It was authentic and loaded with calories.

Elaine: We walked through the busy streets of Pamplona before arriving at our destination in Cizur Menor. We passed a group of school children playing outside during recess. I was carrying my trekking poles for protection in the "big city" and gazing absentmindedly at the carefree children when a little girl, about seven years old with straight, raven hair in pigtails, locked her gaze squarely on mine and cheered, "Hola peregrina!"

I already knew I was walking a pilgrimage, so why did it come as such a surprise to be acknowledged by this small child as a pilgrim?

I think it's because I was walking into this city with a set of assumptions. One, I am a hiker not a true *peregrina* seeking God through my steps. Second, children should not talk to strangers, and I'm clearly a stranger. Third, cities are cold, crime-riddled places where I must keep constant guard or risk losing something valuable, including my life. Despite all that, here was a little girl, boldly greeting me, a stranger, without an ounce of fear. And I was already in the city. The greeting shot through me like a momentary shockwave, plowing through my shortsighted expectations. Next thing I knew, I had naturally loosened my grip and put away my trekking poles, realizing I didn't need them.

The couple from Madrid had commented just yesterday about how crime in Spanish cities is rarely violent. "Yes, you'll hear about how people steal money or pick-pocket items like wallets or phones, mostly from unsuspecting tourists, but you don't see people getting shot or stabbed here...it's mostly petty crimes." Their off-hand comment, in tandem with this little girl's reception today, opened my eyes. I walked through the streets feeling freer and more at ease. It felt so good to let go and just see the city where I'd so often watched the "running of the bulls" on TV. Ernest Hemingway's statue is here by the Plaza de Toros. It's the place where he depicted the Fesitval of San Fermín in *The Sun Also Rises*.

We were now in the very heart of the Basque region, which started in St. Jean for this pilgrimage, and would end for us in Burgos. Pamplona felt like a punctuation mark in Basque country. I hadn't noticed the strong nationalism in any of the other Basque towns before, but I couldn't ignore it here. The Basques are fierce about their autonomy. They are very similar to the French-Canadians in their nationalistic pride. A quick inspection of the graffiti on the walls and sidewalks tells the story: "Pilgrim, you are in Basque Country!" There's a pride in these words and in the people themselves that at first glance can impress as arrogance. Pride, arrogance, patriotism, passion? You decide. But as you're deciding, think about the consequences of that decision on your reaction to the person who passes you on the street, or the bartender who serves you, or the woman who watches you from the second-story window above. You can avoid thinking about the consequences of your beliefs, but that won't stop them from influencing your perceptions. It's like a drop of dye that colors an entire pail of water. Today I'm going to look at everything, even the graffiti on the sidewalk, with compassion. If I use my imagination, it's really not that much different from the 27,000 year-old graffiti called petroglyphs, a part of history we pay money to see today back in the U.S.

Lesson for Today: Cynical judgments can follow us daily if we let them. Challenge them actively. Then prepare for some wonderful experiences.

Chapter 10: Empty Vessels

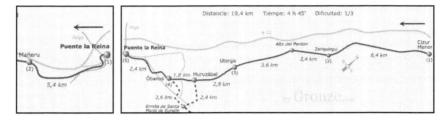

Trail Day 5, Cizur Minor to Mañeru, 25 km

The enjoyment of leisure would be nothing if we had only leisure. It is the joy of work well done that enables us to enjoy rest, just as it is the experiences of hunger and thirst that make food and drink such pleasures.
- Elisabeth Elliot

Joe: It's 5:30 in the morning and the heat from the day before has barely subsided. I'm sitting alone in the dark in a small courtyard. I've just slept with nine women in a ten-person room; married couples are allowed to sleep together, but there were no other married couples in our room. The women were of various ages and from different countries. I'm surprised and impressed at the number of women on the path, young and old, walking alone or in small groups. I also realize how lucky I am to be married to someone who doesn't snore.

Postscript: Elaine says it wasn't just the women that were snoring!

We've met several people along The Way that have done this pilgrimage more than once, some that have been doing parts of it for over twenty years. It gets to be a way of life, a renewal, a cleansing of the body and soul. I'm starting to feel this renewal, albeit slowly. It's directly competing with the aching pain in my feet, legs, back and shoulders.

I'm also surprised how Elaine has responded to the new people we've meet. She isn't feeling drained by the experience, which is her typical response back home. Instead she appears to be gaining energy from it. I'm seeing the real Elaine, not the one that can sometimes be buried under a blanket of anxieties.

As the daylight approached, pilgrims started making their way across the courtyard to the bathrooms. Soon everyone, including us, were packing their belongings and walking out the gate. Elaine and I headed east for the mountains as a long stream of colorful backpacks swayed back and forth in the morning sun. We climbed to the top of the mountains, down the other side into a valley, and kept on walking through miles of farmers' fields. We pushed hard in an attempt to get away from the crowd of pilgrims, wanting a little peace and quiet to recharge from all the geographical and social inputs. Instead of stopping at Puente la Reina, a traditional pilgrim's oasis, we walked further on. Our plan was to find a private place tonight in Mañeru, a small village another 6 kilometers away.

It was a bad decision. What the guidebook had indicated as a nice "forested path" ended up being a scorching march down an open, gravel farm road and up the side of a half-barren mountain. There's a big difference between hiking under shady trees and hiking in open fields when the hot afternoon sun is beating down on your head.

Arriving in the village of Mañeru, we were debilitated and exhausted. Our water bottles were now empty and our shirts were drenched with sweat. The dust from the road had settled into our wet clothing, our hair and our pores. The small village was quiet. We walked through the empty streets looking for lodging while the sun continued to beat down. We saw not a single person. The western edge of the town was fast approaching when we spotted an open barn door. Inside we found a middle-aged couple stacking produce boxes filled with green vegetables.

Elaine poked her head in and asked in Spanish, "Excuse me, where can we find the local albergue?"

The couple was Portuguese and their Spanish was limited. Elaine struggled to understand them. We learned that the local albergue had been closed for over a year. The woman who owned it had taken ill and never recovered.

The husband, Milton, started giving us directions to the next town several kilometers away. His wife, Dora, noticed our dejected reaction to the news as well as our sweat-stained, dusty clothes. Elaine had already taken off her backpack, a sign that she'd had enough. Dora stopped talking to us and turned to her husband, saying something to him.

She turned to us and said in Portuguese, "You're staying with us."

Milton was already pulling off my backpack. He then bent over and picked up Elaine's from the earthen floor and carried them both into an ancient-looking house made of large fieldstone. We were peregrinos and we were in need. We would be staying with them for the night.

Once inside, Dora took us upstairs and pointed to the showers. I don't know if it was out of kindness or because of the odor and dust clouds that were trailing behind us. She led us to the small bathroom at the end of the hall, saying, "El chuveiro." I beat Elaine to the shower but she playfully assaulted me until I gave in.

In the end, our push to get away from the crowd just wasn't worth it. Elaine ended up with an angry blister and the cost to our tranquility (before we met Dora and Milton) was too high. We did learn a lesson, though. If we wanted to prevent a premature end to this trip with the kind of pain and exhaustion we experienced today, we would have to carefully attend to *all* our needs, not just our need for privacy.

Elaine: We hiked some mighty tough terrain today, including the spectacular "rock-stravaganza" just past the Pamplona basin, on the backside of Alto de Perdón (Peak of Forgiveness). Most people know it as the often-photographed panoramic mountaintop with the iron silhouetted statues of pilgrims and their livestock all walking single file. I've never hiked over such craggy terrain before. Some of the rocks were as big as watermelons, and the descents steep and treacherous along an old, washed out road. There were a few times when I thought, *There's no way I'm going to finish this without breaking something.* But I focused on the path and held tight to my trekking poles. It was mostly the poles that helped me make it to the bottom.

There are so many ways to look at the day. The pessimist in me says we should have stayed in Puente la Reina and it was our selfishness, our search for privacy that caused our suffering. After all, that town had a good number of albergues with enough variety that we should have been able to find something to our liking.

The positive seeker and philosopher in me thinks, if we'd stayed in Puente, we would have never experienced the kindness we knew today. The couple that took us in showed such generosity I had to consciously will myself not to cry. Milton and Dora were far from rich, but they shared their home and food freely, making a simple meal of lentil soup and white cheese that restored us.

Although Dora and Milton spoke mostly Portuguese, we communicated freely. I discovered that Spanish and Portuguese are surprisingly similar, with about a 70 percent overlap in the words I could immediately understand. We had fun trying to find common words while in the middle of a sentence. I would start pointing or making a charades-style movement to explain my meaning, and then one of them would understand my message and translate it to the other. It took some effort, but we all seemed to be willing to work at it.

I made a point of expressing our gratitude repeatedly during dinner. Milton said, "I believe it's a blessing God sends. We take care of others and He takes care of us…this is as it should be." He explained that he and his wife use their property as a little produce shop and pilgrims regularly wander in looking for assistance.

I asked, "Do you ever feel annoyed by the interruptions?"

Without hesitation, he answered, "People do not ask unless they need. Why should that bother me?"

I told him we were kindred spirits because I also enjoy performing acts of kindness, and I've always gotten at least as much out of it as the person I've helped. I turned to him in a confiding manner and said, "Look how, even now, my past good deeds are coming back to me." It made us all smile, and we lingered over our food for a few more moments.

That night, I also learned some important hiking tips. Dora and Milton were experienced trekkers with an elaborate morning ritual they had developed for walking long distances. They explained it to us in detail, each taking turns: "First you tape the toes with adhesive tape. Then you put Vicks (VapoRub) NOT Vaseline or Compeed between the toes and over the soles of the feet. Use a lot, and don't be stingy. It avoids blisters," said Milton emphatically.

"And it's very refreshing for the feet. Use it when your feet get tired from walking during the day," Dora added. They swore by this technique and insisted they had not had a single blister during their many hikes.

Our experience reminded me of the parable of the little boy on a beach throwing washed up sand dollars back into the ocean. The boy is stopped by an old man, who says, "Why are you bothering with that? There are thousands of these things on the sand. You can't possibly make a difference." The little boy picks up another sand dollar, throws it back in the ocean and says, "I did for that one!"

It really makes a difference when you happen to be that one sand dollar that's lifted and thrown back into the ocean.

We pounded our bodies in some blistering heat today. For awhile I thought I was going to exercise my option to end the hike, but now I realize that the joy we felt at the end of this day was a direct consequence of all the pain we endured.

Lesson for Today: The good you do comes back to you.

Chapter 11: Accepting Change

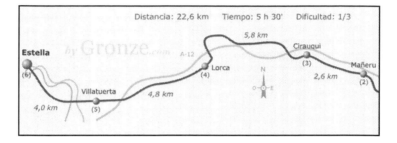

Trail Day 6, Mañeru to Estella, 16 km

It's not hard to make decisions when you know what your values are.
- Roy Disney

Joe: We'd finishing our breakfast and were preparing to leave when Elaine politely offered Milton some money. We weren't surprised when he adamantly declined. Sharing their home and food with us was a gift, pure and simple. We respected his refusal. Our American sensibilities might stress over receiving such acts of kindness from complete strangers, but that was our problem, not theirs.

I walked out of Mañeru with a full stomach and a lightness of heart and headed down the trail toward Estella, 16 kilometers away.

Several hours later Estella appeared around a bend in the river we were walking beside.

"We should take a day off … give your feet a chance to heal. We can explore the town tomorrow."

Elaine replies, "I'm fine. It's okay, let's keep walking."

I say, "Experiences take time. If we rush they'll be lost."

"I want to keep going; we'll get behind schedule."

Again, I reply, "I want to finish the Camino too, but more importantly, I want to experience the journey."

I'd decided we were both taking the day off. We'd drink in the sites and culture while we both tended to our need for rest and repair. I didn't want to struggle against our main form of transportation, our feet. Elaine would just have to go along with it, or at least that's what I told myself.

Elaine: The little town of Estella is the quintessential Spanish hamlet nestled in the autonomous Basque community of Navarre. It was founded in the 11th century and is a real study in contrasts. It has a small-town feel with a handful of trendy restaurants lined up along the square. It also has a relaxed, casual atmosphere highlighted by a band of local musicians who parade through the town on Sundays playing a short, infectious tune, much to the delight of the residents and the visiting pilgrims.

We made a mistake and took a quick nap right after arriving. We'd treated ourselves to a private room in a *pensión*, and the secluded bed was too great a temptation. Afterwards, we hit the streets only to find the stores were closed for siesta. It was 4:00 p.m., and we would have to wait until 6:00 p.m. to find some bandages for the blister caused by yesterday's walk.

Joe insisted we take tomorrow off. He said he needed a break to recuperate. He argued that a day off would provide time not only for rest, but also reflection. We haven't written as much as we would like out of sheer fatigue, and we know we'll forget the little details that, when strung together, can make a big difference in our appreciation of the trip. I know he's right, but I notice some nagging guilt about stopping. I have this internal dialogue running through my head.

Elaine "the goal-oriented": "You probably shouldn't take a whole day off. Have you really walked long enough? It's only been seven days. There are people who are walking longer with sprained ankles, and all you have is a blister! Remember, pain is just weakness leaving the body. C'mon, you do want to get to Santiago some time this *year*, don't you?"

Elaine "the mindful": "There's nothing wrong with taking a break. It's important to listen to my body; I'm tired. This isn't a contest; it's supposed to be a journey, not a destination. Relax, enjoy the time off. You deserve it; you're working hard."

I try to practice the principles from Acceptance and Commitment Therapy, which is the type of behavioral treatment I used in my clinic before I left my job. It requires me to become the "peacemaker" to my own conflicted mind.

First, I summarize the conflict. In this case, my intellect is saying "press on" while my feelings (and body) are saying "rest and enjoy."

Second, I show respect for both positions because even though they are opposing each other, they are still part of me and for that reason alone they deserve my equal attention. In this type of therapy, neither feelings nor intellect are considered superior. They both have value.

Finally, I use "Wise Mind," that part of me that can intuitively see which is the best course and allow it to act as the peacemaker between my intellect and feelings. Often, people will refer to it as the *gut instinct*. It's the part of us that knows what the right action is deep down inside.

In this case, my wise mind or gut tells me to focus on my purpose for this journey.

Yes, I value endurance and efficiency, but I've always been very good (or bad, depending on your perspective) at pushing myself to do things for the sake of achievement. It's like a muscle I've worked out for years; it's strong. What isn't as strong is my ability to see the value in taking care of myself. My purpose for this trip is to break through my anxiety, to learn a new way of living by cultivating a greater appreciation for *experiences* instead of focusing on *things*.

I grew up poor, so I lived much of my life believing I had to have more and better stuff: a nicer house, a luxury car, stylish clothing – anything that others would recognize as a symbol of success. On the way to buying these bigger and better things, I lost the capacity to live in the present and to enjoy simple pleasures like lying on a mountaintop and looking up at the clouds, witnessing the majesty of a great waterfall, or even writing creative stories. I didn't have time to leave the clinic, and when I did, I was too tired to do things to improve my family's and my own health.

When I was "Major Mom" on full-time active duty, after work I'd focus on *things* like cleaning the house, washing clothes, shopping. These chores had to be done after my sixty-hour workweek, so they took up all of Saturday. Sunday was spent making meals for the week and just vegging out in front of the TV as my way of recharging for the grueling week ahead.

I thought that by keeping everything organized, I was adding order and structure to our family life. I believed I was serving as a responsible role model for my sons. Maybe I was. But living in that world where the order and preservation of things had primacy came with a lifetime loan repayment that may have to be paid by my children. I can only see it now in hindsight. My boys could have experienced a very different world if I had placed a greater value on the *experience* of our life together. Like one of the other military moms, who took a push broom to the toys strewn about the living room and in one quick sweep piled them all into a corner and announced, "Now that we're done cleaning, let's go to the park!" I can almost hear the kids shouting "Yay!" Or the story I read of a family that took a yearlong sailing trip to see the world. A year of home schooling never felt so good. After the year was over, they sold the boat with improvements and made all their money back. Those are experiences that allow us to make memories with the people we love. I love money just as much as a Wall Street stockbroker, but the research is clear: past a $50,000 salary, more money does not provide more happiness. Why couldn't I see that before? Is it too late?

Even now, I find myself in an internal debate. Is it really better to make a good salary at work or to spend that same time being creative while I still have the mental and physical stamina? Working on my priorities instead of "working for the man." What value do I want to place on building memories with Joe and on his desire to explore the world while we can still climb mountains, drive the autobahn, and pilot a sailboat?

I don't want to keep saying, "No, I can't do that because I've used up all my vacation days." I want to stop putting off my life pretending I have all the time in the world for the things I want, the things I can't buy. Maybe that's the reason I keep putting off my life; it's like starting the diet "tomorrow." We put off the intangibles because they are harder to get. You can't just plop a good relationship or a meaningful memory onto your credit card. You can't just add some overtime at work to pay for them.

Joe: Elaine agreed to take the day off. She spent the morning in bed, letting her feet recover. I explored. It was an early Sunday morning and the town hadn't awakened yet. I walked the city streets and climbed the long, wide steps to Iglesia San Pedro. The walk, instead of brightening my spirits, dragged me down into a funk; the solitude was depressing. I chalked it up to culture shock and headed back to our room. It was lunchtime by then and wondered if Elaine's ready to come out and play. I realized she's a touchstone for me. I use her to pull me back to the present when my mind wanders off into murky waters.

Lesson for Today: When in doubt, make decisions that will keep your behavior in line with your purpose and values.

Chapter 12: Dark and Cold

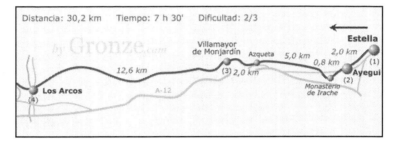

Trail Day 7, Estella to Los Arcos, 21 km

It takes a lot of courage to release the familiar and seemingly secure,
to embrace the new. There's more security in the adventurous and
exciting, for in movement there's life, and in change there's power.
- Alan Cohen

Joe: We wanted to get a head start on the day so we rose early, about 5:30, and left Estella while the streets were still dark. Walking through the city and up into the hills, we didn't see another living soul. The complete emptiness left me feeling very alone. It was cold and windy. We were wearing every single piece of warm clothing we'd brought in our backpacks.

Climbing up and out of the city, we were once again walking through the woods and vineyards, our headlamps lighting the way. We had no one to follow, no one to lead the way. It was difficult choosing the right path; the darkness and the bitter, cold wind forced us to keep our heads down. The day off gave us some much-needed rest. I had the excess energy I needed to push past the cold as well as my sullenness from the day before.

Elaine: Walking in the dark and cold was tough. Our breaths were heavy with warm, moist air that condensed into micro-clouds in front of us. We walked for over an hour before we saw another pilgrim. I could just make out his headlamp bobbing up and down on the trail behind us. The only thing that made it worth the hassle of walking in the pitch black was being able to stand on a mountaintop to watch the sunrise. Then there was also that great feeling of finishing the day before the sun had a chance to scorch us. I had heard about how hot it could be walking the Camino in the summer, but I had no idea the afternoons in the fall would be so blistering. I guess it's the whole pay me now or pay me later thing; freeze in the early morning hours or bake in the afternoon sun. Leaving later is more comfortable at the beginning: sleeping in, coffee and breakfast, sunlight, warmer temperatures. The cost is walking in the midday sun. For now, I'm willing to pay the price of leaving early and feeling cold. We did pay an extra price today though; we missed a little pilgrim's treasure. We completely passed the *Bodegas Irache*, only two kilometers outside of Estella. This was a great disappointment. What better way to celebrate agriculture than a fountain of free-flowing wine? Literally! A free wine tap mounted into a monastery's stone wall.

Joe: I'm tired of the farmland. After awhile it just becomes a blur of dirt paths, farmhouses, and field after field of crops. Walking a total of 21 kilometers, we eventually entered the little town of Los Arcos. The early morning cold transitioned to a mid-morning cool comfort and then to the sweltering heat of the afternoon. We began our daily routine of exploring the town, looking for sleeping accommodations. While stopping for a glass of wine, a patron sitting next to us at the local café recommended the Pensión Mavi. This soon initiated a meandering search through the city streets for the proprietor. Eventually we found her hanging out at the bar at the Mavi Restaurant several blocks down the street...it was siesta time. We followed her back to the Pensión Mavi, where she graciously provided us with the "Santiago Room." She copied our passports, stamped our credenciales and handed us a key before heading back to the bar.

Hanging out at a bar in Spain shouldn't be confused with hanging out at a bar in the US. In Spain, a "bar" is typically a local café that serves drinks and fresh food. Many of these bars tend to stay open throughout the day and this is where people go to relax, drink coffee, read the newspaper and catch up with friends. It's where the young and old, singles and families come to socialize. Drinking during the day is typically a beer that has been watered down 50/50 with lemonade. It tastes wonderful and it's quite refreshing. Elaine and I prefer wine to beer, but no problem: a 50/50 mix of red wine and lemonade is also popular and known as a *tinto de verano*. We're becoming quite adept at hanging out at the bars after our long hikes in the sun.

Elaine: Getting the "Santiago" room was a good omen. I often wonder whether I'll have the endurance to walk the whole 800 kilometers. After arriving and checking into our lucky room, my spirits were high. I invited Joe to have lunch at a restaurant. I'd seen a bunch of locals go into it while we were looking for the proprietor of the Mavi. The menu was hard to interpret because it consisted of only Spanish titles with no descriptions. The waitress was very kind, though; she took the time to repeat the ingredients of each dish since I'd forgotten some by the time she reached the end of the menu. I've noticed this with the other pilgrims as well; hearing several "specialties" in a restaurant is a lot like going to a party and being introduced to a bunch of new people all at once. By the time you've heard all the names, you might just as well have heard none. It's normal, but most of the time I'm embarrassed by it, or I don't want to put the waiter through the extra effort of repeating, so I just take my chances.

I ordered trout and it came fully dressed – head and all! The Spaniards don't seem to mind the fact that their meals can make eye contact! I felt a little uneasy when the waitress served me and it was time to dig in. What is the proper protocol? Do you cut off the head straight off the bat and put it aside, or is it proper etiquette to eat around it? The trout looked so lifelike, it was hard to think of it as a meal. I imagined him talking to me as I tried to figure out how to proceed:

Trout: "I was swimming in the river this morning very close to here before they caught me."
Me: "It must have been painful."

Trout: "I don't think the hook hurt me as much as saying 'adios' to my family, especially my wife and children. But I knew this day would come and I was prepared."

Me: "How could you prepare to become someone's meal?"

Trout: "I never believed my life would go on forever. I have no memory of existing before I was born. While I lived, I swam to hidden places, I laughed and I played with my family knowing each day could be my last. I even taught my children that life must be lived each moment, taking not a single second for granted. I was curious and explored everything around me. Today, for a brief moment, I saw only the bait, and missed the hook."

Me: "I'm sorry you missed that hook."

Trout: "Ahhh…but the taste of that last meal was heavenly. It was my last living memory; charging hard and fast at something I wanted and then realizing the taste of it. It was good, and so was my life."

Me: "I want to feel that way when I die. I'm just sorry you had to go like this."

Trout: "Nonsense! I'm fortunate to share my last act of love with you because you are willing to listen and I believe you understand. I wish you *buen provecho* (enjoy this meal) as my energy merges with yours."

Me: "Thanks for your kindness. I accept the lesson with gratitude."

Once I got over the difficulty of making the first move, I imagined this little creature's vitality passing through me as I savored the taste of my meal. I also realized that this fish was part of the same cycle of life and death I would follow. The fact is, there's no escaping death for any of us. The question lies in what we do to give this life meaning while we're alive. It was worth the struggle to overcome the initial aversion I felt toward this physical display of death before me – the head really did have that much impact. The trout itself was exquisitely tender and moist with a flavor that matched the reverence and gratitude I felt as I ate it. It was the product of a life well lived.

I'm starting to realize that we're learning to adapt to the Spanish culture and reaping the benefits of breaking out of our traditional customs. It requires a willingness to experience discomfort and to leave the familiar behind, at least for a while. Even walking in the dark over completely new terrain takes courage.

Lesson For Today: Be willing to stare fear straight in the eye as you try new things.

Chapter 13: Losing Track of the Days

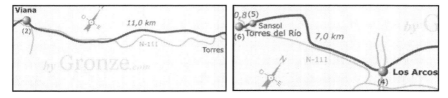

Trail Day 8, Los Arcos to Viana, 18 km

Between stimulus and response there is a space. In that space is our power to choose our response. In our response lies our growth and our freedom
 - Victor Frankl

Joe: I've lost track of how long we've been on the trail and the names of the towns we pass through. The only things I easily remember are the kilometers we've traveled, the kilometers ahead of us...and the people. Our interactions, our conversations with fellow pilgrims and the local Spaniards seem to stick with us, much more than any normal day at home.

We were walking down the road and a car passed by.

Elaine says, "Wasn't that the café owner from the other night?"

I respond, "Yeah, I think it is. Why would we remember that? We barely said a word to him."

Is it another symptom of culture shock? Is my mind on overdrive, sucking up the critical pieces of information I need to survive in this foreign environment?

Everyone I encounter seems to be engaged with life. They are friendly and interactive in a way I'm not accustomed to back home. I eventually realize it's not the people. It's me! Yes, the Spaniards are generally friendly. Yes, our fellow pilgrims tend to be more open than the typical crowd in the grocery store, but the major difference is in me. Traveling in this manner makes me vulnerable. It forces me out of my comfort zone and into a "receptive" mode. My eyes and ears are more attuned to the things around me. They have to be, we are taking risks. Our path takes us through villages, farmers' fields, narrow wooded paths, across bridges and along major roads. Our Way can be easily lost with one wrong turn. So I watch, I listen, I ask, I pause...I question my decisions to ensure we're not stranded on the top of a mountain at the end of the day.

The amount of time available for me to think as we walk has opened up another line of thought. I can sum it up by the old adage "we create our own reality." The idea is that we each see and experience our surroundings and our own lives in different ways. Most of it's based on our attitude...our approach and reactions to the events unfolding around us.

I don't want to get in too deep and start contemplating my navel, so I'll just use an example and move on: After hiking up and down 20 kilometers worth of mountains, we walk into a village. We're tired, sore, thirsty and hungry. We now have to search for accommodations, choosing between a half-dozen different hostels or albergues that are spread throughout the town. We can take one approach, I'll call "reactionary." It's based on worry and anxiety. "Will we find a bed?" "Will it be quiet?" "Will it be clean?" "Will there be bed bugs?" "Will they have hot water?" All these thoughts and more run through our heads and create stress and desperation. We seek out the familiar. We want to stay in our comfort zone and jump at the first place we think is acceptable. Invariably, when we fall into this trap, it's just a little later that we find a more interesting place to stay. One of us will then say to the other, "Gee, I wish we'd taken a little more time to check this town out before we decided."

The alternative approach is what I'll call "inquisitive." It's based on having faith. It's having the courage and the strength to remain open to our surroundings with patience instead of fear. The inquisitive approach would look like this: We enter a village and just relax, maybe wander around a bit, maybe we drop our backpacks and relax with a glass of wine in the central plaza. This requires a leap of faith because we're exhausted and just want to find a bed, lie down and rest. To make it worse, some of the pilgrims we walk in with already know where they'll be staying and are busily searching for their lodging and getting settled for the evening.

Sooner or later, by taking just a little extra time and staying curious, we get the feel of the town. We watch where the pilgrims gather, where the locals congregate, and we allow events to naturally unfold. This method always, always works. Some local resident points us in a direction or even takes us by the hand. We find an ideal place to stay, an exceptional local café with fresh food and good company.

We take the time to learn and explore and this patience pays off because we find a place that is well suited to our desires. Could there have been an even better place to stay? Probably. An even better place to eat, more interesting people to meet? Most likely, yes. Even the place we choose after taking our time could have been the same exact place we saw as we walked into town. But our attitude and our approach make all the difference. Whatever happens is based on an active choice instead of a powerless submission to anxiety due to fatigue and feelings of vulnerability. We no longer feel like victims; we're active participants in how we want events to unfold. We really are creating our own reality.

The pilgrims of earlier centuries had no idea where they were going to lay their heads at night, no idea if they would have a meal available at the end of the day. They risked sickness, injuries, bandits, wars, extreme weather and religious persecution. All they had was their faith in their God and in their fellow man to provide for them when the need came. We sure have it a lot easier in our modern world, and yet we often feel even more vulnerable then those pilgrims that came before us. Simply because we have come to expect a level of predictability they had never experienced.

Arriving in the large town of Viana around midday, we searched for a pensión that was recommended to us by an old man who was handing out flyers. It seems that the capability of these folks to make maps that can actually guide a stranger to a specific place is still evolving. I think it comes with the village culture. Everyone traditionally knows the details of their town because they've lived there all their lives. In many of these towns, the number of outsiders has been very limited before the recent explosion of pilgrims on the Camino. Now that there are thousands of pilgrims passing through each year, the need for additional accommodations and the competition between facilities has also increased. Thus, an elderly man, obviously a farmer at one time by his appearance, is now drawing maps and printing out flyers to guide the tired pilgrim to a warm meal and a soft bed.

As best we tried, we could not find the hostel using the map on his flyer. Meandering through the streets and alleyways, we eventually found the building that coincided with the arrow marked on the map. I knocked at the door but no answer. I knocked again and waited.

A female voice asking, "Quién es?" came booming out of an old dilapidated intercom mounted next to the door.

Elaine explained that we had used a flyer to direct us to this building and asked if this was a hostel. Seconds later, the door was unlocked and there stood a middle-aged woman, holding a dishrag and a ladle, obviously preparing dinner in her *private* home. Elaine self-consciously explained why we were knocking on her door and without knowing the language I could tell she seemed to be apologizing profusely. The woman just smiled as we stumbled with the awkwardness.

She said in Spanish, "You're at the wrong house. My son, Ivan, will show you the way back to the center of town."

She then turned around to her son standing behind her. "Ivan! Make sure they make it back to the town square before nightfall!"

She turned back to us with a smile. It was mid-afternoon and the square was only five minutes away. Within minutes we found ourselves being led back to the central square by our teenage guide.

Ivan was tall with curly hair and eyes so dark he appeared to have no pupils. He was clearly the neighborhood Don Juan. He led us back down the streets, greeting and briefly chatting with every attractive girl we passed. They all knew him and seemed happy for the brief attention he paid them. Once we arrived back in the center square, he walked us up to another couple, two Canadians waiting in front of a large door. The Tourist Center was closed for siesta.

Elaine: The different realities we've experienced in searching for accommodations, just by changing our attitude, strikes to the core of this Camino for me.

Growing up in New York City, a town where our motto is "don't make eye contact," I've been brought up to believe that people are either prey or predator. As I noted in Pamplona, unless I actively fight the fear, the habit of worrying about city crimes and dangers will always win. I've missed out on some decidedly sensational experiences because of it. Each time I fight the desire for security, I receive an insight. When I'm really lucky, it takes me to some eye-watering sight that makes me think, "I could die right now and be happy."

Today, we'd walked into the town of Viana feeling perfectly lost. There were so many buildings, people everywhere, so much unfamiliarity mixed with my own tension that I just gave up on the idea of taking our time and letting things unfold.

"Joe, we've tried it your way with that whole 'inquisitive' thing since we got here. Tonight I just want to find a place, any place as long as it gets us out of this crowd!"

I insisted on going to the Tourist Center right away. "We can get some quick hotel information there." Joe reluctantly agreed.

It was closed.

While we waited, Joe struck up a conversation with some Canadians who were also waiting for the Tourist Center to open. They'd completed their Camino and were hoping to get some information about their follow-on trip to Sicily. The couple soon grew tired of waiting and after some more chatting, they decided to move along. Now it was just Joe and me. I was still insisting we find *any* room, while Joe argued for resting at a local bar to buy us some time away from the busy streets. I'm not sure how this looked to the strangers around us, but we suddenly had one step forward to interrupt our bickering. She was a primly dressed woman who appeared to be in her nineties.

She asked in Spanish, "Are you going to Mass?"

I curtly answered, "No!" still heated from our debate. I immediately checked myself. Then I tried to explain more gently that we were waiting to ask about local accommodations. As we talked about the town and our failed attempts with the map, this wizened and frail woman offered to take us to her house and have us stay with her family! I could not believe what I was hearing. I quickly declined, afraid of imposing, but I could see she was offering from her heart. It's as if she had stopped being an "elderly woman" and transformed into a ministering angel on the Camino. She was barely able to walk, using a cane for balance, but she gently touched my arm and said,

"Don't worry, I will take you to find a place to rest."

Even now, as I lay on this bed in a quaint and comfortable room, I still can't get over how we got here. Did our friend, Pete, have similar experiences? Is this why he believed that everything here happens for a reason, with a purpose? I had my own lesson to learn today. I had given up on my intention to stay in the moment and observe. I lost patience with Joe and let circumstances dictate my behavior.

I told Joe, "I let my fear take over today. I felt like I had to get back in control when all that crowd in the central square started closing in on me."

Joe looked at me and just smiled.

I pressed, "What?" I know he's sitting on one of his little mental gold nuggets.

Still silence.

"C'mon, you know you want to tell me, so just spill it."

Joe finally budges. "Do you think it's a coincidence that just when you lost your faith, when you made that choice to go against your intention for this Camino, God sent a messenger to pull you back?"

Lesson for Today: Making a leap of reason or faith requires both feet to be off the ground at once. The action is the same whether jumping off a sidewalk or the Empire State Building; the difference is intention.

Chapter 14: Having Faith

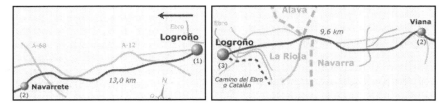

Trail Day 9, Viana to Navarrete, 22 km

Nothing can cure the soul but the senses, just as nothing can cure the senses but the soul.
- Oscar Wilde

Joe: We walked up and down rolling hills and into the large and beautiful city of Logroño. It was the most modern-looking city we'd seen since we started. It was lunchtime and the streets were busy with businessmen and women. We felt a little out of place with our clothes and backpacks covered with a layer of grit as we wandered through the streets. Both of us were hungry so we stopped at a wine bar popular with the business crowd. They served us wonderfully delicious pinchos and a fine local wine.

"Why don't we spend the night here?"

Elaine replied, "Let's keep going. I feel good this afternoon."

I was hesitant. Elaine's feet had been very tender during the morning walk. I countered, "It's probably that glass of wine that's talking."

As we walked out of the city, I repeatedly argued against it. Elaine insisted.

Elaine: Logroño has a vitality and diversity I wasn't expecting. It's the capital of the La Rioja province and combines the modern amenities of a city with bars that are intimate but crowd-pleasing. The city was recently awarded the "2012

Gastronomic Capitol of Spain" by the Capital Española de la Gastronomía. The wine is world-famous, but a glass can be purchased for only 2.50 euros, even in this cosmopolitan enclave. It appears that today is all about delighting the senses. I'm surrendering to every pleasure: tasting, seeing and smelling the savory food and wines; the bright red tomatoes bursting with flavor; the green pickled *guindilla* peppers; sweet black pudding; the rich aromatic smell of the coffee; and the whispers of spice permeating the deep burgundy Rioja wine. To round out the senses, I attended to the voices and frequent laughter of the locals socializing around me. I felt the hot sun, the bar's hard wood surface, and later, Joe's warm hand on mine as we walked. It's strange to hold someone's hand while you're both wearing backpacks. I imagine we look like two lumbering turtles up on hind legs, the backpacks like two heavy shells attached to our spines and causing us to waddle more than walk because our hands are joined. I share the image with Joe.

"Well, we may look like two turtles, but at least we still care enough to maintain human contact," he says, then playfully squeezes my hand.

Joe: Each day I'd ensured we had the right amount of water to drink. I hadn't even been aware of it. Too much and it's an extra load on our bodies. Too little and we become dehydrated, drained of our energy. By the time we reached Navarrete, we'd completely drained our water bottles. I think it's a survival instinct that drives me to control our pace. It was also my own pain from watching Elaine suffer. I didn't like it one bit. We pushed too hard and it was obvious to me that we'd have to take another day off. We soon checked into an albergue and Elaine crawled into bed to rest.

A number of people wouldn't even attempt to walk the Camino, they'd be afraid of the pain and discomfort. These fears prevent people from living. Elaine would never have attempted this journey if not for me. Now that we're here, her fear has come true: excruciating pain. There's something strange about it though; her fear is gone. She is fearless. She suffers every day, but she's the one who pushes, telling me, "I'm fine, let's keep going." Well, I'm not fine.

"Elaine, I'm tired, I really need to take a day off."

She replies with a smile. "Okay, I'll do it for you."

Ahhh, now I know the trick, tell her it's me that needs to stop.

Elaine: I woke up this morning with my feet swollen, and feeling as if they were being torched. Just getting out of bed was like walking on hot coals and the heat seemed to transform into shards of glass where my heels used to be.

I tell Joe, "I don't think I can do this anymore."

"What about your decision to stay open and let things unfold?" he chides.

I reply, "Well, you said I could pull the plug at any time."

I pause, waiting for his excuse, his counterargument. But the sly dog answers, "Okay. When do you want to leave?"

Damn! Why does he have to be so supportive? I don't really want to leave. I just can't use my feet to get to Compostela. There's no way Joe would ever take a taxi, so I don't even ask. It goes against the whole idea of our pilgrimage anyway. I picture myself saying, "Hi, God, I finally made it to Compostela! I'm here to be pardoned for all my sins. You know, the ones where I did what was good for me and decided to ignore your rules, but I just didn't enjoy the walking so I decided to catch a cab to pick up my plenary indulgence. That's cool with you, right?"

What I really say is, "But Joe, I don't want to quit; I just can't use my feet anymore."

He's the engineer; maybe he can figure something out. Joe sits on the bed and rubs my feet with oil. He's thinking. Joe's always thinking.

"What about the naproxen, are you taking it every day?"

I say, "I'm taking naproxen *and* fish oil, but it's not enough. Look at my feet; they look like two red water balloons!"

Joe has been watching me wince as he rubs my feet and seems convinced that more drastic measures are called for.

"I hear the pharmacies here are pretty liberal compared to the States. Let's go visit one to see if we can get some different inserts for your shoes or medicine to take down the swelling."

As I dress for going outside, my feet are too swollen to fit into my size five shoes, so I leave in Joe's size eleven Crocs – really attractive.

At the pharmacy, Joe met a familiar pilgrim and they started a conversation. I was happy for the chance to peruse freely. I made a point of speaking to the pharmacist in Spanish, asking about shoe inserts and pointing to the various Compeed products, hoping to build up the courage to ask about stronger drugs, more than just NSAIDS. The pharmacist was very friendly and she seemed to understand my Spanish easily, but she kept showing me ointments and topical NSAID like diclofenac, and, of course, ibuprofen. After pretending to be interested for a few more minutes, I finally compressed the air in my lungs and shot out the words, "Tienes oxycodono?" I held my breath, and then I held my swollen foot up trying to prove to her that I wasn't an addict looking to get high from opiates.

She seemed genuinely sorry when she explained, "Esa medicina se vende solamente con prescripción." ("That medicine is sold only by prescription.") She said it so apologetically I didn't even feel uncomfortable. But I could see she had an "aha" moment and she dashed to the back room, returning with a slim little box labeled *codeína*.

"We normally prescribe it for cough, but you could use it for pain," she told me. "We also have prednisone for very bad inflammation."

Before my decision to buy, I debated taking this drug for my pain. I remembered a Chinese doctor, an expert in Qi Gong, who once told me, "You doctors in the West see pain and you give pain *killer*. In China we see pain as language of the body. Body is communicating. Saying something is wrong. Chinese medicine try to understand the message, to work with it, not kill it."

Then I thought about what Joe would say: "Do you really need that?" They are simple words, but they feel like a stern admonition from him. I consider the walk back to the room, and even worse the walk of shame back home because I "couldn't hack it." It only takes a second for me to decide, "Screw it! I'm going to kill that pain." I look straight into the pharmacist's eyes and ask, "Cuánto?" (How much?)

It's also good to know the prednisone is there too. It's one bad mammy jammer of a drug. I know it can have some pretty significant adverse effects on vital organs like the liver and the body's ability to fight off infections. Then again, nothing else, especially in the non-steroidal family, even comes close. Prednisone is a straight-up steroid; there is no "non-steroidal" about it. I won't even consider that one today, but I will file it for future reference since it requires a prescription in the States.

I walked out of the pharmacy, but Joe was out of sight. I didn't even take three hobbled steps before tearing through the box and breaking the blister pack to expose one innocent little codeine tablet. *Should I take one or two?* I ask myself. They're 30 mg apiece. I should only take one to be safe. But I don't want to chance the walk tomorrow. I pop two in my mouth.

One hour later, I'm lying in bed, feet propped up and writing. I'm feeling a warm glow. I've never felt any effect from codeine in the past when I've taken the liquid formulation for strep throat pain. Why is it so different this time? My body is changing, and maybe my metabolism is too. No more two-pill doses for me. But I do notice my feet feeling closer to normal. This is good. I'm going to add it to my daily regimen: Naproxen 500 mg, Omega-3 1000 mg, Codeine 30 mg.

Should I tell Joe, or will he judge me? He'll probably say its wrong to kill the pain instead of resting more or buying different shoes or inserts. Also known as *listening to what my body is telling me.* I know I should do all of these things, but they take too long. What if my body is telling me "I can't do this?" And besides, medicines are made for a purpose, in this case to relieve pain. What's so wrong with that if it works? My conscience answers, *What's wrong is you could be doing some long-term damage by not listening to your body when it's telling you something.*

Uggghh, I've got to get off this mental roller coaster. I've decided. I'm taking the codeine and I'll accept the consequences.

Lesson for Today: Practice letting go of the mental chatter and stop "shoulding" on yourself.

Chapter 15: Searching for Hidden Gems

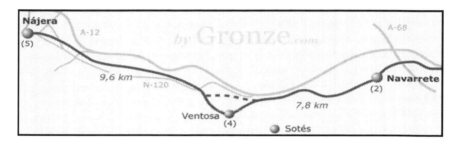

Trail Day 10, Navarrete to Najerilla (Najera), 16 km

If everyone is thinking alike, then no one is thinking.
-Benjamin Franklin

Elaine: Do you know there are hidden dining treasures in Spain? If you are the average tourist like me, you can easily miss them because it's so easy to find an open table along the sidewalks and riverbanks. These tables are easy to spot, typically in places where you can just sit, relax and watch the world go by. This quick and easy culinary experience can be quite satisfying and can offer some good people-watching opportunities. But Joe and I discovered a very different side of Spain that is even more meaningful to us because it meshes with our philosophy of having faith and taking the time to blend in with the local people in the places they call their own.

We arrived in Najera just in time to discover that there was "no room at the inn." There was an agricultural fair going on for the weekend and the place was packed with people. It will come as no surprise that Joe and I implemented our practice of checking our worry and taking our time. It worked like a charm. We wandered some more and found a quaint little hotel near everything, that is, after we figured out where everything was. We settled into our room and decided it was time to eat. Walking through the winding streets, we passed many of the obvious riverbank restaurants where the pilgrims were devouring the standard pilgrim's meal. We walked past them, enjoying the scenery, choosing to explore with the faith that things would work.

We happened upon a small restaurant off the beaten track with a bar and a few small tables. The menu looked good and the prices even better: 10 euros for three courses and a bottle of wine. We're starting to become more expert at sniffing out places where the locals hang out, and even though this place was small and pretty empty, we decided to go on in and test it out. Not more than five seconds after announcing we were there for dinner, we were whisked down to the cellar where the place was absolutely booming with Spaniards. The outside of the restaurant had given us no clue to what was inside. There was no printed menu and the waitress spoke only Spanish. It seems they have no need for multilingual menus because there are no patrons who require translating in these sequestered spaces.

The wine in this region is from the Rioja valley, produced from the very vines we've been passing and sampling for the last several days. These grapevines are as thick as an elephant's leg, and the grapes are dark purple, plump and bursting with succulent sweetness. They've consistently revived us as our energy wanes from all the walking. The grapes can be purchased anywhere. The Spaniards appear to love their produce; even the smallest grocery stores are filled to capacity with fresh fruits and vegetables.

It's also clear that the people here are unabashedly proud of their wine. So much so that the waitress was offended when we suggested we might want to try a wine other than a Rioja today. "All our wines here are the best; you are in Rioja," she sniffed.

We quickly checked ourselves and offered, "Of course, we would love a bottle of Rioja" and all was right with the world again. Even the stuffed red chili peppers were fresh off the local vines with an earthy, organic flavor that can only come from just-picked, ripe, local produce.

By the time we finished dinner, it was dark out and the locals had come out to visit the fair. I kidded with Joe, "I'm from New York City. What do you wear to an agricultural fair?" We both laughed because we knew I only had one change of clothing.

It was dark, but lights shined on each visitor reflecting every age and color in a scintillating constellation of skin tones and dermal creases. One thing was the same for all of them: a love of food. I'm not used to seeing people in their 80's mixing in with teenagers and adult couples and babies on a Friday night. But there they were all together, ordering chocolate crepes, plump sausages and cold drinks side by side. There was no awkwardness, no one visibly impatient when the elderly required more time to complete their transactions, meticulously counting pennies from their purses. There was no one clutching a purse or wallet in fear. We stayed out later than our typical pilgrim bedtime of 10:00, but that's okay.

Lesson for Today: Take time to find cultural and culinary treasures; a warm, local bistro or a local food festival can rival travel pictures for creating cherished memories.

Chapter 16: Walking Our Own Camino

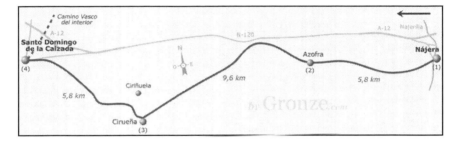

Trail Day 11, Najerilla to Santo Domingo de la Calzada, 21 km

The cost of a thing is the amount of what I will call life, which is required to be exchanged for it, immediately or in the long run.
- Henry David Thoreau

Elaine: We had a particularly late start this morning. The breakfast and the company were so inviting we lost track of the time. Sitting at the table next to us were two unfamiliar pilgrims, Patty and Len from Canada. They were walking at about the same pace as us, having left on the same day from St. Jean, but we hadn't crossed paths before. They freely shared some of their history. He operates their campground in Calgary and she is a former paralegal.

Patty had no trouble disclosing, "I lost my job clear out of the blue."

She explained that being unemployed had allowed her time to walk the Camino but, "It's the lack of income that's getting to me. I don't want to be spreading A-1 sauce on dog food when I'm older because I can't afford to eat steak."

She peers across the table expectantly and waits for laughter. I know she is making an effort to take the edge off her own worry. So

I laugh even though I'm starting to wonder which brand of dog food taste closest to real steak...just in case the same thing happens to me.

Patty was so open about losing her job I found myself eagerly sharing how I had left my own job with the military.

"I just couldn't listen to the soldiers without feeling angry and nervous. I knew I definitely wasn't feeling hopeful, so the whole 'instilling hope' thing stopped being believable even for me. I lost the hopefulness," I reiterated for emphasis.

"But now," I confided as if I'd known her for years, "I feel guilty because I know there are so many people I can still help. These people *need* me and I'm walking away."

Then I swallowed hard and finished it: "What's even worse is I don't *want* to go back."

Patty listened, and I could tell from her squinting, pensive look that she was thinking very seriously about her answer.

Then she gave a little head bob as if the thought had finally settled. "Can you really help someone to move out from that deep dark place when you're stuck yourself? I mean stuck and without a flashlight?"

Her eyes held my gaze, and there was no hint of doubt to the answer. She expected me to say, "No" and we both knew it.

I hesitated, but she pressed her advantage. "Leaving a job or even retiring doesn't mean you stop working, Elaine; it means you get to stop long enough to figure out what you need...without having to apologize to a boss."

I could feel the knot in my stomach, the one I feel whenever I think about my job, start to loosen, and I wanted her to keep talking.

"It's your time to be creative: to paint, to write, to...to get out and walk the Camino!" She laughed heartily.

Then she reached out and touched my hand, "Let yourself enjoy this time before you decide what to do."

I think Patty understood what I needed because she was working through the same worries. But, there was an important difference between the two of us, she knew what she wanted.

"I want to start a business selling organic cosmetics. I've already developed some products that are selling faster than I can make them, but we just don't have the money for any kind of big production."

This didn't seem to dampen her excitement though. "I know it's going to work if I can get some investors because my customers are actually driving for hours back to our campground just to get more of the lotions I've made. I think it's because of the essential oils I've been experimenting with."

Len overheard his wife's last comment and noted lovingly, "It's true. Just the other day one woman's husband drove sixty miles just to get one of the lotions Patty made. He said it was for his wife's birthday and it would make a great present because she was convinced it improved her age spots."

Patty appears to be a strong woman who follows her dreams. I resolved to spend more time with her.

We also met another pilgrim this morning. Her name is Susan and she's walking the Camino alone. Susan had arranged before the trip to have her backpack sent ahead each morning to the next place she'd planned to stay.

"I want to enjoy the walk, not the strain," she pronounced.

She's the kind of woman that's used to getting what she wants, and she shared her opinions openly with an air that suggested she always knows best.

"The Camino does not have to be grueling."

Susan is a successful civil rights attorney and she decided to walk the Camino as a break from her demanding life. It's ironic how she brings her regimented schedule with her on the Camino, a journey she's using as a means to de-stress.

"At 8:00 a.m. I have my breakfast. By 9:00 a.m., I've taken my Omega-3, DHA, CoQ-10, Ibuprofen, calcium and multi-vitamin. Then I'm out the door."

Susan told us she had all of her hotels booked before she left Canada and knew where her luggage would be delivered at all times.

She explained the itinerary she and her luggage followed, as a teacher would review a lesson with a pair of slow students: "The luggage is not always delivered to my hotel. Sometimes it has to be sent to a nearby bar or restaurant where it sits until I can retrieve it."

When we asked if Susan took any unplanned days off for rest or relaxation, she looked mortified. "All my reservations are booked way in advance. Any time off has to be scheduled or it would throw off every other reservation I've already made."

She had made a point of picking only the best and safest hotels right from the beginning. It was ironic when she shared her irritation over a bed bug infestation she had fallen victim to at one of the tour-approved establishments.

"I didn't just get bitten by bed bugs; I had a terrible allergic reaction that landed me in one of the local clinics."

She received an antihistamine shot and the swelling subsided, but she quickly got back on the trail to keep up with her luggage. Susan was clearly a woman who would not be deterred. We finished breakfast and wished Susan, Patty and Len a "Buen Camino" as we headed out the door.

Out in the daylight with our bellies full and the day's hike ahead of us, Joe and I were glad we had no plans and no schedule. After our conversation with Susan, it seemed like such a luxury to go at our own pace and carry our own backpacks. I pictured Susan as the rabbit from *Alice in Wonderland* walking the Camino, all the while exclaiming, "I'm late, I'm late…for a very important date." I could not be relaxed with that kind of pressure. But I think Susan has found her own zone. It would probably have been too alien for her to have no schedule. The Camino was taking her outdoors and out of her high-powered law practice. She was getting exercise, fresh air, meeting people with different perspectives, seeing and photographing breathtaking sights and eating splendid meals for a full thirty days, even if it was on a fixed schedule. In fact, the schedule may have been the familiar handle she used to start this foray into the unfamiliar.

Joe: Our path took us through more desolate fields of recently harvested crops. The earth had turned to hard clay with layers of dust on top that slowly migrated up over our shoes, eventually covering our pant legs. The farm roads cut through the small hillocks of the reddish-brown earth, exposing several meters of strata. I poked at it with my trekking pole to test its consistency. It looked like packed earth but felt like solid rock. It must have been here for several millennia. My mind wandered down ancient paths, images of farmers a thousand years past, breaking the earth of these rolling hills with pick-axes and horse drawn plows. Looking closer at the strata, I wondered if there were buried artifacts inches away, waiting to be discovered.

I started thinking about my dad and how he would have loved this trek. He loved the outdoors and spent most of his life outside. He had tough, leathery skin that told anyone who saw him that he was a man of the earth, a man that worked and played under the sun, the wind and the rain. I pictured him ambling down the road beside me, telling jokes or just teasing me about one thing or another.

I slowly drifted away from Elaine as we walked. Fifteen minutes later, she noticed that I'd fallen behind and stopped to wait for me.

"What's wrong?"

"Nothing!" I replied and pushed on.

I realized I was in a foul mood: feeling impatient, bored. I was tired of the slow, methodical, incremental steps and this monotonous landscape. I just wanted the day to be over.

We climbed several more hills over the next few hours, eventually reaching the peak and the anticlimactic outskirts of Cirueña. Apparently, modern-day developers had attempted to build an American-style community of townhomes, condos, and a golf course, complete with an uninviting concrete clubhouse. It was an abysmal failure; a ghost town of unkempt lawns, empty houses and "Se Vende" (For Sale) signs everywhere. I don't think the Spanish culture was ready for this onslaught of modern suburbia.

I turned to Elaine, "This would make a perfect minimum security prison."

She nodded in surprise. "I was just thinking how that building over there reminds me of every penitentiary I've ever seen on TV."

She smiled. I didn't.

The mild and sunny weather of the morning had turned into a cold drizzle as we entered the development. I didn't want to stop. It was almost scary: the emptiness, the desolation. The gloom was as thick as the wet, cold air blowing around us, blowing right through me. We bundled up. I looked down at my feet and kept walking.

We left the failed suburbia behind and entered the original town of Cirueña, the old stone buildings welcoming us back to Spain. At this time of year, after the harvest, it's quiet. A few farmers worked on their machinery inside their barns and an occasional pilgrim walked by. We sat down on an old, unpainted wooden bench and pulled out some stale bread and cheese we'd been carrying for several days. We shifted closer to each other in an attempt to stay warm and ate our meal in silence.

It was difficult to take a break from the walking, to rest when it was so cold. We were just trading one form of discomfort for another. After about five minutes, the chill started to set in.

I looked at Elaine expectantly. "Are you ready?"

She nodded her head, and we slowly got up from the bench.

Elaine said, "I think my body is reacting to that haunted town; my legs are feeling like lead!"

"C'mon, it's just the cold," I said.

I knew she was trying to break the shroud of disenchantment we were both feeling, but I wasn't ready. We stretched our legs and torsos as much as the rain gear and backpacks would let us and headed further down the road.

We stepped onto the wet dirt farm roads that separated the large square plots of barren fields. A long line of pilgrims spread out ahead of us, heading for the top of a wooded hill on the horizon. Their heads were lowered, their parkas blowing in the wind. All of us were heading northeast, but it was like trying to move a rook diagonally across a chessboard. First west for several hundred meters, then north for several hundred more and then west again, weaving around the square plots of land. A younger and more energetic couple passed us.

I had an idea. Turning to Elaine I said, "Follow me!" As pilots like to say, "We'll go 'VFR direct.' We'll make better time than that pair."

I lacked the patience for humor and wasted steps. We stumbled through a drainage ditch that separated the field from the road, slipping on the wet grassy slopes as we moved. We entered the barren field and headed directly for the line of pilgrims disappearing over the next hill. I'd outsmarted them.

As we walked through the field, I started to notice a slow but steady heaviness in my footsteps. The soft, recently plowed ground was a bit more difficult to walk on than the hard-packed roads. We marched on. My feet were still getting heavier, and I looked down. The dust covering the fields had turned to mud, and a thin layer stuck to the bottom of our shoes like glue. Each step we took added a new layer to the last and before long, it felt like we were wearing heavy snowshoes. I glanced over at the younger couple still taking the long way around. They were beating *us*! We struggled through the field, having to stop repeatedly to scrape the mud off our shoes with our trekking poles.

Elaine's only words were, "That's what we get for cheating on the Camino."

I realized that the shortest distance between two points isn't always a straight line and I drifted off on a mental exercise about physics, wormholes and the lost art of being a couch potato.

Walking into the town of Santo Domingo, we were wet and feeling miserable. Okay, I was miserable. Elaine, despite her aching feet and wet clothing, was in a good mood as we wandered the streets, exploring and searching for an albergue. We walked toward the center of town and noticed a large, thick wooden door that looked hundreds of years old. It was mounted with heavy wrought iron, black hinges and had an array of iron studs and a sign that read: "Abadia Cisterciense." We entered the small courtyard and walked through the main entranceway. Behind the counter at the end of a short, narrow hallway was a small, elderly nun. She welcomed us into their faithful community for the night. I was very tired. Elaine and I quickly settled into our room and then did some clothes washing by hand. Afterwards, I crawled into bed. It felt like such a luxury, the old mattress on top of the steel bed frame felt like a soft cloud of down. I drifted off into a deep sleep. It was 7:00 pm.

Elaine: I just returned to our communal sleeping area after a raucous dinner party. I walked over to Joe, curled up in his sleeping bag, and whispered,

"Are you awake?"

No reply.

The dinner I'd just come from could have been cast straight out of the movie *The Way*. He would've loved it.

We arrived in Santo Domingo de la Calzada late in the afternoon and decided to stay in an albergue run by Cistercian nuns. The ancient structure is attached to the village church and feels just like a convent. On the ground floor is a communal kitchen and eating area with stonewalls, a wood-beamed ceiling and a huge fireplace with giant logs burning in it. After reaching our individual beds, I laid down to rest and journal, but there was no way for me to relax or even keep writing with all the noise. A bunch of pilgrims were downstairs bursting into loud spasmodic fits of laughter, their voices rising and falling like a roller coaster.

I was heading downstairs to find out what the ruckus was all about when I met a middle-aged redheaded Australian woman named Trisha. She wore a grey wool fedora hat with a tiny red feather and several Camino pins embedded in its black headband. She had the look of a seasoned trekker.

"We're having a pilgrim's dinner. Why don't you come? You can have a glass of wine with us."

I wasn't sure if I was ready to mingle with such a raucous crowd, so I hesitated. She stopped in mid-step,

"Oh! I forgot the wine. I was so busy arranging for my bags I forgot to grab it."

Trisha had a British accent, not a working class Australian accent like the one you might associate with the famous Crocodile Hunter, Steve Irwin. I didn't know that Australians had different accents.

I asked, "Do you need any help?"

But she was gone.

I walked into the crowded dining room alone, feeling tentative. I didn't know anyone, so I decided to hang back by taking a seat on the other side of the dining room. This gave me a full view of the long wooden table overflowing with peregrinos from all around the world. They were laughing, eating, and drinking wine out of a leather "bota bag," trying to see who could take the longest swig. The laughter was ear splitting with frequent clapping, picture taking and overall rabble rousing.

On my side of the room were the still interested but more sedate pilgrims like me. I think we liked the euphoria, but from a distance. One woman in her late 60's, who was doing her second Camino, introduced herself and explained she had first walked the

Camino because she was at a "crossroads" in her life. This was a recurring theme. One young man from Ohio who was sitting with us had just completed his two-year Peace Corps commitment. Another couple we'd met earlier that day was just starting retirement, and yet another pilgrim was recovering from a divorce.

Is it true that the Camino calls to people who are trying to make an important life decision? If so, why? What is it about the Camino that is so attractive during times of grief or uncertainty? The obvious answer is that it's a perfect time to seek a closer relationship with God. But most of the people I've talked to so far have expressed little desire to commune with God. Even I haven't done much more than attend a few Masses so as not to feel guilty about receiving my plenary indulgence.

As we discussed some of our theories around the fire, there was a consensus that the Camino brings us closer to our most basic form of existence: finding food and shelter, and lots of movement. We're all pushing our physical and mental endurance, testing our limits of pain, joy, and sometimes boredom.

It's as if we're working from the bottom rung of Maslow's hierarchy of needs. It's at this very core, at this basic foundation, that we can begin to construct the lives we intend to build. The Camino first strips us down to mostly physical beings with some brief flirtations with the spirit. At first we dream about how simple our lives can be, but these are merely punctuations in the running cacophony of burning feet, brain-numbing fatigue and the persistent inner battle over what to eliminate from our backpacks. As we continue walking, we're forced to realize how many of our material possessions are simply unnecessary.

The backpack is a good example of the axiom "that which you own, owns you." The Peace Corps pilgrim talked about a quote from Thoreau that says something to the effect that your material possessions do not only cost what you paid for them, but also what you give up in order to have them. I've heard uniformly from other pilgrims that the Walk of St. James teaches you just how little you really need to live a happy life and maybe that's what draws us closer to the spirit, to a more lasting peace. As I glanced over at the joyous crowd eating a simple meal of stewed olives, onions, tomatoes and pasta, I think, *Thoreau would have enjoyed it here.*

And speaking of a simple life, it's close to 10:00, way past this pilgrim's bedtime.

I lean over and kiss Joe goodnight. He looked sad today. I guess our load can also become heavier from the emotions we carry. I make a note to remind him tomorrow to practice releasing some of the feelings he seemed to be clinging to this afternoon. Then I silently crawl into my bed and drift off to sleep while listening to the distant sounds of laughter echoing up the stairway from the floor below.

Lesson for Today: The lighter the load, the greater the freedom.

Chapter 17: If God Really Wanted Us to Fly

Trail Day 12, Santo Domingo de la Calzada to Belorado, 23 km

Habit is habit and not to be flung out of the window by any man, but coaxed downstairs a step at a time.
- Mark Twain

Elaine: Why do people like to travel? Think about it. If God really wanted us to fly, he would've made it easier to get through airport security.

Given that I'm primarily a hermit, I'm trying to draw on my own perspective to understand what keeps many of us at home and away from the airport. Personally, I feel safer in my familiar spaces, especially since I have an exceptionally bad sense of direction. Always knowing where my two favorite places are, the bedroom and the kitchen, gives me a warm feeling of security. There's little planning required for my basic needs: food, water, shelter and cable. I rarely wander very far from any of them. I usually don't feel a great need to socialize, so I don't feel I'm missing out on the world by maintaining my privacy and avoiding strangers. If I feel a great need for the exotic, there's always Netflix, Amazon, TED Talks and Chinese delivery.

So what the heck am I doing here on an 800-kilometer pilgrimage in northern Spain? Why did I leave my job with great pay, flexible hours, and a beautiful house on the water in a perfectly warm and sunny climate?

I know it's important to have a partner who pushes me out of my comfort zone from time to time, but that can't be the whole reason. I wouldn't feel so happy on this pilgrimage if I were purely doing it for someone else. Oh, and I do feel happy. I sing on the path every day with zeal and outright abandon that I had no idea I was capable of – especially since I have a lousy singing voice. Trisha, the Australian pilgrim I met last night, says she also sings at the top of her lungs (at a safe distance from the others). "Follow the Yellow Brick Road" seems to be an all-around favorite.

Another added incentive is cost. Given Spain's economy and the declining euro, it's very reasonable to travel here. Joe and I are picky about some things. For him, it's good food and coffee. For me, it's occasionally staying at a quiet, private place to rest and unwind at the end of a 25-kilometer day. Despite these somewhat stringent requirements by Camino standards, we're spending less than 75 euros ($100) per day total, much less than most vacations would cost. Some who are traveling with us are spending less than half of that. They are staying at the communal albergues every night for around 8 euros, buying food at local grocery stores and eating only pilgrim's meals, all adding up to less than 30 euros per day.

I'm learning that not just every day, but every hour can be a new adventure. Today we climbed a mountain, walked through a pine-scented forest where we stopped for a picnic lunch and listened to nature's equivalent of a crowded housing project with about a hundred birds in one tree all singing and chirping at once. And that was all before noon!

This afternoon was just as entertaining. We sat and discussed politics with some Brits, Germans and an Australian. One of them asked, "Is it true that 90% of Americans don't own a passport?" I couldn't answer that question, but I did say, "It wouldn't surprise me. I didn't get mine until I was forty."

I guess this brings me back full circle. I'm not sure why some people have the wanderlust and take to traveling like fish to water. Is it genetic, an uncommon level of curiosity? Is it confidence in their navigation and problem-solving skills? Perhaps it's a desire to meet people of diverse thoughts and cultures? I imagine it's all of these. But, as a person who does not like to travel, I can declare firsthand that you don't need any reason to find yourself singing "Follow the Yellow Brick Road" in a totally unfamiliar country with complete strangers.

Lesson for Today: If you keep doing what you always did, you'll keep getting what you always got. So why not try something new and get something you've always wanted?

Chapter 18: Fouling Up

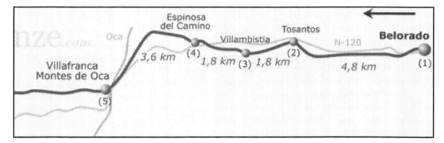

Trail Day 13, Belorado to Villafranca de Montes de Oca, 12 km

Even if you stumble, you're still moving forward.
- Victor Kiam

Elaine: We walked only three hours, reaching Villafranca de Montes de Oca before lunch. It was billed in the guidebook as an untidy, noisy, trucking route of a town. Most of the pilgrims we walked into the town with had already decided they would only stop for lunch and quickly move on. But we had a mind to explore.

We strolled less than a kilometer before hitting pay dirt. It was a Camino trifecta: a pilgrims' albergue attached to a luxurious hotel, the "Queen's Hospice," nestled just above the ancient Romanesque Church of Santiago. Both of us knew instantly we wanted to stay there for the night. After settling into the albergue, we decided to take a tour of the hotel, starting with its coat of arms displayed proudly at the entrance. We'd only gone a few feet when we saw Patty and Len, the couple from Canada who we'd met at breakfast in Najera three days before. Then in walked Trisha, the Australian woman from the bota-wine-dinner-fest in Santo Domingo de la Calzada. I felt instantly comforted. It's strange how the Camino can work as a catalyst for friendships. I'd talked with these people for less than three hours total and none was American, but seeing them was like running into long lost friends.

We all talked for a while about our sore feet and the accommodations we'd chosen for the night. We were each staying in different spaces. Trisha was a purist. She would only stay in albergues for the entire trip. Patty and Len would only stay in private rooms. Joe and I balanced out the two, preferring to alternate depending on the circumstances.

Joe offered, "Elaine and I are headed for the church, but why don't we all meet for dinner later tonight?"

Trisha answered, "I'm going to the church as well, but I prefer to go by myself. I'd be happy to meet you for dinner later, though."

Patty wanted to go straight up to the hotel room. "It's pretty ritzy up there. I wouldn't normally stay in such an expensive place, but Len says he's paying!"

Len looked at her with a shocked expression, and we all laughed.

After touring the majestic hotel grounds, we worked our way over to the church to ask about evening Mass. The church was closed. As we stood there admiring the architecture, we began to notice a flurry of activity. About ten senior women, who looked between sixty and eighty years old, started converging on the church courtyard. Several were carrying canvas bags. They opened the bags and started pulling out and aligning a bunch of wooden pins at one end of the courtyard. Then they placed a single pin at the other end. Some of these women were actually hobbling to take their position; arthritis, bad hips and stiff knees weren't going to stop them. A large wooden ball then appeared out of a younger, blond woman's bag; she was the referee. This same woman hiked up a scoreboard and hung it on the church wall for all to see.

While she was placing the scoring tiles on the board, I asked, "Qué hacen ustedes? (What are you all doing?)

"Vamos a jugar bola." (We're going to play ball.) she answered, plainly assuming anyone would know just by looking.

I had never seen anything like it. The game can best be described as primitive bowling. There are two teams of these matriarchal women taking turns throwing the heavy wooden ball at perfectly aligned wooden pins. After careful aim, the ball is first thrown at the cluster of pins right in front of the bowler with the object of knocking down the most pins. The ball then continues to roll to the opposite side of the court, with the aim to precisely knock down the one pin placed there. It's a game of maximum precision and dexterity played by two teams of post-menopausal women. I was awestruck. Forget tai chi, yoga, mahjong or knitting. These women were out for blood!

I was so taken with the competition, one of the team leaders noticed and asked if I wanted to play. At first I felt hesitant, but I decided to try anyway. After all, if an eighty-year-old woman can play this, I should be able to blow the competition away.

When I got up into position, ball in hand, I took it so seriously that when I finally threw the ball, I simultaneously lowered my team's average and life expectancy. I threw the ball so hard it rolled through the church grounds and down into a crowded truck crossing, almost causing the death or at least dismemberment of some poor, unsuspecting motorist. It took several minutes to retrieve the ball from the busy street, that is, after our hearts resumed beating. I assumed the women's age and physical conditioning from so much bola playing is what allowed them to laugh it off. In fact, I'm sure that is what must have happened after they personally escorted me off the church property and got back to their game.

Lesson for Today: Take a chance; losing is more fun than sitting on the sidelines.

Chapter 19: Stepping Back in Time

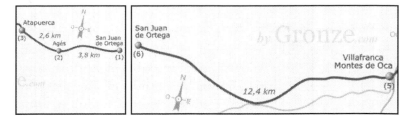

Trail Day 14, Villafranca de Montes de Oca to Atapuerca, 18 km

Travelling is almost like talking with men of other centuries.
- Rene Descartes

Elaine: We walked into the birthplace of European civilization today, Atapuerca. It's a UNESCO World Heritage Site because it was here they discovered bipedal primate fossils and stone tools dating back 1 million years. These early human fossils predate Neanderthals by over half a million years and offer a rare glimpse into the objects and culture of the earliest human communities in Europe. It's hard to miss the importance of this town. A huge signpost of a primitive man staring out at each passerby marks its entrance, as if to say, "Jurassic park has nothing on us."

I learned a few things today. First, there are nine UNESCO World Heritage sites on the entire Camino (four on our current Camino Frances) including several cathedrals, a suspension bridge, Roman walls, Paleolithic art, a monastery and the city of Santiago de Compostela itself. Second, I learned that there's a time apart from the traditional AD and BC, called "BP." It stands for "before present." Archeologists and other scientists use BP as a convention for marking time, using the year 1950 as the reference date. So if something is dated 4250 BP it would mean 4250 years before 1950. We non-archeologists would know it as 2300 BC. How much more can a hiker ask for? Great sights, exercise and an education in our human evolution. There's even a Human Evolution museum that links to the Atapuerca mountain dig site and an archeological park. There are places along this hike that beg for exploration. Atapuerca is one. All this and we're only a third of the way through our pilgrimage. I suspect my mind and body will be in top shape before this is all over, unless they both collapse from the strain.

Lesson for Today: Time travel comes in many forms.

Chapter 20: Unconventional Travel, Uncommon People

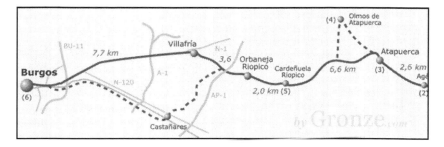

Trail Day 15, Atapuerca to Burgos, 20 km

If in the last few years you haven't discarded a major opinion or acquired a new one, check your pulse. You may be dead.
- Gelett Burgess

Elaine: Burgos is officially one-third of the way to Santiago. It's also the largest city we've encountered since starting the Camino. After walking the last 100 kilometers through bucolic pastures and vineyards, I felt an unnerving sensory overload when I first set foot on hard, concrete pavement. The bumper-to-bumper traffic and honking horns filled me with a sudden sense of urgency. I now understand how noise can be categorized as a type of "pollution." It felt like I was going from a sensory deprivation chamber into a thunderous, crowded nightclub. We heard the same story from other pilgrims we talked to about the trek into the city. Basically, "It was grueling."

Once we got past the initial shock and away from the rush-hour traffic, the experience changed. The scenery near the central plaza was very much like an outdoor museum. There were the statues you'd expect, depicting historical figures riding horses or standing proudly. But there were also amusing statues of average people doing ordinary things. Like an elderly couple resting on a bench staring out at the square, or a middle-aged man, appearing to be engrossed in a rather thick book, sitting near the cathedral. These statues showed up in places you would normally see real people doing the same things, so for a brief moment it was easy to feel confused about whether they were real people or statues.

During our walk through the city, we ran into Trisha, who was busily working through a map to see where she might reunite with her backpack. She believes, like Susan, the attorney from Canada, that the Camino is for pleasure and should never be a burden. "I'm not a snail; I don't need to carry my belongings on my back," she said with a resolute tone. We sat down at an outdoor café and ordered drinks.

As we worked to solve the case of the missing backpack, the waiter brought us free appetizers and three chilled *tintos de veranos*, which seemed especially exotic after drinking warm water all day. As we relaxed and shared our plans for finding shelter, Trisha offered up a great piece of advice,

"The two Brits I've been walking with told me the new albergue in Burgos is the best municipal you'll find on the whole Camino."

She went on with assurance, "They said it's modern and clean, and for 5 euros you can't beat the price, now can you?"

We helped Trisha formulate a list of potential backpack locations as we finished our drinks. The conversation drifted into relationships and Trisha's decision to walk the Camino alone.

"My husband has a great job making lots of money so I don't have to," she said with a forced smile.

Trisha has her own consulting business and takes off for as long as she cares to without any worries about money.

"So why do you only stay at albergues?" I asked.

"Staying at the albergues isn't about money. Oh no, not at all. The albergues are how I prove to myself that nothing matters."

It seems Trisha's life philosophy was distilled down to pure vapor: "We think so many things deserve our attention, but none of it's worth a moment's worry because everything happens as its meant to, no matter what one does."

Joe and I continued to listen silently. I looked at her, feeling puzzled. She continued,

"I just take each moment as it comes and I make a point of enjoying where I am *no matter* where I am."

I liked the carefree attitude she was describing, but something about it bothered me. Was it because it painted life with too broad a stroke? Or maybe it was the fatalism. If everything is going to happen as it was meant to, then why bother doing anything proactive or preventive?

Her words brought back the philosophy of the soldiers I'd treated who'd completed several deployments. If you asked them, "Are you worried about dying when you're out there on the convoys, or looking for IEDs (improvised explosive devices)?"

The answer was predictable. There are multiple variations, but the theme is the same: "Nah. I figure when it's my time there ain't nothing I can do to stop it, and if it's not my time, then it doesn't matter what happens 'cause I'm not going anywhere."

This fatalistic view of life adopted by many service members is usually the result of watching unexplainable events. One soldier told me how he and his buddy had flipped a coin to decide who would man the turret on their armored vehicle. His buddy pulled heads and took his position at the turret. Within seconds, he was shot; his blood and brains spraying everywhere, including on the soldier who won the toss. "That could've been me." He said.

I also heard about a Staff Sergeant who worked in EOD (Explosive Ordinance Disposal) for a full year's deployment, then came home and was shot and killed in a drive-by shooting in Camden, NJ.

Military members share these events with one another and it forms their impressions of the world.

Sometimes for the good: "Why worry if you ultimately have no control over what happens?"

Sometimes for bad: "Why bother if you ultimately have no control over what happens?"

I think both are extreme positions, and I've tried to weave a balance for my own worldview.

We said goodbye to Trisha and headed for the municipal albergue. The advice was good. The place was so big it had elevators! There was an Internet café, laundry facility, balconies on every level, and even a communal room on the top floor with a view of the city. A group of pilgrims had already banded together up there, playing guitar, singing, sharing laughter, food and evidently some thrilling stories. One quick glimpse into the room revealed a tale of the Camino's strength. The scene was an inventory of vastly different people, all ages mixing in a way that seemed to honor their differences. There was no great age divide like I often see back home. In the US, whether I'm watching TV, looking at magazine covers in the supermarket or going out to a nightclub, the message is clear. Youth is cool, attractive, and vibrant. Old age is invisible, even distasteful.

Before I left my job, I was worried about signs of aging, believing they would push me toward insignificance, especially as a woman. It reminds me of the old button that reads, "Life sucks, then you die." Except in this case it would be "Old age sucks, then you die."

The behaviors between the old and young here seemed to say, "I see your worth, and I know I can learn something from you." This is a recurring scene almost everywhere we go on this Camino, old and young, professional, artisan, even the homeless, all teaching one another we're more alike than different. Is it because unconventional travel tends to attract uncommon people? Is it our shared suffering or our dependence on one another – kind of like marine boot camp, which famously creates friends for life through shared adversity? Whatever it is, I like it. It looks and feels like something you'd experience in a utopia.

Burgos had a couple of more surprises for us. It turns out this city has one of the most lavish Gothic cathedrals in the world. It's another UNESCO site, and once you've seen it, I guarantee you will have some kind of strong reaction. Some of the visitors said they were awe-struck by the beauty and grandiosity. They said that this cathedral had "ruined" them for any other church they would see along the way to Compostela or perhaps the world.

Others had a completely different opinion. We bumped into Patty and Len on the way out of the cathedral. As we walked, Patty described her reaction: "It was like eating too much candy at once. It tastes good at the time, but I don't think I'll want to visit another cathedral for a while." Patty and Len had booked a hotel in the city several days earlier, fearing they would have trouble finding something nice in their price range. We described the exceptional albergue and how pleased we were to have discovered it.

"And it only cost 5 euros." I was now bragging and didn't even try to stop myself.

Patty said, "I would've considered it if I had known how cheap it is, but I'm still not sure I can sleep in a room with so many people snoring and coughing...you know, all that commotion."

Len had found a perfect set up for a sardonic remark. Turning to Patty, he said, "You didn't seem too concerned about money when you almost hailed that taxi coming into Burgos this afternoon."

Patty didn't miss a beat. "I told you I'd just as easily take the bus." She turned to me and confided, "The walk into the city today was so exhausting I would've ridden anything with wheels, but Len is so stubborn he just flat out refused. He thinks we should walk the whole way."

Patty and I spent the next few minutes walking alone and marveling over the differences between men and women. Then, Joe called out to us,

"Hey how about some dinner? I just read about the number one restaurant in Burgos and I think it's pretty close to here."

After stumbling around lost for a bit, we made it to the inside of a mobbed Spanish tapas restaurant called Cerveceria Morito. Forget tables: there was no standing room! We figured we'd be waiting for hours, especially since the Spanish savor their conversation as much as their food. But this is where Joe's "road-less-traveled" philosophy saved us again. He spied an old spiral staircase in the back leading up to the second floor and decided to take a look. Next thing, Joe bolted back down the stairs, signaling excitedly for us to follow him.

"The upstairs is empty, I got us a table!"

We were the first diners upstairs as the waiter seated us, but within ten minutes the entire room was packed.

We spent the rest of the night sampling huge-portioned appetizers of all varieties: calamari, octopus, mushrooms with bacon, ham, tomatoes in olive oil and balsamic vinegar, eggs served with crispy French fries. All fresh and steaming hot. They used a dumb waiter to haul the food from the kitchen on the ground level up to the second floor as soon as it was ready. We took turns sampling each other's menu choices and washed it all down with huge pitchers of Sangria. Finishing the meal, we then realized just how late it was. We barely made it back to the albergue before the doors were locked at 11:00. The last thing I remember before falling asleep was the sound of a guitar serenading a family-style gathering of pilgrims upstairs.

Lesson for Today: If you want to love and understand yourself better, seek out unfamiliar people in unfamiliar places.

Chapter 21: Emotional Insurance

Trail Day 16, Burgos to Rabé de las Calzadas, 13 km

You can avoid reality, but you cannot avoid the consequences of
avoiding reality.
- Ayn Rand

Elaine: We had an exceptionally late start this morning. Our tardiness set us on a path that intersected with an Australian named Stan, and he was in trouble. Stan couldn't speak Spanish and his girlfriend had a respiratory problem. Stan was so big and hulking, when I first saw him I thought, "This guy could take down a sumo wrestler!" He had the accent I've come to expect and love from Australians since seeing the movie *Crocodile Dundee*. He even looked like the stereotypical Australian sportsman: burly and bearded. That's why I was so surprised when he started talking to Patricia, the only staff member still there at the albergue, with mounting helplessness. Stan was stumbling over his words, flipping through phone cards, insurance cards, credit cards and any other physical prop he could find to try to get her to understand his girlfriend needed help. Patricia told him, in Spanish, that she couldn't help him because she didn't understand what he was saying.

I had been watching this scene unfold trying to stay out of it. I have a tendency to get overly involved when people need help. I've learned the hard way that it's just as important to allow others to struggle long enough to succeed on their own. But I had held my tongue long enough. I plunged into the rising commotion. "I speak Spanish and English. Can I help?"

Stan explained about his girlfriend; she was still lying in bed upstairs and unable to walk because her breathing was labored. He wanted help getting her to a doctor but didn't know how to dial local numbers in Spain from his Australian cell phone. I explained his dilemma and Patricia bolted into action. First she tried calling the number he provided from his cell, but when that failed, she gave him her own phone and even handled the appointment and transportation for him.

I don't normally diagnose on the fly, but I could tell Stan was a worrier, like me. As we waited for their transportation to the hospital, he explained how well prepared he was for any eventuality on the Camino,

"I have insurance in case I get sick and in case my phone gets stolen. I have accident insurance and traveler's insurance."

Stan's insurance would even pay for him to stay in a five-star hotel if he got sick on the Camino and needed to recuperate as an outpatient. I couldn't help but think that Stan probably wished he had learned some basic Spanish before his trip to Spain.

I pointed at his little insurance card and playfully taunted, "I bet you wish you had translator insurance."

This got him to relax and laugh for the first time, and when this guy laughed, the walls shook. I guess we were bonding through crisis and gallows humor. Stan was clearly a good-natured guy with an equally sardonic sense of humor. We stayed long enough to make sure he and his girlfriend were squared away then headed out for our destination, a town that was described in the guidebook as "sleepy" and "permanently on siesta." I wondered what that would feel like after our "Burgos cityscape" high.

Lesson for Today: If you are worrying about things that could happen, save energy by focusing on problems with the highest probability of actually occurring.

Chapter 22: A Sleepy Town

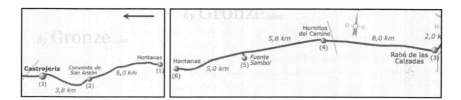

Trail Day 17, Rabé de las Calzadas to Castrojeriz, 28 km

Tell your heart that the fear of suffering is worse than the suffering itself.
- Paulo Coelho

Joe: I've slowly turned into a walking, eating, sleeping machine. We average about 20 kilometers (12 miles) a day at a speed of just over 4 km/hr. Over the days and weeks, my pains have slowly diminished and become more generalized aches. I've grown accustomed to it, learning to identify the pains that require immediate attention compared to the daily ones that go away after a couple hours of rest. Feet and shoes are a daily discussion between the two of us as well as with the other pilgrims. This is where the rubber hits the road, so to speak, and I've heard many stories over the last couple weeks about short-lived pilgrimages due to persistent blisters, ankle sprains, and knee problems.

We take special care of our feet and pay close attention to any hint that they might be failing us. The first thing every morning, I coat them with a heavy layer of Vaseline. Elaine had started using Vicks VapoRub since we'd met the Portuguese couple back in Mañeru. Either way, the petroleum base minimizes the friction between our feet and our shoes; friction is our enemy, the major cause of blisters. We then slip on two pairs of merino wool socks. We never use cotton; when it gets wet, it stays wet. Wool wicks away the moisture and continues to insulate your feet in cold weather. It's also very durable. After washing, the SmartWool socks dry in just a few hours.

We walked for hours across the quiet *meseta*, a high central plateau. Only the sounds of nature were pervading our solitude. There were few pilgrims on this leg and the vast expanse of rolling landscape left me feeling isolated from the rest of humanity. I sank into my thoughts and walked on.

Elaine: The guidebook was right; Castrojeriz is one *sleepy* town. It was a little eerie walking into the village with the sun still blazing but not a single living creature around except an occasional dog. Every now and then, Joe would walk ahead of me and I would feel like I was entirely alone. The only thing that reminded me there was still life on the planet, ironically, was a text message from my son, Ben, back in the states. He wanted to know if I would buy Joe a birthday present instead of a gift for him. Ben and Joe both have the same birthday. After I agreed to his request, Ben swore me to secrecy. "Don't tell Joe!"

Then it happened. Ben's selflessness in the midst of my solitude in these arid surroundings brought tears to my eyes. I hadn't expected any contact from him on the Camino, and I was dehydrated which made my tears even more of a surprise. I read about people suddenly crying on the Camino. It seemed to happen when they witnessed some beautiful scene, or something so exceptionally meaningful that the tears flowed without warning. I had wondered if something like that would happen to me, but I thought it would be related to my Catholic upbringing. I assumed I would see some religious artifact or spiritual symbol that would bring me to tears. Instead, it was a text message from my soon-to-be twenty-one-year-old son. His selfless act of love on the rise to manhood filled my heart with joy and sorrow. He was clearly a good man, someone I would like to know even if he weren't my son. But he was no longer a boy, no longer *my little boy*.

I had worried a lot about being on the other side of the world and away from family. But this event served as a reminder that allowing our loved ones some time alone to find their own way, just like allowing others to suffer so they can succeed on their own, is painful but necessary. It reminded me of the maxim that there can be no growth without pain. I amused myself with the thought that if I could make it to the end of the Camino, it would be impossible to stuff me back through that hatchway on the C5 we flew in on.

When I caught up with Joe, neither of us had yet to see a single person. A little way farther into the town, we found a patron-less bar. It didn't matter that the bartender was nowhere to be found; it was a sanctuary and there was a little white dog there to greet us. We spent five minutes looking for the bartender, then after finding him sleeping way in the back of the building, the three of us sat and laughed about the town's sleepy reputation.

The whole time we were there I worked hard to contain the flood of feelings pushing me to share Ben's kindness with Joe. After all, how would Ben even know I told him? The gift was especially meaningful because of Joe's late entry into our family's life. We married when my two youngest sons were already in their teens, one of the hardest times for a man to take hold of the reins of a new family. Although my oldest son, William, had already finished college; he had come back home to live temporarily. My high schoolers, Ben and his younger brother, Andrew, were at the age when even the healthiest kids are turning away from family and toward their own independent lives. Joe's climb was probably the steepest with Ben because, as the next oldest after William, he had already adopted the role of "man of the house." He was the quintessential "alpha male" and the idea of a new man in his mom's life was completely unacceptable. Ben never disguised his feelings that I shouldn't be dating. He said things like, "Mom, you're too old to be picking out an outfit for a date...it's creepy." He was mortified when we decided to marry.

I don't know how Joe pulled it off, but he became a father to each of my boys, including the least willing of them all, Ben. That's why the act of giving up his own birthday present in order to make sure Joe had one was completely inconceivable, even now. How the heck did Joe do it? And doesn't he deserve to know? But we were on the Camino scrubbing our spirits, and I had promised not to tell.

I bit my tongue and sipped my wine, in the middle of nowhere with Joe and a bartender I barely knew, but my soul was dancing with such an unbounded happiness that I don't think I could have ever experienced that kind of joy in any other moment or place.

Lesson for Today: The fear of leaving loved ones in order to travel can blind us to the benefits. Separation requires new ways to communicate and helps us appreciate the closeness we already share.

Chapter 23: Skin Hunger

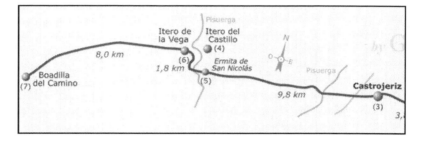

Trail Day 18, Castrojeriz to Boadilla del Camino, 19 km

One of the main points about travelling is to develop in us a feeling
of solidarity, of that oneness without which no better world is
possible.
- Ella Maillart

Joe: It's my birthday! It was exactly one year ago when I was
celebrating it by sitting at a café, eating dinner in a little town in
the northern mountains of Slovenia. I was alone and very tired,
and I hadn't slept since the day before. I'd taken an overnight flight
from New York City to Venice, then rented a car and drove north
out of Italy and up into the Slovenian mountains.

Tonight, my birthday is quite different. Elaine is curled up in
her bunk, fast asleep. I'm sitting at a table in a small, enclosed
courtyard of a *refugio*. It's in the town of Boadilla del Camino.
There are nine college students sitting around me. They are from
all over the world, including three musicians from New Orleans
(with guitars) and a beautiful young Argentinean woman. Her
voice is so sweet; it melts the ice in the drinks of the young men
listening to her. They're all singing "Happy Birthday" to me. I'm
laughing while drinking some powerful local Spanish liquor called
"orujo" that's flowing freely around the table; it's made from the

residue of wine production and goes down my throat smooth and very warm. I've decided to fight fire with fire and drink away this melancholy mood that has been overtaking me for days.

Our trek today had led us down a long, dry, dusty trail. After several hours we reached the top of a hill and just by Camino luck we saw Stan and his girlfriend, Barb, standing with Len and Patty.

"Hey guys!" I said as we walked up to them.

They all smiled and we decided to have a seat at one of the nearby tables on the side of the dirt road. Barb had fully recovered and everyone seemed in great shape and good spirits.

We were sitting in the shade of some trees at the top of the meseta. Some local residents had set up a small refreshment stand next to a fountain. Thinking what a wonderful enterprise for them to make a little extra money, I approached the makeshift table to purchase some drinks and snacks. I selected a couple of Cokes and a homemade sandwich.

I asked, "Cuánto?"

The two middle-aged men shook their heads. "No, this is free, it's already paid for by local supporters of the Camino."

I don't know why, but I was caught off guard. I just looked at them, obviously farmers, judging by their clothes. I didn't know how to respond.

Why haven't I learned to expect this generosity? Have I already forgotten about Dora and Milton opening their home to us on that blistering hot day two weeks ago?

These local volunteers had taken time out of their day to load up their van and drive five kilometers out of town to provide free refreshments for us. I felt completely humbled. I wasn't even sure what to say. I mumbled a "Gracias" to the farmers and dropped a few euros into a donation cup set aside for those people that just can't receive a gift from those who have such meager financial resources. I then joined our newly assembled group of well-to-do pilgrims. But now I wonder...which of us are really the "well-to-do?" Is it the six of us or is it these humble supporters, so rich in love and faith that they spend both freely in support of a world full of peregrinos? It's another lesson for me in accepting kindness. I'm a pilgrim, a poor sinner that needs, that should, that must welcome gifts from strangers.

Elaine has been worried about me. I've been withdrawn lately, feeling like there is something missing on this path, but I just can't figure out what.

I'm not going to worry about it today though; it's my birthday, damn it!

Elaine: We'd now fallen into a pattern of walking with Stan, Barb, Patty and Len. Stan had owned a large vineyard back in Australia. He used to grow grapes for Shiraz, and exported them all over the world. After his wife died five years ago, he sold all his belongings, including the vineyard, and moved out of the family home.

"I kept going into the kitchen expecting to see her. I looked every day, but she wasn't there. I think I was going batty," he remarked with an attempt at humor, but he sounded more sad than amused.

He had met Barb on the Internet the year prior after giving himself permission to date again. It was the first time he was able to feel a connection to someone else. It scared him but despite the feeling, he moved closer.

Barb, who is also Australian, is twelve years younger than Stan and although they come from the same country, her accent is completely different. Her words and her actions were all blue-blooded, aristocratic. The kind of accent you'd expect from upper class Brits. When she spoke, it was like walking next to the Queen of England. Her actions were slow and graceful, but somehow she ended up meters ahead when we least expected it. She has some kind of special position with the Australian government but doesn't like to talk about it, so I don't pry.

Barb lost her husband many more years ago than Stan lost his wife. Her grief is still fresh though, kind of like she got stuck in the depression stage and couldn't reach out or get any closer to acceptance. She still idolizes her dead husband, referring to him in saintly terms, "he was the light of my life." I noticed she tended to avoid getting too close to Stan, referring to him as a companion instead of as a partner or boyfriend. Contrary to Stan, Barb's fear acted as a force field, preventing her from drawing closer. She'd move away from him even as they walked. When we ate together, they kept a strict account of their finances, both making sure they were paying exactly 50-50.

While walking, we talked about "skin hunger," that human need to be touched that seems to grow in direct proportion to the time we spend completely alone. Barb chimed in on this topic with personal knowledge,

"After my husband died, I spent all my time alone. Then one day, I decided to treat myself to a manicure. It was just a whim. I didn't think much about it at all until the manicurist began massaging my hands and forearms. His skin was soft and he stroked my hands and fingers in such a soothing manner that I couldn't help it...I began weeping right there in that very chair. It had been so long since anyone had touched me. I had no idea how much it mattered until that very moment."

We all nodded in profound agreement. Apparently we each had our own skin hunger stories.

Len and Patty caught up, and we all talked effortlessly. It happened so naturally, I'd started to wonder how many permutations were possible between us. There were six of us, so about fifty-seven different combinations. I guessed that was right, depending on repeats and such (I always hated probability theory). Sometimes I'd walk with Patty, then Barb would join in, and we'd talk together. Then a spontaneous switch would occur, one of the guys would slow down and join us. We just kept talking until the subject or the group composition shifted again. Next, it would be just Len and me talking. These changes were so unplanned and effortless that I didn't think twice about how they happened or how instantly the conversation changed. I just marveled over how broad the range of topics could be: from where we'd stop for lunch, to the best ways to parent, to the death of a spouse. It's rare to get along so seamlessly with four completely different people, and yet here we were sharing the terrain and our lives as if we were all long-lost friends.

I'm also impressed by how easily the men can describe their emotions out on this trail. It's so different from the military guys I'd been treating. Warfighters, and men in general, are more likely to suffer from "alexithymia," which is the inability to label feelings. Most men can identify feeling "pissed off," "aggravated," "frustrated," "furious," "annoyed," or "irritated," but it's not so easy for them to describe feelings like loneliness, sadness, helplessness, fear, worry, or affection.

In therapy, I would often ask the men with alexithymia to imagine all of their emotions had been poured into a blender. The blender takes the original emotion, no matter what it was, and converts it into one identifiable feeling: anger. The blender is always set to automatic so it takes an act of will to purposely shut if off and keep the primary emotion. I even used a list of cartoon-style feeling "descriptors" (think emoticons with feeling labels) that they could point to as I asked them to describe specific events and their emotional reactions to them.

We'd have fun trying to find the right emoticon with its associated feeling label, and it was liberating for them to share emotions that made them feel more human and less frustrated. As one of my former patients described it, "I was always ready to explode because that's all there was...I couldn't say I was scared. Who's going to respect a guy that says something like that?" This soldier did not walk into my office voluntarily. It took the threat of divorce and a restraining order for him to finally ask for help.

Some of my patients would latch on to the exercise so strongly and take it so seriously; they would look at the feeling labels and say, "Well, I guess I was feeling suspicious, jealous, guilty, sad and worried." They would pick out so many feeling words I would literally have to stop them in order to get a handle on the situation they were describing. It was like a kid with a new toy, but the toy was a language - a treasure chest of feelings.

Why was it so easy for the men I was walking with to open up so naturally about a variety of feelings? How did we build this level of trust so rapidly? Is this what the "real" world, the world outside of therapy and the military looked like? Or was it the Camino?

Our walking led us into the village of Boadilla del Camino. Stan and Barb had reservations at an exquisite pensión and split away from us. Patty and Len had reserved a private room at the town's albergue. We followed Len and Patty in hopes that we could share both the camaraderie of the albergue while enjoying the luxury of a private room.

There's one word I would use to describe our night together, "Abundancia!" From the moment we walked in the door until the minute we walked away the next morning, the family who owned the place showed generosity like no other I'd seen. We ordered drinks but no one kept tabs. Trisha arrived and joined us for more cold drinks. We then all sat at a communal dinner table where we received food in huge steaming pots with ladles for serving as much as our stomachs could hold. No single-serving deck-of-cards-sized portions here.

The wine and conversation flowed freely among the pilgrims sitting around us. Trisha drank more than we'd seen since she started the Camino. I chalked it up to her decision yesterday to quit smoking.

"I quit many years ago and for some blasted reason started up when I got here. There's no reason for it."

She leered at a group of musicians from New Orleans smoking with abandon. It seemed like she'd order a drink every time one of them would light up a new cigarette. As the dinner progressed, Trisha told the story of her first day hiking up the Pyrenees. She was almost a different person, behaving like a stand up comedian, even using dramatic gestures and audience participation. The sequence of events she described for her first day on the trail was as unpredictable as they were funny. Her eyes were on fire and her cheeks flushed crimson. I believe she was conscious of her hold over every one of us at the table. Sometimes, she would even take a little bow like a Buddhist stage actress, but she did it with such humility it just made her more endearing and fun to be with.

The night was filled with spice, not just in the bountiful food streaming endlessly across the tables, but also via the exceptionally handsome Don Juan-type character who took care of us at dinner. It was clear from his confidence, lingering playfully with each woman in the room, that he believed he could have any one of them at his pleasure. Although he flirted shamelessly with all the women, it was done in good taste, and most of them playfully returned the happy banter. But with Trisha, it was different. Their eye contact lasted longer. Her expressions of admiration for him were especially effusive and stretched past the average praise you might see between customer and server. I wondered how often the *Don* used his looks and personality to gain special favors with his visitors. The entire evening was filled with hints of romance and little moments of electricity between the sexes that I hadn't noticed at any of the other albergues. What a relief. I thought the Camino would prove too exhausting for romance, but here was a place that scoffed at such an idea, and all it took was one person to ignite the fires that yearned for expression in each of us. After dinner, Joe went outside to hang out with some guitar players from New Orleans. I said my own "good nights" to everyone at the table and went to bed.

Joe: The warm liquor gave me just the right amount of courage to pull a guitar from the willing hands of one of our musicians. I started singing and strumming an old Neil Young tune. Some of the older pilgrims knew the words and joined in. It had been a long time since I'd played, so I was a bit rusty, but everyone around me seemed to enjoy it. We then swapped our individual stories of the Camino while pouring and toasting liberally. The New Orleans musicians were the stars for the night. I was the honoree, and judging by the attention the beautiful Argentinean woman was receiving, she was the MC. What an oasis of laughter and music, of people and companionship. Speaking of companionship, I'm starting to miss Elaine. I stand up tenderly on my swollen feet. Handing the guitar back to our musicians, I bid everyone a hearty, "Thanks for a wonderful birthday! Buen Camino!" and hobbled to our room.

Elaine: I was just rustled awake! Joe's back in the room now. He's glowing from all the unexpected communal support for his birthday and the passion he shared playing guitar with the band tonight. His excitement is still at a peak. It's hard to believe, but our room in the albergue is completely empty. Everyone is enjoying themselves outside. It's even more surprising how romance sparks and the body revives when there's a threat of being discovered.

Lesson for Today: One person can change the experience of many.

Chapter 24: Touching the Spirit

Trail Day 19, Boadilla del Camino to Carrión de los Condes, 24km

Know that everything is in perfect order whether you understand it or not.
- Valery Satterwhite

Joe: We walked out of Boadilla del Camino with a spring in our step and encountered a section that evidently had some money poured into it. The path runs along a busy road and it's been freshly graveled and bordered with numerous Camino pylons displaying the familiar scalloped-shell emblem. Although obviously expensive, the path was ugly, too commercial, too sterile. I'm sure it was done with good intentions, but they could've done better with a simple path, well away from the busy roadway. As a poor pilgrim, I know it's better to accept the gift with gratitude and not judge. Our next stop was Población de Campos, 4 kilometers farther down the trail.

We came upon Patty and Len, and our path led the four of us further on to Carrión de los Condes, where we set off in search of lodging. Choosing one of the many interesting pensións, we climbed the flight of stairs up to the lobby. We found Stan and Barb standing there at the desk with their luggage. We're no longer surprised at such things; we just smile broadly in acknowledgement of each other.

I'm amazed at the amount of luggage that Stan and Barb have with them. This is the first time I'd seen all of it. It will take a couple trips for Stan to get it all up to their room. I guess that's why they take taxis so often, to keep up with their caravan of luggage that moves ahead of them. It reminds me to keep things light, not only on our daily walks but also in our lives.

After getting settled into our room and dropping off some laundry, Elaine and I headed out to explore the town. As we are walking the winding streets, we come upon Stan having some beers with a couple of other pilgrims at an outdoor café on the edge of a large courtyard.

Elaine says, "Hey, Stan, are you coming to church with us?"

She knows his answer is a definite "No." He's not the church-going type; she just wants to joke with him a bit. Stan laughs. He looks embarrassed and shakes his head in a shy, side-to-side weave.

"No, thanks, not tonight," he says with a smile.

I'm feeling pretty exhausted and sit down to join them. Stan introduces his new friends.

"This is Jim and Dawn from Australia."

We shake hands and I introduce us. "We're Joe and Elaine from the States."

As pilgrims do, we quickly start talking about our Camino experiences. While we're talking, Elaine looks across the courtyard and says, "Oh, look, Joe, there's the church and it's almost 7 o'clock."

I look over at the tall, stone edifice and then back at the cold beers sitting on the table, their sides dripping with condensation even in this dry, dusty weather.

"Sorry, darling, I'm just not up for it."

She's standing behind me giving my shoulders a deep massage, "It's not like you have to walk very far; it's just across the courtyard."

I shake my head. "I just can't do it."

I still don't know where Elaine gets the energy to go on like this. How can she be so energized while I'm so drained? I'm in better shape than anyone around me, but I just want to go to bed. Elaine suffers excruciating foot pain all day, but once we reach our destination she's a party animal, well, church-wise that is. Elaine walks away, disappointed, and heads toward the church.

The waiter comes walking by and I call to him, "Señor, una cerveza, por favor."

Elaine: The connection I felt with our little group and our discussion about skin hunger yesterday was a perfect set up for the Mass I attended tonight at the Santa Maria church in the center of Carrion de los Condes. I had asked Joe to come with me but he was uncharacteristically obstinate and refused to move from his chair at the outdoor café.

"C'mon Joe, puhleeezz," I implored. "It's not like you have to walk very far; it's just across the courtyard."

By close, I mean our waiter could have tripped and landed in one of the pews.

Joe could only say, "I just can't do it," and went back to his conversation.

I've noticed today that his mood has been changing. He didn't even seem excited when I told him Ben had bought him a professional-quality camera for his birthday and it would be waiting for him at home when we got back. I had found a Canon D1 online and ordered it while we were at a bar with Wi-Fi.

I was still nagging him to come to church with me when four new pilgrims joined our table and I realized I couldn't keep begging without being rude or sounding whiney. I worry. *Is he upset with me? Have I been callous in some way that has hurt him?* I start to run through the different events of the day but can't pinpoint any one thing I did that would cause this kind of reaction. Why am I suddenly feeling abandoned and unloved just because Joe doesn't want to go to church with me?

Geez, get a grip, Elaine! I scold myself. *Talk about pathetic.* I start to feel my mood plummet until my Wise Mind steps in and says, *Hold on. It doesn't help at all to call it pathetic. You've been divorced, and heck, that's all about feeling unloved and abandoned. The feelings are just that, feelings. No more and no less. They don't get to define reality. You've known Joe long enough now to have some faith. If he's not going with you it's probably because he needs to recover somehow. Church is probably the best place for you to go right now, even if it's by yourself.*

I grudgingly listened to my Wise Mind and headed for the church alone. I walked through the courtyard and realized I knew one of the pilgrims. She was just opening the door to the church. It was Barb. By the time I entered the vestibule, she had already found a pew and sat down. I headed straight over and sidled in next to her. She acknowledged me, patting my shoulder, silently smiling. I needed that.

I found myself daydreaming through the Mass, mostly because of what happened with Joe but also because all the services here are in Spanish, and if I don't pay close attention, I lose the message.

Then, just after the Mass ended, something very special happened. The priest explained a Catholic ritual he was about to perform for the peregrinos, the *laying on of hands*. He described how we each have a need for spiritual and physical healing and how the laying of hands is a special blessing that combines the two through direct contact with the Holy Spirit. At the end of the Mass, he specifically asked all the pilgrims to rise and come forward. Once we'd all reached the altar, he deliberately placed his hands over each of our heads while reciting a special blessing for healing. I had never experienced anything like this before. Such a personal expression of love and compassion for the pain we're all enduring on this pilgrimage, whether physical or spiritual.

The personal contact through the hands of that priest was a healing experience for me, and from the expressions I saw on the other invigorated pilgrims' faces, it was for them too. As we walked back to our seats, I could see that the priest had touched a chord in each of us. I couldn't stop the tears from welling up in my own eyes. It felt so meaningful; this holy man's willingness to individually recognize our pain and to physically reach out to us through our growing identity as pilgrims.

How amazing! We talked about skin hunger yesterday and tonight we encounter the laying on of hands, all this at a time when I'm feeling particularly vulnerable, even unlovable. I wonder if it would have felt so healing if I hadn't been alone, separated from the person I have the closest relationship with. Stepping out on my own to attend tonight's service brought me riches I hadn't expected. It was a reminder that a pilgrimage has got to be personal in order to be a true spiritual journey. Joe has to find his own way, not mine.

I can hear Pete's voice in my head: "There are no coincidences on the Camino.'" It's fascinating how much Pete has been following me like a sprite on this Camino. I wonder if he knows the impact he had in just those few minutes we spent together in Westover.

Lesson for Today: There's a spirit that calls us toward a singular path, a path meant for no one else. Our relationship with that divine voice is like any intimate bond; it thrives on love, trust and respect. The language may be different for each soul, but the inspiration is there for those who are listening.

Chapter 25: Symbols of the Camino

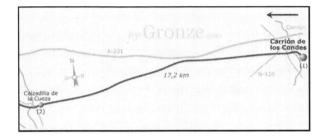

Trail Day 20, Carrión de los Condes to Calzadilla de la Cueza,   17 km

Dogs are our link to paradise. They don't know evil or jealousy or discontent. To sit with a dog on a hillside on a glorious afternoon is to be back in Eden, where doing nothing was not boring – it was peace.
>   *-Milan Kundera*

Joe: Elaine and I ate a quick breakfast of toasted bread and espresso at the café adjoining our pensión. The owner was in the kitchen making sandwiches for us, which means French bread wrapped around a pile of Iberian pork, cheese, fresh green peppers, and Spanish onions, all doused with a homemade marinade of olive oil, balsamic vinegar and Mediterranean spices. We had a long 17-kilometer stretch in front of us without a single village to provide food or drink. The meal he eventually carried over to our breakfast table could have kept us going for a week.

Elaine worried about our water supply, so I offered, "How about I get a bigger bottle, twice the size?"

It sounded like a good idea until I added the larger container to my backpack. I immediately noticed the added weight. I said "adios" to the owner of the pension and we headed down through the city streets and crossed the Rio Carrion out of town.

An outsider might think that our close-knit group of six would automatically plan our departures each morning so that we could all walk together. We've had such meaningful conversations, freely opening our hearts to each other and now we were even in adjacent rooms in the pensión. So why not arrange a simple starting time together? It's because the Camino is too strenuous for such luxuries. Coordination with other people requires too many compromises. Attempts to conform to each other's schedules and abilities can surprisingly affect both our physical and mental strength. Each one of us is on a personal journey and the effort for just Elaine and me to work together can be exhausting at times. This is not a team sport and each of us understands that when we part ways after our evening meal we may never see each other again.

The Camino amplifies our strengths and our difficulties. We're exposed and vulnerable to a constantly changing outdoor environment as well as to the shifts in our physical and emotional health. A wrong turn that takes us down longer paths or causes unexpected delays can have a surprising effect on our mood. The opposite is also true. The simple gifts that we give each other every day are much more significant when each of us is trying to regulate our reserves of energy. "Honey, will you get me a cup of coffee?" has a lot more meaning when the simple act of standing and walking across the room to the counter causes pain to radiate from swollen joints and exhausted muscles. But the love and appreciation I see in Elaine's eyes when returning with these simple acts of kindness more than makes up for the temporary discomfort.

About an hour after crossing the Rio Carrion, we noticed Stan and Barb a short distance behind us. We'd had few opportunities to walk together, just the four of us.

I yelled back to them, "G'day!" and they eagerly joined up with us.

We could already tell it was going to be a long hot walk. Our destination was Calzadilla de la Cueza. The dirt farm road we walked on was straight as an arrow and wider than most any we'd walked. We wondered about this until an hour later, when we heard a noise approaching from behind. It was a huge combine barreling down on us, leaving giant plumes of dust in its wake. It didn't slow down and it didn't move over. It was going about 40 miles per hour as it passed us. We had to step off to the side of the road and wait to be enveloped in the thick clouds of dust trailing behind it. Several of these bright green machines passed us during the morning. By lunchtime, we were covered in a thick layer of dust.

We stopped at a small shaded picnic area for an early lunch. An excited, white and brown wire-haired terrier greeted us as we entered the little tree-covered oasis. Judging by the collar that was practically cutting off her air supply and the lack of any buildings for miles around, she was obviously homeless. She was also making out exceptionally well with the pilgrims. I immediately started removing the un-tagged collar from around her neck as she jumped from side to side, playfully chewing on my hands. The collar was so tight that she choked when I slightly tightened it to release the catch.

Once free, she seemed to enjoy the liberation by jumping right up onto our picnic table to inspect our slowly emerging sacks of food. Living a hard but obviously well fed life, our canine companion was a solid mass of twisting muscle. I picked her up from the table and returned her to the ground. Unstoppable, but also intelligent, she got the message and controlled her begging by keeping her hind legs on Mother Earth. The rest of her was fully engaged in catching an unending stream of morsels coming her way from every direction.

I think we enjoyed it as much as she did. We knew her game and she knew ours. Our mission was to give food and receive entertainment. Her mission was to receive food and provide entertainment. And she provided it with glee. She'd twist and turn and jump into the air like a gymnast. She'd snap at food with such ferocity and speed that it caused me to worry about losing a finger. But, the occasional times she did manage to grab the food before I had time to release it, she throttled back so fast that her teeth gently held my hand like a mother carrying her pups. She ran in circles and did somersaults in the grass. I didn't even know dogs could do head-over-heels somersaults.

After our communal meal, we got up from the table and started packing up. She wasn't happy. She knew the routine and bit my shoes and pants to hold me back. She curled herself around my leg and I rubbed her dusty belly, her newly liberated neck and the top of her head. As I walked away, she took a running leap and grabbed at my shirt cuff. I pulled away just in time. Lowering my hand, she securely took hold with just the right amount of pressure. I then lifted her into the air by her teeth, her tail wagging the whole time. I did this a couple more times before releasing her and we continued on with our departure.

"I would love to take her home," Elaine said.

I kind of liked the idea and started wondering about the logistics of bringing her with us.

Before we could make it out onto the road again, she once again grabbed hold of my heel and I dragged her several more feet toward the entrance of the picnic area. At its threshold, she released my foot. She gave a quick little bark then turned away, running for another picnic table holding three women who'd been watching our antics with big smiles on their faces. It was their turn now.

Walking back down the road, we spent a good ten minutes conjecturing about the abandoned pup's history as well as her future employment as a circus performer, cattle rustler or con artist. About an hour went by when we walked past a small farm. There were a dozen cattle in the pen next to the barn. In the pen with them was another white and brown wire-haired terrier running and barking and jumping with way too much energy for the midday heat. He could've been our lunchtime companion's brother. Maybe our new friend really did have a home after all and just loved eating with the pilgrims.

By 3:00 pm the four of us were once again walking into another one of the little farming communities in search of lodging. It was siesta time in this hot, dry ghost town of beige, brown and white adobe buildings. We searched up and down the empty streets until we reached the far side of the village. The town appeared to be completely empty. I was about to say that we'd have to walk on toward the next community when Barb spoke up. "There's something, see it? Over there!"

She pointed down a side street. There, in stark contrast to the rest of the town, were some brightly colored red tables and chairs.

They were sitting in the hot sun by the front door of a newly painted two-story building.

Red tables and chairs, with Coke or beer logos on the back, are the second most sought-after signs on the Camino, second only to the yellow arrow blazes pointing us toward Santiago itself. They can be spotted from a kilometer away and guide the tired pilgrims to a temporary sanctuary, just like humming birds to nectar.

These low-cost red plastic tables and chairs mean sustenance. They signify cold drinks, fresh food, and possibly even lodging for the night. They provide rest for our aching legs, a lightening of the load on our backs, and fresh air for our throbbing feet as we sit and slip off our trail shoes. Most important of all, these simple, economical furnishings offer community. They offer laughter and the discovery of new friends, lighthearted banter and deep philosophical discussions about religion, society and the differences between our countries.

In our "normal" lives back home, these everyday examples of cheap, mass-produced plastic furnishings would've meant little to us. We wouldn't have given them a second thought. Not here, not now. We've changed. In each of our lives, important, meaningful beacons call to us every day and in very simple ways. All we have to do is pay attention. The Camino teaches us to pay attention, to look for the signs.

This time though, we slipped right past the patio furnishings and into the cool, dark interior of *Hostal Camino Real*. Resting at a table just inside the entrance were Patty, Len and Trisha.

"What a coincidence!" I said playfully.

The three of them had arrived an hour earlier and were already checked in.

Elaine: If you're ever looking for a place to be alone with your thoughts, consider walking the stretch from Carrión de los Condes to Calzadilla de la Cueza in mid-October. For a while there, until we met up with Barb and Stan, it felt like a walking solitary confinement.

When we finally reached the pensión, it was "old home" week with Trisha, Len and Patty there to meet us. I took the opportunity to check in with Trisha about the other night as she was walking out for a smoke.

"That good-looking owner's son the other night seemed to have you in his sights. Did you notice?"

Trisha lit up a cigarette and blew the smoke out from only one side of her mouth, saying,

"He was a cheeky one, wasn't he?"

"How cheeky are we talking, Trish?" I asked expectantly.

"Well, let's just say we spent a little time together alone."

"I knew it! I saw you two walk out of the albergue headed toward that party going on in the barn and I knew he was going to hit on you."

Trisha looked at me vacantly for a moment, then crushed her cigarette decisively,

"He didn't come on to me. I was the one making advances."

She looked away. I hung on to what I was hoping would be a therapeutic silence.

"Actually, I'm quite ashamed of myself. I was drunk and behaved stupidly."

I was still listening but not ready to offer any thoughts. I believe she took my silence as disapproval because, rather than say any more, Trisha hurriedly grabbed her cigarettes, coins and lighter, stuffing them all in her pouch and stood to leave.

"Trisha, do you really have to go? I know the other night was super-charged, that whole place was like a fantasy. It was like some kind of secret garden. We were all feeling it."

I was struggling to help her relax the grip of self-recrimination she was caught in, but the look on her face told me it wasn't working. Trisha looked at me but no longer registered me. "I've got to go, I'm supposed to Skype with my husband before dinner." And then she was gone.

Lesson for Today: If you ever get stuck and wonder what it looks like to be free of anxiety, find a dog and take a lesson on staying in the moment with a curious, non-judgmental mind.

Chapter 26: Strong Women

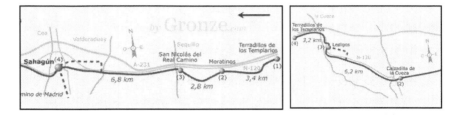

Trail Day 21, Calzadilla de le Cueza to Sahagún, 22 km

> *I'm convinced that material things can contribute a lot to making one's life pleasant, but, basically, if you do not have very good friends and relatives who matter to you, life will be really empty and sad and material things cease to be important.*
> *- David Rockefeller*

Elaine: I think of walking as a "moving meditation." I'm not very good at it though. I suffer from perpetual "monkey brain." My mind wanders, swinging from limb to limb, while judging my every move. My version of mindful walking started out today with me telling myself: *Just let go of all judgments and watch the world with a completely loving heart.* The other part of meditative walking is to use as many of the senses as possible. I focus on the feel of the ground under my feet, the smooth pavement, the shifting gravel and slippery wet grass. I breathe in, checking for any hint of vegetation, flowers, and in this case, the ever-present smell of cow manure. I listen to the birds in the trees and the voices of Joe and the rest of our group behind us. About a minute goes by and I can already hear the chatter in my monkey brain: *I wonder how long we'll be walking before we can stop today? Why do I get tired so quickly? Everybody else makes this hike look like a cakewalk and my feet are already aching. I should have spent more time preparing for this. Will I be able to finish?*

Then I reprimand myself. *Focus! Get back to the ground, the sights, the smells!* I start to breathe in again...there's the cow dung. Then, *What if I have to go to the bathroom and there's no place to stop? Do I have to go now?* My meditation is lost.

I'm in luck, though. Trisha is up ahead and she's stopped for a smoke. She likes to walk alone, but every now and then she slows down to tie her shoe or take a picture. This gives me an opportunity to catch up. It's a chance to make up for trying to act like her therapist last night.

I tell Trisha about my problem with the walking meditation. "Joe reminds me to just observe the thoughts as they flash through my mind, and not let them hook me. I already know it, but I get hooked anyway. So I start all over, and then I get hooked again."

Trisha advises, "Try turning around on the path every now and then. I've seen some beautiful scenes that I would've easily missed if I focused only on what's ahead."

I immediately respond by turning around. I watch our little colorful group: Patty, Len, Barb, Stan and Joe in animated conversations a few hundred meters behind us. I walk on with Trisha, neither one of us getting too deep. I remain careful about not probing into last night.

As we continue to talk, I notice that Trisha seems distracted and sometimes curt in her responses to my questions. I wonder if this is her way of suggesting I should leave her alone. I haven't known her for very long, so it's difficult to know for sure. Normally, I would react to such aloof behavior by backing off and giving her space. I don't know why I did it, but instead of backing off, I pressed forward.

"Trisha, are you upset with me about yesterday?"

Based on her progressively tight-lipped and sour replies this morning, I was fully prepared to hear her tell me to go away. But just as soon as I asked her, it was clear that she had been holding back tears. My question had scaled the barrier she erected and left her surprised and momentarily exposed. She quickly wiped away the tears using the heel of her hand.

"I've decided I'm not going to reply to my husband's phone calls."

I listened, but this time I asked, "Why?" immediately. No pauses.

"I'd planned to walk the Camino for over a year. I talked about it constantly. And yet, he let me come alone even though he knew I wanted him here with me."

She stomped the ground. "I've always supported his dreams! This was supposed to be my turn. But all he did was complain about how it would be impossible to take a month away from his job. How he would lose too much money."

Trisha had discovered such great beauty during her walks. When we sat and rested earlier, she'd been so happy to show me her exquisite photos. She had a good eye: a natural artist. But there was something wrong with one of her pictures. It was the metaphorical image reflecting her married life. In it, she was mostly alone.

We walked and talked about the reasons her husband gave for not coming, about his fear that he wouldn't be able to afford the bills if he took two weeks of unpaid vacation. His concern that his clients, or worse yet, his boss, would perceive him as "not invested" if he left work for a month.

"Do you think he's afraid he'll lose his job if he's gone that long?" I asked.

"I know he is. He even told me so: 'If they can get by without me for a month, why not a year, why not always?'"

Trisha shook her head sadly and asked if we could sit down. After we'd settled onto a low rock wall next to the path, she pulled a cigarette from the little pouch attached to her belt and promptly lit it. She took a long, sober drag. I could tell she'd been pondering these next words for a long time.

"You know what bothers me? I've come to the realization that he is more afraid of losing his job than losing me."

The words lingered, floating like a spirit in the smoke between us.

She then went on. "I decided to walk this Camino to prove to myself that I can go on with my life without him. That I don't need him to be happy."

Trisha's Camino was no longer a path to Compostela; it had transformed into a symbol of her future. It was a test of her marriage, of her capacity to find happiness on her own. Trisha had nursed her feelings over her husband's absence, and instead of finding happiness; her feelings had grown into a bitter resentment.

I've seen this many times in the patients I treat. It usually occurs around mid-life when a simple question rears its head: "Is that all there is?" It's the fear that time is running out. Running out for happiness, for physical attractiveness and mental dexterity, for realizing the dreams that would make them feel fulfilled. Many people in their forties, fifties and sixties don't even stop to update their dreams. They're still running on the same aspirations they had in their twenties: "I've got to have a good job. I've got to make more money."

By all accounts, Trisha's husband seems to love her. He looks after her when she's sick. He encouraged her a year ago to push her boss to let her work from home and offered to support her if she lost her job because of it. She won a great deal of independence when she took that risk.

Her husband always remembers her birthday and their anniversary with a nice gift and dinner out. What Trisha's husband had failed to do was check in on her updated dreams. He probably wasn't even checking in with his own evolving needs. Was it still a fitting goal to own the best car, the biggest house, or make the fattest paycheck? Could he benefit from completing an inventory of his forty-six-year-old values? They've most likely changed over the years. If he did perform the inventory, he might discover his purpose had grown with the wisdom of midlife. I decided to share my thoughts.

"I think getting older is hard on our memory; we become more forgetful. But there's one very good thing that happens. We get better at seeing the big picture and sidestepping the traps. Even our motivations change. Maybe yours have changed and his just haven't caught up yet."

Trisha agreed with the part about her motivations but was more leery about having hope for her husband.

"I'm much more worried about staying healthy than he is. His family has heart attacks early and his father died of Alzheimer's disease. But he doesn't want to work out with me. Even though back home I walk every day."

She continued, "And it's not just about physical health. I'm doing charity work now that I've reduced the hours I used to travel to work. The Camino was supposed to help me walk and be more creative."

She had taken a photography class before she booked her travel and had learned techniques she would use here specifically, like how to best capture the changing terrain by getting the camera lens down on the ground level so that she was peering up to the foot standing above the earth. While her husband was still back home trying to keep up their comfortable lifestyle, Trisha was opening the door to a different life.

Erik Erikson, a developmental psychologist, described midlife as: the phase of life in which "generativity" must prevail for healthy growth. It's the key to growing old successfully. It requires us to extend our personal goals beyond ourselves and our immediate family and friends to include the greater needs of the world and humanity. For most of us, this desire grows proportionally to our age and our emotional maturity. For others, it leads to what Erikson called "stagnation." These individuals remain self-absorbed on material goals and experience little desire to guide the next generation or to contribute to the greater society. They lose ground and fail to establish a creative and meaningful life beyond establishing successful careers.

Trisha was wrestling with the anxiety that she would have to spend the rest of her life in a marriage where her dreams would die of neglect. She wasn't ready to accept that this was "all there is." She knew time was running out, and she would have to take action on her own in order to break through the inertia of the unfulfilling existence she and her husband were living. I guess that's why she chose to walk the Camino alone.

Trisha finishes her cigarette and we rise from our perches on the stonewall. While shouldering our backpacks, she says, "Thanks for listening to me. If you hadn't asked how I was feeling, I probably wouldn't have even brought it up. It's hard to admit we're having this trouble, even to myself."

"I have the feeling you're going to find a way to salvage your marriage, Trisha," I say. "You're strong and you haven't given up on your dreams. Plus, it's clear you still love your husband and he loves you. Divorce is the last option, only after you've tried giving it everything you've got. Believe me, I know."

Trisha's decision to walk the Camino without her husband had already proven that she could take care of herself. She could use that same strength to teach her husband. I've been watching women like her, so strong, walking hundreds of miles alone. They give me hope that some day I might have the same kind of courage to just be myself.

Lesson for Today: It's scary to be middle-aged and alone. It's even scarier to be middle-aged and trapped.

Chapter 27: Stone Cold Sorrow

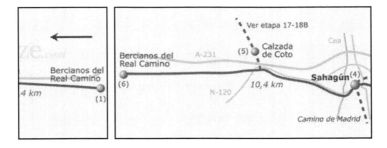

Trail Day 22, Sahagún to Calzadilla de los Hermanillos, 14 km

Remembering that I'll be dead soon is the most important tool I've ever encountered to help me make the big choices in life. Because almost everything, all external expectations, all pride, all fear of embarrassment or failure, just fall away in the face of death, leaving only what is truly important.
- Steve Jobs

Elaine: It's often said: "Be careful what you pray for." I learned today just how very true this statement can be. As we've walked, I've prayed for a better understanding of why I'm doing this pilgrimage. Today, I received it. While Joe and I sat on the front porch with our friends sipping cold drinks, he received a text message. Leaning over, he whispered into my ear, "You need to look at this." It was from my sister, Janet. It simply stated: *"Pop is sick, the doctor thinks it's cancer."* Joe and I excused ourselves from the group and bolted upstairs to our room to start making phone calls.

Joe: The six of us walked together, reaching Calzadilla de los Hermanillos around lunchtime. It was a short day of 14 kilometers when we entered the small farming village growing out of the flat, chalky plains. It wasn't even marked on our map. There were no obvious cafés and the one grocery store was the size of a walk-in closet. The pensión we found at the edge of town was quite wonderful though, and completely unexpected in this ancient little community. We all checked in to our rooms and agreed to meet later on the patio. A half-hour later, Elaine and I walked back downstairs. The young proprietors were husband and wife. She focused on our comfort and preparing our food, while he focused on making us laugh. We took our seats at one of the red plastic tables sitting on the front porch. Everyone in our group was there and we ordered cold drinks with lots of ice. Our drinks were being served when I received a text message.

Elaine: I called Janet and asked what she knew. She said, "The doctor's 90 percent certain it's cancer. He says it's probably terminal because Pop's lost a lot of weight over the past month." To make matters worse, they had detected a sizeable mass with imaging studies. She did not want to alarm my parents by telling them about the doctor's opinion and implored me to keep it to myself.

I hung up and immediately felt nauseous.

Pop's eighty-one years old and has been having stomach issues for the last year. It sounds serious. My immediate reaction is to stop the Camino and jump on the next flight back home. Joe starts checking on flights and we soon discover it would take several days to get back.

"Thank God it's not a life and death emergency," I say, but I'm already feeling like it is.

"I've got to call my parents! I've got to go home!" I'm practically screaming the words.

Joe is quiet. I'm completely irrational and I know it. It doesn't matter though, because I'm running purely on fear. I don't *care* whether I'm making sense.

"I'm in the middle of nowhere and my father is dying and there's no airport here. We don't even have a rental car!"

Joe is very soothing. "We'll get a taxi to drive us to the airport. It will only take thirty minutes. Then we can get on standby for the very next flight out. "

He's slowly peeling me off the ceiling with his calm, logical approach.

Joe goes on, "The airport just seems far away because all we do is walk. If we got in a car right now, we could be there in 30 minutes."

This little assurance of hope gives me the strength to call my parents to get their thoughts on what's happening. I exhale as a cue to relax and slow my breathing, then I dial their number.

After speaking to my mom and pop, it's clear that no one has told them about the "90 percent" part. Just that the doctor thinks there could be a number of causes for his weight loss. Since my sister has sworn me to secrecy, I say nothing, but I still question my mother about returning home.

She tells me, "I think you should finish what you started. There's no reason to come home yet. You don't have that much longer to go anyway."

My father says, "I've lived a good life. We all have to go sometime and we still don't know what's going to happen."

They both encouraged me to "wait to see what the doctor says" before I try booking an emergency flight back home. My mother finished off with some more advice: "I had cancer and I recovered. People don't die from cancer overnight. Your father still looks healthy, and he's eating. You should continue the peregrinación."

I think about their advice and how much the reality of death has been nagging at me for the past few months.

I know it sounds morbid, but every day, even several times a day, I've been thinking about my own death and how I will face it. I picture myself embracing the final moment. So much so that I've mentally practiced what it would look and even feel like – physically. For instance, just today when Joe and I checked into our room, Joe filled the bathtub with cold water. As I tentatively started submerging my burning feet into that freezing liquid, I immediately remembered how one author had described the moment of death. He'd compared it to jumping into a pool of cold water, but said that once you embrace it, the pain is over. I thrust my feet down into the water and tried to accept it when my feet were feeling stabbed by thousands of needles. The pain didn't stop no matter how much I tried to let go and "embrace it." I wondered whether that author had any real clue about death. I guess none of us really does.

I'm wondering...all this thinking about death and then I get the message about Pop. Have I been doing this walk with the right spirit? Have I been devoting myself to this journey with the right faith, or have I been in the wrong mindset? I know I can't stop my father's, my mother's, or my own death. The ruminations about life and death are happening for a reason. I can't help thinking about the words of Princess Isabelle in the movie *Braveheart* when she stands at the bedside of the dying king and whispers in his ear, "You see? Death comes to us all."

Just two days ago, Len told me about the loss of his mother. Len looks like a tall, ruddy-faced Canadian Teddy bear. He speaks gently and there's a warmth about him that attracts strangers to become his instant friends. We were walking ahead of the others when he told me his mom had died a year ago. "It was right in the middle of a family reunion that she had put together for all of us." Len knew it was coming; she had been in poor health for a few years, but he never expected it to happen during their party.

"I guess in a way it was perfect for her because she got a chance to be with all the people she loved on the day she died." I said this hoping to soothe him. But the thought of losing his mom was still too raw for him to hold in his mind.

I can still hear his soft words, "The death of someone we love is very hard to accept, eh?"

His words spoke such a simple truth. He added, "I just want to reach out to her...just a phone call, but she's not there." I think his words are the definition of grief. We want to reach out, but the space is empty where it was once filled with love, with support, with some simple words of encouragement, or at the very least, with a living being that meant something to us. Every time we reach out, the emptiness reminds us we're missing something important that we still want and can't have.

Pop is alive, but this is another reminder that I will soon enough lose everything in this world including this body I'm using to carry me to Compostela. Can I use the rest of this pilgrimage as a spiritual journey, focusing on the Church and the symbols of life after death as a means to deepen my own faith? Can I stay on this path and focus on the reason we've been placed on this Earth despite the transience of our existence? I certainly won't be the first, but rather the millionth or so pilgrim to use this walk to deepen my understanding of life and God. Is that what God is encouraging me to do through this additional suffering, through this contact from my sister?

I'm now praying about this and trying to be a better listener. My path doesn't seem clear. I don't know if I'll finish this pilgrimage or go home for my Pop. Before I make such an important decision I'll have to give myself a chance to think, to listen and to choose a spiritual path regardless of whether I fly back or continue walking Santiago's way.

Joe went downstairs to meet everyone for dinner while I withdrew under the covers of my bed and into my thoughts. He quietly returned shortly afterwards. Thinking I was asleep, he tiptoed around the room as he got ready for bed. As he crawls in next to me, I realize he's been very quiet throughout all of this. *There's something going on for him too.* I immediately think it has to do with the news today, with my father. But that doesn't feel entirely right either. I'm too tired and too emotionally depleted to talk to him about it now. Instead, I curl up against his chest to bridge the gap between us and try to fall asleep.

As I lie there awake, I hear a steady humming sound. I wonder which electric appliance is running in this barren little room of ours. Then I yawn and the humming stops. I decide to use a monotonous form of repetition as a tried-and-true method for relaxing: *1, 2, 3, 4, 5, 6...* I usually get to 100 and start over again until the regulator in my brain kicks off like a thermostat that's reached the set temperature and I fall fast asleep. I start mentally counting and the humming starts again. "What is that?" I say it out loud, and as soon as I open my mouth I realize what it is. It's the sound of my jaw clenching!

Lesson for Today: No matter how much we prepare for the inevitable reality of a loved one's death, the first experience of grief feels raw and painful. Accepting this truth helps to separate our pain from unnecessary layers of suffering.

Chapter 28: People of Our Camino

Trail Day 23, Calzadilla de los Hermanillos to Mansilla de las Mulas, 20 km

Ordinary riches can be stolen; real riches cannot. In your soul are
infinitely precious things that cannot be taken from you.
- Oscar Wilde

Joe: Elaine and I quickly outdistanced our companions. With the worries about her pop, Winslow, she had withdrawn and was out-walking me as she pushed forward down the path. Her eyes were focused on the ground, her trekking poles stabbing furiously at the earth. I'd had breakfast with our group a couple hours earlier and told them about her father's illness and our need to walk our own path today.

I knew that Elaine just wanted to be left alone with her thoughts, so I quietly walked beside her without saying a word. Occasionally looking behind us, I noticed our increasing distance from the group. I wondered how they felt about being left behind. An hour of walking down the dirt road passed before Elaine's pace slowed. She raised her eyes from the path just in front of us and looked up at the horizon.

Breaking the silence, she said, "I'm getting tired. Can we find a place to sit down?"

Up ahead, about a half a kilometer away, I saw some green trees and tall grass growing out of the barren farmland. This signaled the location of an occasional stream that meanders through the mesetas. I nodded my head, pointing my trekking pole at the oasis in the brown, broken countryside. Elaine nodded her head in agreement and we walked on.

I've noticed over the last week that I've become more introspective. I've been withdrawing from people, including Elaine, and I seem to have switched roles with her as far as socializing with others. Aside from my ad-hoc birthday party, I've been keeping to myself. I've detached emotionally and the news of Winslow's sickness has brought a cold feeling to my heart. I still worry about Elaine. I know what I need to do to help, to support her, but on the inside I'm just numb. How does any of this matter? We live. We die. We're forgotten. Life goes on.

As we headed toward our oasis, I tried to shake out of my depression. I needed to be there for Elaine, I knew she would want to talk when we sat down to rest. Watching our slow separation from the rest of the group, I thought about how everyone travels the Camino at different paces: some are on schedules and have to get back to the "real world," some have no immediate commitments and are leisurely taking each day at a time. Other pilgrims are uncomfortable with the day-to-day search for a place to lay their heads, so they've made reservations several days or even weeks ahead of time that requires them to stick to a schedule. No matter how we go about it, though, it still comes down to putting one foot in front of the other, at different speeds, with different strides and at different times, but all with the goal of reaching Santiago.

During our walk we'd reunite with pilgrims we'd met days or weeks before. It's a nice little surprise. From our frequent meetings with Stan, Barb, Len and Patty, it was apparent that our progress along The Way was quite similar. We all got along quite well, so it was an unspoken decision that we would be traveling together for a while. But it's purely circumstantial. Even today, Trisha walks alone and she's apparently gotten ahead of us.

As we walk, we learn a lot about each other. We talk about our backgrounds, relationships, and why we're here. Elaine, being a natural-born therapist, asks those personal questions that draw people's feelings out into the light of day. It's a fairly safe environment to talk freely, being separated from our family and friends and our normal routines. We have an abundance of time to reflect as the kilometers pass under our feet.

These discussions eventually led to the deaths of loved ones. I explained to the group how my Camino had come about due to the death of my father on the Appalachian Trail. Stan talked about the death of his wife several years ago and his struggle to recover from the emptiness in his life. Patty reflected on the death of her ex-husband and Len described his difficulty accepting the loss of his mother just a year ago. Elaine gently prodded each of us to reveal more, using examples from her past as well as explaining the various stages and psychotherapy techniques for dealing with grief.

I can't help but be amazed by the level of openness and trust we'd already shared with each other in such a short period. We'd only been together for a few days and yet we were discussing topics and shedding tears with one another in ways many of us don't even experience back home with our closest friends and relatives. I can see how "Camino friends" can become friends for life. Is that part of how the pilgrimage becomes a spiritual journey? For many of us, God is at the center; but perhaps this is His way of speaking to us directly. These pilgrims help to center and balance our lives by sharing the pain we often cover up with our daily routines back home. Here on the Camino, our feelings are splayed open with a faith that they will be held gently by our fellow peregrinos. But I guess I'm not ready to be splayed open quite yet.

Elaine and I approached the little green oasis that was intersecting our path. We dropped our packs to the ground and sat down in the lush, green grass on the bank of the stream. Through the clear rushing water, I could see small colorful fish darting back and forth in the current, weaving in between the swaying, multicolored water plants.

Elaine said, "It's not fair for me to leave our friends out...they've shared so much with me...I feel bad for leaving them behind."

I nodded my head in agreement. "Maybe we should wait for them."

She sat quietly, looking at the clear water flowing just below our feet and then back down the road at our companions a kilometer behind us. Elaine then stood up and started walking back the way we came.

"What are you doing?" I asked.

She yelled back, "It's not enough to just wait for them."

It's an unwritten rule on the Camino: no wasted steps. It's just too damn long. I don't know if she realized that retracing her steps like that carried a lot of meaning.

Len and Patty are typical Canadians; they love the outdoors and have more energy and endurance than we do. To look at, to even listen to Barb would bring back memories of your favorite schoolteacher. She's gentle and soft-spoken with a beautiful English accent. She's doing the Camino because she loved doing it so much last year! You will not see me doing 800-kilometers a second time. Then there's Stan, a large man who's in his mid-forties. Take Paul Hogan (of *Crocodile Dundee* fame), double the size of his chest, legs and arms and you have this classic Aussie. He's tough, worked outside most of his life, but is the gentlest, politest tree trunk of a man you'd ever meet. When he's walking with Barb you might be fooled into thinking he's out of shape because of his slow, ambling gait.

When we first got together as a group, the women naturally tended to walk and talk together more often. This allowed Stan to open up, and I'm not talking about words. I'd be out in front of the pack, taking the lead as usual, and the next thing I know Stan is walking beside me. A few minutes later I'm starting to notice my breath rate increasing; I've unconsciously picked up my speed to stay in the lead. Another few minutes go by and I have to accept the fact that Stan wants the lead and he'll let me walk a half step behind him and no closer. Every time I go toe-to-toe with him he takes it as an invitation to pick up the pace some more. Several times a day, Stan and I would leave the pack far behind as we discuss the intricacies of wine production, the design and construction of cast iron machinery or the differences between life in Australia and the US.

I sat and watched Elaine for several minutes heading back down the road toward the group. Stan was in the lead with Len close behind him. Elaine reached them and they stopped for a moment and talked. Then the three of them headed back to my resting place by the stream. I couldn't believe my eyes and ears as they approached. Elaine and Stan were in full-fledged crying mode. The tears were streaming down this big Aussie's cheeks and

I couldn't understand a word either one was saying in between their sobs. Their conversation then paused for a moment in an awkward silence. This gave Elaine the opportunity to turn away and head back down the road again toward Barb and Patty several hundred meters behind. Again, as they returned, all three women were crying and hugging and laughing and crying again. Len, the only stoic in the bunch, silently pulled out his handkerchief and blew his nose, complaining of allergies. I was actually feeling a little left out but at the same time relieved that I had been spared any more tears. The night before, Elaine's despair over her father had been pretty rough on me. I was feeling powerless, empty, and drained of emotion.

We all rested quietly by the flowing stream, occasionally picking up pebbles and throwing them into the water, watching the fish first dart away and then return with curiosity at the disturbance. Fifteen minutes later we were all once again ambling down the Camino together.

Elaine: I knew exactly what it meant to retrace my steps on the Camino. In fact, one of my favorite phrases while walking was, "No extras!" and I do mean steps. You might say this is a pitiful phrase to have on a journey of the spirit, and you would be right. That is exactly why walking back in atonement for leaving my friends was so significant. I knew there would be no peace for me if I shut these people out of my pain.

Walking back was more than a physical challenge. Would they be angry with me for leaving them behind? Would they feel awkward about my situation? Of course, these were four different people, each with unique reactions and personalities. It didn't matter. I had no control over any of those things. The only thing that mattered was doing the right thing: apologizing. If they were angry or rejecting, I would deal with it.

I stepped toward each one of them and said, "You shared so much with me on our walks, it was wrong for me to walk away. I should have had the courage to take the same risks you did."

I hoped that duplicating my steps would show them how sorry I was.

The first time I said it, I braced myself for dismissal. But by the time I got to the last person, Patty, there was no more fear, only gratitude. Instead of four different responses, I got unanimous support from all of them. At that moment, there was no stopping it. The tears came flooding down and I didn't even try to stop them. It may sound trivial, but I'm so proficient at remaining impassive because of my profession and overall guarded nature that I can actually cry out of only one eye. I didn't even know this was possible until I sat watching a movie with my family one day, some dramatic tearjerker. I didn't want anyone to see me crying and the next thing I knew, I was crying from only one eye, the one on the side where no one was sitting. I'm embarrassed to admit this, but it's true. The freedom I felt to cry openly with these individuals told me something was changing in me. There was no role to play, no false beliefs about what it meant to be strong here in this place. It was like finding out you've been wearing a 100-pound suit of armor for years and then suddenly realizing you could take it off without being attacked. I'd like to say I will never pick it up again, but I don't know if that's true. I can say I know how liberating it feels to drop it and experience the lightness of just being me.

Lesson for Today: Avoiding others when we feel vulnerable is as natural as using a strong, well-formed muscle. The real emotional strength training occurs during the effort we make to lift others into our private space.

Chapter 29: Saying Goodbye

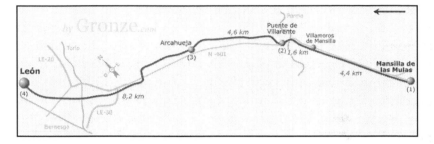

Trail Day 24, Mansilla de las Mulas to León, 18 km

Things derive their being and nature by mutual dependence and are
nothing in themselves.
- Nagarjuna

Joe: Stan and Barb bade us goodbye early this morning as Elaine and I searched the empty stone streets of Mansilla de las Mulas for an open café. They were worn out and decided to take a cab to our next stop, the grand city of León. We waved goodbye as they climbed into a taxi and rode away. I wondered if we would ever see them again. We walked farther on through the town, eventually finding our coffee and croissants at what appeared to be the only establishment open. Patty and Len soon appeared, and after about 1000 calories worth of sugars, fats and carbs, I felt ready to go. It was four of us now as we walked out of town and across the medieval bridge spanning the Rio Esla.

Our walk was uninspiring. We journeyed down the busy highways and streets that fed León. The rush of cars, the industrial complexes, the suburban sprawl depleted me.

I notice that my mood lifts as the architecture ages. It's a Friday afternoon and the beginning of a long holiday weekend. The people were festive as we mixed and jostled along the sidewalks of the city, feeling like part of the crowd instead of foreigners on pilgrimage.

León is the capital of the León province and famous for its 13th century Gothic cathedral, Pulchra Leónina, filled with ornate displays of stained glass windows and the Basilica of San Isidoro, housing the Tombs of the Kings. It's Friday, the 12th of October and we'd been warned that it was a national holiday; all the pensións would be booked. Concerned, I'd tried to make reservations online even though it went against our "no plans" philosophy. The warnings were correct; there were no habitaciones anywhere. We headed for the Santa Maria de Carbajal, a Benedictine monastery and albergue just off the Plaza de Santa María del Camino. Stepping off the busy street, we entered through a passageway into a quiet central courtyard. We found a dozen or so pilgrims standing at the reception desk. It was all very organized and peaceful; the sheer presence of the monastery brought a hushed tone and gentleness to us all.

We were soon meeting other pilgrims and telling our individual stories while waiting to check in.

"Hi, I'm Joe from Massachusetts," I say to a small group sitting at a picnic table.

Jim, Ellen, and Nancy are from Texas. They'd been on the pilgrimage for two weeks. Nancy, a pretty woman with long auburn hair, says that she's here with her teenage son.

Jim speaks up and says, "Well, he's somewhere on the Camino, who knows where."

Nancy nodded and had just started to walk away when it struck me.

"Oh, by the way, Nancy, I have a message from your son."

She turned to me and gave me that all-knowing sneer that every man is quite familiar with. It's the one that says, "I've heard that line before, nice try." She walked away again, knowing that some complete stranger isn't going to come walking up to her out of the blue to deliver a message.

I tried again, speaking confidently to her back. "His name is Peter."

She stops and turns. Her expression is mixed between amazement and suspicion. She's thinking, "Either this guy's really good or I'm having a Camino moment!" She turns back to the table with a questioning look and I know my guess is correct.

I continue on. "We ran into Peter a couple days ago. He was heading to a pharmacy. He's fine and wanted me to tell you not to worry."

He didn't really say that last part, but mothers always like to hear it. Never expecting to meet this woman, I had filed Peter's request away in the back of my mind, about assuring his mom he was okay. *What were the chances?* The Camino takes care of that, though. We just have to take the steps to let it unfold. We all parted company after getting checked in and Nancy appeared to be a bit happier after hearing that her boy was okay.

This was the first time that Patty and Len were staying at an albergue. They were visibly nervous about the whole idea. They'd had an unpleasant experience during their first night on the Camino. Arriving late in the evening to the Roncesvalles monastery, they found it had no room. After one of the most brutal days of the Camino, they were without a bed. They had to walk the dark streets to find a taxi that would take them to another town for lodging. Ever since that experience, they'd always made reservations to avoid a similar occurrence.

The hospitaleros gave the four of us a quick briefing on the facilities, the rules and the etiquette. Since it's an active monastery, the male and female sleeping quarters are separated; men upstairs and women downstairs. Patty was a little shocked at this; she was already nervous about being packed in to a huge bedroom with a bunch of strangers. Now she was going to have to do it without Len.

The hospitalero continued: "Breakfast is at 0800. There are laundry facilities and there's someone to do your laundry for you if you wish. There are kitchen areas and free Wi-Fi, all for a donation of 5 euros. There's no judgment; if you can't afford the 5 euros, you are just as welcome."

They then showed us to our assigned beds.

Len and I settled into our dorm and changed out of our dusty trail clothes. He was worried about leaving his backpack unguarded in the barracks-style lodging.

I understood his hesitation and said, "It take's a little getting used to, but it really is safe. It was hard for me at the beginning to let go and just have faith. Besides, if it's something I can't afford to lose, like my phone, I just take it with me."

A half hour later we were cleaned up, and Elaine suggested we visit the church. I wanted to support her and go along, but I was feeling completely exhausted. I didn't know why. I was in great shape, and my feet and legs were strong and pain-free. On the trail I'd even run on occasion just to get my heart beating a little. But I was lacking energy at the end of the day, more than what I'd expect for normal fatigue, more than the rest of our little group. Maybe it was my frame of mind. Winslow's illness might have been having a bigger impact on me than I thought.

I walked out of the monastery with the others, but my heart just wasn't in it. How could Elaine have so much energy?

As we walked, she urged me to walk faster, saying, "I need to see the church. Let's eat quickly so we can move on. Maybe we'll find Stan and Barb if we keep moving."

Something is happening to Elaine and I'm not sure it's based on her father's illness alone. She looks like she's suffering physically, more than I've seen during this entire trek. She'll ask me to tie her trail shoes tighter, saying, "Pull them till they're ready to snap, Joe." Before this, her goal was to let her feet breathe as she walked. I'm worried she's pushing herself too hard as she wrestles with her decision about going back home.

I've started carrying most of the gear in Elaine's backpack. I began the Camino with twenty-two pounds, but I'm now at thirty-five. It's a constant battle with her. She's too proud for such assistance and I have to be persistent. "Elaine! You're not only slowing yourself down with this painful struggle, you're slowing me down!" After another hour or so she'll finally relent and I can load up. She doesn't believe me when I say, "I don't even notice the difference," but the fact is, I don't. If anything, it helps because I don't have to "check" my stride as much with a little extra weight on my back. My comfortable stride shortens down a bit to better match Elaine's.

Sometimes, when she is being especially stubborn, I have to sneak things out of her pack when her back is turned or when she's gone into a café to grab something. She eventually catches on, usually when we're in our room and she's looking for some item.

By then it's too late and she can complain all she wants. I just smile at her.

Lesson for Today: It's easy to worry about being too dependent until you realize a healthy relationship runs on a thermostat constantly adjusting to the changing needs of the other.

Chapter 30: A Horse of a Different Man

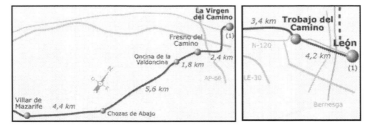

Trail Day 25, León to Villar de Mazarife, 22 km

Some people see things that are and ask, "Why?" Some people
dream of things that never were and ask, "Why not?" Some people
have to go to work and don't have time for all that.
- George Carlin

Joe: Breakfast at the monastery was a madhouse as Len and I
entered the crowded little room filled to capacity. It was hard toast,
jam and instant coffee. We didn't last very long in the press of the
crowd and worked our way back out. The search was then on for
our wives, who were still sequestered in the female sleeping
quarters. Len was hesitant to enter the women's quarters, so I
ventured in alone to face a barracks full of half-dressed women. I
found Elaine completely dressed and ready to go, but Patty was still
sound asleep despite the hustle and bustle of pilgrims getting ready
for the day. The sight of her lying there still sound asleep was quite
comical. Throughout her trip she's been worrying about not being
able to sleep in an albergue because of her need for privacy.

I asked Elaine, "Should I wake her up?"

She shrugged her shoulders. "Maybe we should give her a
little more time."

I departed while trying not to stare at all the bare skin and
went in search of Len. He was in the courtyard talking to several

other waiting husbands. I told him about Patty's state of consciousness and he asked me to return and wake her up. He was nervous about going in, but I was told it was all right when I'd asked one of the hospitaleros about Internet access. In order to get to the computers, everyone had to pass through the women's dormitory.

"It's a tough job, but I'll go back."

Returning to Pat's bunk, she was just opening her eyes to the new day and strange surroundings. She smiled at me and I could see she was well rested. When I smiled back, she knew exactly what I was thinking and said, "I guess I was more tired than I realized, eh?"

An hour later, the four of us were heading out of León and up another series of rolling hills. We walked only a few kilometers before Elaine's pain returned with a vengeance. This was going to be a very tough day for her. We were worried about even making it to the outskirts of León. We had to do something to fix this, but what? We'd tried everything.

Elaine: I saw something today that made me think of the freedom we lose when we try too hard to stay in control. The Camino is meaningful because of the demands we leave behind in order to stay on the path to a stronger spirit. By stepping into this simple world of walking, eating and resting, the pressures of the life we leave behind are less stark, less in-your-face. For many of us, walking the Camino means setting aside our job, kids, the house or now, in my case, my Pop's health. All those things we believe we have control over. Back home, we accept these as responsibilities, never questioning and always feeling an obligation to keep them in play like a juggler with so many balls up in the air.

Today, I saw something that changed all that.

While sitting outside resting my throbbing feet at a small sidewalk café in the city, we watched a man walk up and tie his pony to a lamppost only a couple of meters from our table. He turned and walked into the café as if he'd just parked his car. The pony had a birdcage strapped on its back with a single yellow cockatiel perched securely inside. The bird had its own little mirror and a bell for entertainment. The pony was so close; we reached out and petted him as we drank our coffee. He was surprisingly calm amidst the interested roamers that stopped curiously to investigate, petting him lovingly. Cars passed by, then bicycles. There were all sorts of distractions that normally spook prey animals like him, but he remained utterly calm. Even the bird was unusually placid. It seemed both the owner and his animals had broken from their normal conventions. It was as if they were all saying, "We're a family. We live on our own terms, whether it's making our way through a bustling city or ambling down a dirt path. We accept all risks because it's the price we pay to live as we want. So laugh, scorn or love us. None of it matters. We define our own lives."

We saw this merry little troupe later on again as we walked into the town of Chozas de Abajo. The man was offering a local woman the opportunity to take a picture of her little boy on the pony. Was this man rejecting society or finding his special place in it. Either way, his lifestyle was his own and it was a good reminder of how often we follow convention without considering the range of wildly different alternatives available to us. What would I do differently if I didn't have to think about how other people would react? Or, if I released my belief that I can control people and events? I don't see myself walking with a horse and a bird, but maybe I would sell my house, keep a few personal mementos and explore the most scenic parts of the world. As I walked today, this man and his traveling companions solidified in my mind, the understanding that the only thing I can truly control in this life are my actions.

Since I'd gotten the news about my father, I'd been going to church before Mass to pray, and each time I stumbled onto an active novena. A novena is a supercharged prayer. At church it's all the more powerful because there are several voices all rising in unity on the same path to God's mercy. Believers follow the Rosary bead by bead saying the corresponding ten *Hail Marys* and a singular *Lord's Prayer* and *Glory Be* per decade of the Rosary. I join in immediately because I've been part of novena gatherings since I was a kid.

In my teen years, I rejected my Catholic identity and later, as an adult, I turned away again after my divorce. They didn't want me because I didn't get an annulment and so I decided I didn't want them. But the novena was different. It stayed pure because I learned it through the good-hearted women who visited my childhood home and used it as a direct line of communication to God. Walking in on a novena each time I've stepped into church for the last two days, especially when I'm so conflicted, is a sign from the Holy Spirit. I know it is. Today, I started saying my own novena without a rosary during our walk. I'm praying for my father's recovery using every single step as a tag for every word in my prayer.

Patty, Len and Joe have slowed their pace for me. I'm getting better at letting them. It helps me stay balanced while I wait for news about my father's diagnosis.

Lesson for Today: The power to control life, death and the people around us is an illusion that takes us on the path of Sisyphus.

Chapter 31: A Bittersweet Promise

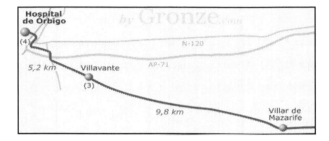

Trail Day 26, Villar de Mazarife to Hospital de Órbigo, 16 km

I went to the woods because I wished to live deliberately, to confront
only the essential facts of life, and see if I could not learn what it had
to teach, and not, when I came to die, discover that I had not lived.
- Henry David Thoreau

Joe: Somewhere along this desolate stretch of road we crossed an imaginary line. It marked 500 kilometers since we departed Saint-Jean-Pied-de-Port. It seems so long ago. I've changed. My body ignores the temporary pains; it's grown all too familiar with them. When my mind says, *Stop, this is enough!* I keep walking.

Patty, Len, Elaine and I worked our way farther west, pushing for the town of Hospital de Órbigo. The terrain was reasonably flat so we were more relaxed, more able to walk together and talk as a group.

Patty brought up her idea about starting a cosmetics business. She'd been experimenting with different formulations of natural cosmetics and toiletries as a hobby. She said they'd gotten quite popular with her friends, neighbors and their customers at the campground.

She said, "I'll need to invest a lot of money for production. I'd really be stepping out on a limb with our savings and the equity in our home. We'd have nothing to fall back on."

Elaine said, "That's a tough one. What about getting a business loan? Finding backers?"

Patty replied, "Oh, I can do that, but that's not the problem. The reason I'm bringing it up is because I have huge anxiety about money. Just thinking about it scares the hell out of me. Here, Elaine, take my pulse, you'll see.

Elaine took Patty's wrist in her hand and looked at her watch. After fifteen seconds she released her hand.

"Wow, Patty, it's at 130 beats."

"Yup. That's not from this leisurely walk we're taking. It's just from thinking about spending money, even someone else's like you just said! How ridiculous is that?"

I'd only been passively listening to Patty's words while enjoying our walk, but her last statement sank in. For some reason, it was really important for me to understand what she was feeling. I can see where a fear of heights can come from, but fear of spending money? Why? And is it really "ridiculous?" As usual, my way of dissecting this is to make some bold statements to see if they hold water.

"Patty, your fears, even if they are a bit exaggerated, aren't ridiculous."

Because of my mood, I'd been pretty quiet all morning, keeping to myself, so this catches her attention, as well as everyone else's.

"As far as your body is concerned, these fears are real. You're obviously having a strong physical reaction. Labeling them as ridiculous is like sweeping them under the rug; they don't go away. Anxiety has a strong biological basis. It's a survival instinct. It's a response to some threat to our safety. The problem is that we have the instinct, but we don't have much in the way of real threats anymore. Our modern society has taken care of that for us. Compared to 1000 years ago, even 100 years ago, most risks to our safety have disappeared."

I noticed Patty looking at Elaine; she wasn't expecting me to be the therapist. Elaine didn't interrupt, so I took it as a sign to keep going. "Elaine's taught me a lot about anxiety; we've talked about it for hours. She says it helps to get an outsider's opinion and I'm really motivated to understand it. It has such a huge impact on my life." I glance over at Elaine with a smile.

Patty said, "That's hard to believe. You have anxieties too?"

"No, actually, I'm the opposite; instead of amplifying my fears, I amplify the threat."

Elaine said, "There's a grove of trees up ahead and it's getting close to lunch time. Let's sit down for something to eat, then Joe can give us his thoughts."

Everyone agreed and I silently appreciated Elaine for putting off something I wasn't sure I wanted to continue talking about or had the capability to verbalize. As soon as I'd said "I amplify the threat," something clicked inside. It opened up a door, but I wasn't sure I wanted to go through it.

We continued walking the rest of the way to the grove while a thousand thoughts ran through my head: fear, anxiety, risk, passion, death, God, discontent, depression, pain, suffering...peace. PEACE! When will I ever find some peace? That's my problem here on the Camino, I'm not finding the peace I usually find during my journeys. Even if it's only short-lived, even if I sink into a depression every time my journey is over, at least I find some temporary peace. But not now, not here on the Camino.

Why?

We dropped our packs and sat down on a bed of pine needles underneath the trees. Pulling out some snacks, we shared them back and forth between the four of us. We were all in a bit of internal reverie, and not much was said for a while. Elaine finished her food and pulled off her shoes to massage her feet.

Len encouraged me: "We really do want to hear what you think. We won't give you any peace until you're finished."

I want some peace and now Len tells me I won't have any until I explain myself. Maybe he's right.

"Okay, I'll try to make some sense of this. I push myself to take risks. I think sometimes it's the only thing that keeps me sane. And the risks aren't always about life or death; they are always about pushing my limits. I expose myself, I make myself vulnerable, risking failure or embarrassment or pain. I create threats to my safety, either real or imaginary."

"You've heard Elaine and I say, 'Our plan is not to have a plan.' That's a nice little cozy philosophy that I can just picture on some stupid slideshow on the internet with pretty pictures in the background of couples sitting in hammocks on a tropical island."

"In reality, our 'no plan' plan puts us at risk. We don't know where or when we'll be sleeping tonight. It's not life or death, but it pushes us outside of our comfort zone, especially Elaine's."

I think to myself, *I've been doing this all my life, but I've never stopped to ask, "Why?" At least, not until now.*

Patty says, "Joe, I hear what you're saying, but my fear is about money. What does your risk-taking have to do with my anxiety over money?"

"It has everything to do with it. Your anxiety and my need to take risks are two edges of the same sword. And that sword is engraved,

THREAT

"It's our fight-or-flight mechanism. Your anxiety is a 'flight' reaction to the threat and my passion for risk-taking is a 'fight' reaction to the threat. Both of them are important reactions for our survival. It's the whole duality thing, yin-yang, masculine-feminine philosophy. And the important part to realize is that we often manufacture the threats when they don't really exist."

They all seemed interested, so I continued.

"Over the last 50,000 years we've gone from being cave dwellers to a highly sophisticated society. Along the way, we've understandably made our lives more comfortable. We're more secure. We're safer. It's a survival instinct: we created this safe environment for ourselves. But, there's another survival instinct that's just as important and we can't ignore it: it's being able to respond to threats in our environment. We have to keep our skills honed so we can survive. We're like the house cat sharpening its claws on the living room couch. The cat has no threat to its safety, but it still hones its ability to respond. The cat will sometimes run and hide, other times, it'll attack. It's the two edges of the sword and we've all seen them do it."

"Let me give you an example: Patty, you are afraid of heights, right?"

"Yes."

"Can I assume that the first day on the Camino was hard on you because you were climbing up some pretty high mountains?"

She nods in agreement.

"Why did you do that? What drove you to risk your life like that?"

"Well…my life wasn't really in danger; it was just my anxiety."

"But, as far as your body and your emotions were concerned, you were making a life-or-death decision. Why bother? You could have stayed home."

"Well, I wanted to walk the Camino. It's a challenge."

"Exactly. It's the challenge; it's about creating a threat and then reacting to it. You could have run from the threat of falling off a mountain or you could attack, you chose to attack. They don't have to be life-or-death threats; they're just threats to our comfort, to our feeling of safety and security. And they're instinctual; we're genetically wired to create threats and react to them."

Patty says, "So you are saying that our instinct has to be satisfied, people need to create these threats every day."

"Yes. The four of us are doing it right here, right now. We manifest it differently. You have these accentuated anxieties you respond to, like heights and finances. I have these challenging situations that I navigate through like sailing, scuba diving or riding motorcycles. But it's all the same. Even the physiology is the same. The best doctor in the world would have a tough time differentiating the physical responses between anxiety and excitement. The important thing is to realize that we are building our skills right now, we are practicing our responses to threats and feeling more secure because of it."

We all got up from the ground and hoisted our backpacks. I was still missing something, though. All this talking and I still hadn't stepped through that door I'd opened. So Patty and Elaine create their threats in one way and I create them in another, big deal. Why were they so cheerful and I so sullen?

The farm road meandered through the rolling countryside and the din of highway traffic slowly emerged from our quiet surroundings. Our path led us to a high overpass where we would be crossing a busy highway. The rush of cars and tractor-trailers was an assault on our senses. All our intellectual discussions of the day didn't prevent Patty from withdrawing with a worried expression as we approached the incline that would lead us up to the bridge. She didn't hide it: her fear of heights was intense. She'd been struggling with every piece of the Camino that led her through steep mountains or over bridges. Today was different though: Elaine had been coaching her for the past few days. Instead of asking Len for his hand, Patty motioned for him to keep walking. Elaine pulled out her iPhone and set it to the video mode to record the event. She also secretly knew that the video recording would distract Patty from the fear.

Elaine then said in an encouraging voice, "Ok, Patty, I want you to just follow me, and do like we talked about."

Len and I walked across the overpass and watched from the other side. I've noticed that the heights of guardrails on overpasses in Spain are different from American standards. They are apparently designed to prevent cars from going over the edge *not people*, especially people carrying heavy backpacks. The top of the rail was below the level of Patty's hip and the psychological impact on this cold, windy day with a rush of cars and tractor-trailers passing below us was frightening her.

Patty stepped forward with determination and my own fear started to climb with hers. She carefully put one foot in front of the other as her hair streamed to the side, wet with rain and perspiration. Her jacket rippled in the wind. Elaine was walking backwards, cradling trekking poles under her arm while watching the screen on her iPhone and saying soothing words to Patty. "Remember the breathing we practiced, feel your trekking poles in your hands."

Elaine waited a little, then said, "Think about your goal for why you're doing this. Yeah, that it! You're doing it! It's all just like we practiced!"

"I can't watch this," I said to Len. "It's starting to make *me* anxious."

I turned around and walked on. They reached the other side safely with a cheer and started laughing at how silly they must have looked to all the oncoming traffic.

Patty said, "I think the only serious risk was to the cars that might have drifted off the road from watching our bizarre display."

Energized with some fresh adrenalin and a feeling of success, we continued on to Hospital de Órbigo.

We crossed a long, stone footbridge and entered the center of town. After asking for guidance from a local pedestrian, we found a perfect place for the night. It was a casa rural called "El Centro de

Turismo." We were too late for lunch, so the search was started for anything open with the promise of food. We dropped off our backpacks and walked back to the center of town.

Len quickly spotted a small pastry shop. I'd read that this area was famous for it's desserts and I needed a coffee so we made a beeline for the shop. I reached it first and turned the handle. Just as I was swinging the door, I heard a booming voice with a strong Spanish accent shout, "Closed! Come back later!"

I continued on inside.

A large elderly man, obviously the owner by his countenance, walks out from behind the counter. Len starts speaking Spanish to him in his typical calm, friendly manner. Judging from the little fragments I could pick up, Len was explaining that we just wanted a quick snack to walk out with.

The owner, Manuel, says gruffly in broken English, "It's siesta, store is closed, be quick."

Crowding up to the glass cases filled with sweets, our wives proceeded to fawn over the huge variety of desserts as Len and I pushed our luck and ordered coffees. The pastries were in fact, miniature works of art, all different, all mouth-watering. We surveyed the variety of candied, moist, and creamy concoctions on display and forgot all about Manuel's time admonition.

"What are these?" Patty asked, pointing to a flaky, buttery cake.

"Those are *bizcochos*." Manuel replied tersely.

Len prompted, again in Spanish, "Senor, your pastries are fit for the gods. You're a real artisan."

I could see Manuel's expression soften. "I make these every day. Yes, they are my little *obras* (works of art)."

He continued, "I do not let them get old, only fresh. Many days I give them away because I will not sell old *postres* (desserts)."

The worry over time slowly melted away for Manuel as we each questioned him about his obras. He made all of us coffees as we continued to browse the showcase. He was lost in a baker's world, describing his creations: the puff pastries, the jellied tarts, and cakes drizzled with honeyed syrups. We learn the name for the spongy pound cakes called *mantecadas*. I have my eye on a particularly tempting chocolate dessert covered with dark cream beneath a fresh dusting of cocoa.

Thirty minutes and two coffees later, we were all sitting around Manuel's dessert bar laughing and telling stories like old friends. He seemed oblivious to siesta as the time drifted by. His wife joined us in eager acceptance of this unusual and unexpected diversion from their afternoon break. But was it really? Siesta is about relaxing, sharing, communing with family and friends. I realized that they were treating us like friends, not foreigners. Elaine and Len acted as translators as the six of us continued talking, translating or miming to get our points across. Manuel then told his best pilgrim story while his wife listened intently, inserting an occasional detail here and there:

Two years ago an elderly pilgrim walked into my shop and asked to use the phone. The man, looked like he was in his eighties. He tells me that he calls his son every week to let him know that he's safe and well. I don't like to use my line for long distance, but he was an old man and I know the importance of family so I gave him the phone. I hear him talking, "I'm doing just fine, Son." "Don't worry about me, I feel great." "Only two more weeks to go."

The old man hangs up and sits down for a cup of coffee and a pastry. He tells me he's walking the Camino as a "promesa," a promise he made to his wife while on her deathbed. They were planning to walk the Camino together, but she took ill before they could go. He vowed to God and to his wife he would finish the pilgrimage for both of them, for both their souls. He pays his bill, he even pays for using the phone and he leaves. I wish him a "Buen Camino" and to "Go with God."

Two weeks go by when I get a worried phone call from this man's son, "It's my father! I haven't heard from him since he called me from your number. Have you seen him? Can you help me?" I explained that his father had walked out soon after the call and I hadn't seen him since. I told him his father would be fine and that I would pray for him. The son thanked me, said he would keep looking and hung up. This bothered me, and all the time I wondered, "What happened to the old man?"

A year goes by and I'm here in my shop. It was a cold Saturday morning in November when a middle-aged pilgrim walked in; he sat down for a pastry and café-con-leche. As the man sipped his coffee, he kept a curious eye on me. I feel that he has some reason for being here.

He does not finish his breakfast. He just looks at me and I'm thinking he wants something. Then he says, "Excuse me, but I called here just over a year ago looking for my father. Are you the person I talked to?"

I replied, "Sí, Yes, Yes! I've wondered all this time what happened to him. How is he?"

The son, Thomas, explained to me that on his mother's deathbed, his father had promised to walk the Camino in her name. I told him that indeed his father had told me about the promesa. The son explained that after he called me looking for his father, there was no more word of his whereabouts, no success in finding him. Then, he received a phone call from Santiago a week later. His father had died of a heart attack, just three days after finishing the Camino.

I watched as Manuel's wife reached out and gently squeezed his hand. Then she softly declared, "But he finished it. He kept his *promesa* to his wife. Is there any better way to leave this Earth?"

Manuel bowed his head and nodded. Then he continued:

"That morning, Thomas told me that he stopped here in my shop out of respect for his father. He decided he, too, must walk the Camino as a sign of love and respect for his departed father and mother."

Manuel's story touched us all. I sat there silently looking down into my empty coffee cup. I thought about my dad, John, and his awareness that his time here on Earth was coming to an end. Did he already suspect that the Appalachian Trail might be his deathbed? Did he wonder if he'd made a big enough difference in this world? Was he ready? I think about my mom, who's now in her eighties, and how she's had to deal with his loss as well as facing her own impending mortality. What will I do when she's gone? I'll have no parents left. It scares me.

I watch Elaine deal with her anxieties and pain in such an open, exposed way every day. She actively shares them, challenges them, exposes them to the light of day in front of our fellow pilgrims. In comparison, I'm one of those cold stone statues standing outside the bakery window in this small plaza. My own anxieties are buried too deep; they define my character. My constant motion, my passion for travel, my pursuit of adventure, it's all just my attempt to escape the inescapable.

My anxiety is the fear that I will not be remembered when my life is over, that I haven't done any good in this world at all. I'm afraid that at the end of my days I won't even care. I'll just sink into apathy, dying some miserable death and believing in nothing. And I don't see *that* anxiety going away anytime soon.

Throughout our journey Elaine and I have been passing small memorials, plaques, and crosses in the most obscure places along the trail. Some of them commemorate those who were not able to walk the Camino; some honor those who died on the Camino. Manuel's bakery is a living memorial to the memory of a husband, his wife and their son. A witness to commitment, sacrifice and love. Their story will be carried forward in our most basic and oldest traditions, the spoken word. I know that he will repeat this story to as many pilgrims as will listen, and they in turn, like me, will repeat it to others.

Manuel's story brought calmness and a serenity to our little siesta. We took the silence as a signal that it was time to move on. We paid our bill and shared our appreciation with Manuel and his wife for opening up their shop and their lives to us. We said, "Adios" and walked out the door. The rain was gently falling, a veil shrouding each of us, hiding our personal reactions to his story.

Two unexpected friends were placed on our path. I could have walked away at that first sign of brusqueness – actually, some would call it flat-out rejection. But my growing faith in finding lessons around every corner propelled me through the door of that closed pastry shop. Well, that and my insatiable sweet tooth and coffee addiction.

We walked back down the cobbled street to our beautiful casa rural with its wood fire burning in the hearth and a welcoming family. Home is where my heart and my mind dwell and, even in my depressed mood, they're still right here with me on the Camino.

Elaine: After listening to the moving story of a husband who died on the Camino in honor of his wife, we all walked back in silence. The town and our walk had greater significance now. We were becoming part of a walking history.

"How was your walk through town?" the owner asked me in Spanish as she spread out a pillowcase and passed an old-fashioned steam iron over it. This was no average iron; the steam came from a separate reservoir the size of a fish tank several feet away. It sent plumes of mist rising above her head with a hiss of heat on each sweep. I told her about the story we had heard at the bakery and the spectacular confections.

"Oh, if you thought those were good, you're in for a real treat tonight. My daughter, Carina, is also an artisan."

I smiled and half-heartedly nodded, assuming she was like every mother I'd ever befriended: a one-woman pep squad for her little girl. I reminded myself to say something kind at dinner. I stood up to leave and she called out, "Dinner will be ready at 7:00." She was already done with the pillowcase and reaching for one of about thirty hand towels still to be ironed. I could only marvel at how quickly she seemed to be disappearing amidst an ocean of white smooth linen and creased towels.

At dinner, we met our illustrious chef, Carina. She was about twenty-three years old and strikingly beautiful with long blond hair, a clever expression, and an air of grace that far exceeded her age. Her movements were nimble and confident as she doled out plate after plate of uniquely exquisite courses. We ate stewed codfish with paprika, savory pork medallions, tender white asparagus and rich garlic, and lentil soup until it hurt to keep eating.

"I think you will like the dessert. I try a new recipe every night." Before I could beg, "No mas," Carina had already brought out a perfectly formed, volcano-shaped dark chocolate mother lode of delight. As if to drive home a culinary morality play, she had placed the decadent dark concoction, complete with fresh strawberries shimmering on top, above a cloud of sweet Chantilly. There was no denying it; this young woman had rivaled the artisan baker forty years her senior. How'd she do it?

When other girls her age were dreaming of dates with boys and starting families, she was fantasizing about her next delectable masterpiece. Some people live to eat. Carina lives for self-expression and cooking is her medium. The Centro de Turismo turned out to be an extraordinary find with no fanfare to prepare us on the way to the town. It's not on the popular American websites or guidebooks. We could have easily passed it, having no idea what we'd missed.

Carina was kind enough to provide two of her favorite recipes:

Cheese Flan

Ingredients
Sugar
Whipped Cream, 1 pint
Cottage Cheese, 1 cup
Milk, 1 cup
Cream Cheese, 12 oz

Caramelize sugar in a 9" baking dish (can be done in a microwave). Swirl around the bottom and sides of dish. In a separate bowl, mix whipped cream, sugar to taste (approx 6 Tbsp), cottage cheese, milk and cream cheese. Cook while stirring until the mixture gets thick. Place mix in the caramelized baking dish. Cool on a rack then turn onto a large serving dish and you have a simple cheese flan!

Cup Of Tri-Colored Chocolate

Ingredients
White Chocolate
Milk, 1 cup
Whipped cream, 1 cup
Cottage Cheese, 1 cup

Dark Chocolate
Milk, 1 cup
Whipped Cream, 1 cup
Cottage Cheese, 1 cup

Milk Chocolate
Milk, 1 cup
Whipped Cream, 1 cup
Cottage Cheese, 1 cup

In a pot, mix the first four ingredients and heat until it starts boiling, then place in glass. Do the same with each of the other ingredients separately and pour on top of the white chocolate first and then the milk chocolate last on top of dark chocolate. Cool in refrigerator and top with strawberries or favorite berries...Serve and enjoy.

For pictures of her many wonderful confections visit:
Centro de Turismo Rural (Carina) on Facebook.

Lesson for Today: Travel is often scary, but it carries us far beyond geography. It allows us to live on through the stories we make, the history we create.

Chapter 32: There Are No Coincidences on the Camino

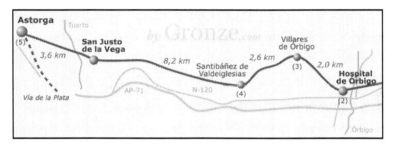

Trail Day 27, Hospital de Órbigo to Astorga, 16 km

Each friend represents a world in us, a world not born until they arrive, and it is only by this meeting that a new world is born.
- Anais Nin

Joe: Due to the limitations in Patty and Len's schedule, they wanted to move on this morning, to take a taxi to the next town where they hoped to catch up with Stan and Barb. They were at odds on the decision. Len wanted to continue walking and Patty wanted the taxi in order to get back on schedule. They were split between staying with us on the slow walking route or taking the easier road ahead. It was a hard decision and we'd all been tempted at one point or another. I knew in my heart that I wanted to walk, but if Elaine decided she'd had enough of the pain I would've gladly hailed the next car that happened by. We said goodbye to them as they loaded their bags into the cab.

Elaine and I walked the next 16 kilometers alone, to the large city of Astorga with its famous 15th century gothic Cathedral St. Marta and Gaudi's Bishops Palace. It was cold, windy and rainy as we entered the city and climbed up the steep streets to the center. It was siesta time again and most of the cafés and all the stores were closed. Everyone had gone home to sit in front of the fire or curl up in his or her beds for a nap.

Unsure of where to go or what to do, Elaine and I stopped and stared into the window of one of the closed stores. Displayed among an array of hiking boots were some cushioned high-tech winter socks. I lusted for them; this is what our world had come to. We were completely alone, in a strange city in northern Spain, in an empty plaza over two thousand years old, and the rain was still coming down. We were wet and cold and tired, but all I wanted to do was stand and stare at a pair of comfortable socks.

Out of the corner of my eye I noticed a stranger walking toward us. He was obviously a pilgrim from his dress and backpack. He had a hood pulled tightly over his down-turned head. As he reached us, still looking down at the ground, he spoke in perfect English, "Joe, can you tell me what time it is?"

I instinctively looked at my wrist, which had no watch on it. The stranger lifted his head and smiled. We were absolutely shocked. "Pete!" we both said together. It was Pete, our Camino guide from Westover AFB. The man who introduced the Camino to us, who was instrumental in helping us prepare for this pilgrimage. Pete was the one responsible for Elaine's efforts to speak openly to everyone she meets because of his simple belief that we are purposely placed on this path to learn and to teach.

As Elaine and I stand there in mutual shock, Pete explains, "I've been with my girlfriend in Germany for the last several weeks and decided to come back to hike the last portion of the Camino one more time. I arrived here in Astorga by bus and missed my connection that was going to take me closer to Santiago."

Pete had been wandering around the city for the last hour in a bit of a funk until he happened to spot two wet, wretched-looking souls staring in the front window of a closed backpacking store. The chances of him running into us within an hour of stepping off a bus in Spain were infinitesimal!

The three of us all start talking at the same time. Elaine's explaining how the Camino has just brought us all together at the perfect moment, Pete's trying to ask how we happened to be here at this moment and I'm trying to say, "Let's go find a warm café somewhere."

Everyone heard my words. We walked away from the storefront and unexpectedly found an open café just around the corner. We entered its warm interior, ordered drinks and sat down to catch up. Over the course of the next half hour, we explained the details of how each of us came to be here. Elaine and I convinced Pete to put off taking the next bus heading west so he could travel with us for a few days. He agreed. We were all convinced the Camino had brought us together for a reason.

Elaine: Ok, I've decided: there are no coincidences on the Camino! Meeting Pete in a large foreign city when none of us had any idea of where the other was at any given time was too uncanny to be a coincidence. I know it meant that Pete had more to teach us and maybe there's something he needs from us. Either way, we know this time is meant to be spent together; otherwise, Pete would be in Germany right now preparing his new apartment with his fiancée.

As we spent the afternoon walking through Astorga, I watched Pete. I wanted to learn more about how he thinks. His gaze sets briefly on a statue of Quo Vadis (the pilgrim), then on some interesting architectural detail of nearby Roman ruins. A second later he's greeting a fellow pilgrim with "Buen Camino" the same as if he's taking a breath. He's nimbly observant of the people and spaces around him, soaking up the smallest details, whether it's stopping to consider the size of an apple tree or reading a memorial left to commemorate a fallen pilgrim. I saw him patiently listen to one peregrino describing his stay at a local albergue, and later, he privately told us he'd already stayed there. "I just wanted to hear what that fella saw when he was there."

Physically, Pete is in incredibly fit shape for any age, but it's even more impressive given that he's ramping into his later sixties. He sports thick, white tufts of hair and looks out into the world with curious crystal blue eyes that are sharp in their focus and warm in their gaze. He makes off-handed comments like, "It looks like the Camino has taken hold of you," and "The Camino will change your life." He can say things like this and mean it because he believes in the power of this pilgrimage. For him, it's a means of transformation; the Camino changed *his* life. He's a perfect example of the axiom, "You find what you are looking for." Pete

193

looks for purpose and meaning in life, and every day he finds it. I know with Pete by our side, we're about to see a whole new Camino. I secretly thank God for bringing Pete to ease my worries.

While on our way to the albergue we stopped to pick up some snacks. The albergue kitchens are set up with the basics for food preparation; like pots, pans, utensils, and cups. Nothing fancy and definitely nothing beyond salt for seasonings unless others have left some behind. Pilgrims who want to cook their own meals bring food from the local *supermercado*. The meals they prepare can range from a simple boiled egg to three or four-course banquets. There's no telling what will be put on the table. Joe, Pete and I kept it really simple – cheese, bread, salami, rice pudding and some cooking sherry I had mistakenly bought, thinking it was wine.

Once settled into our albergue, we sat around musing about our unexpected reunion at the communal table. We promptly met an attractive couple from Germany. They spoke enough broken English to share that he was an engineer and she was in her last year of medical school. She had two months before her boards. They had decided to hike the Camino for three weeks as a way for her to recharge before hitting the books for the final comprehensive exams. The two had just moved in together and were clearly in that *twitterpated* state you see when it's springtime and love is in the albergue.

As the five of us ate together, casually discussing our separate plans for the Camino, another pilgrim approached holding a frying pan. He asked, "Would you like some chicken wings?" This man was about forty with a dark tan, piercing black eyes and wild, long curly brown hair that he tamed away from his face into a thick pony tail. Joe and Pete piped up quickly, "Si. Gracias!"

I have a bit of a germ phobia so I opted out of any food I hadn't washed or prepared myself. My contamination anxiety causes me to miss out on some once-in-a-lifetime offerings, like this one.

The man introduced himself as Cristiano. He served a generous portion of the wings on a simple ceramic plate and made sure to dole out an equally ample, vibrant red sauce he had stewed up as a complement to the wings. Joe was so impressed he asked for the recipe. Without hesitation, the man responded in Spanish, "Salt, pepper, paprika, garlic, tomatoes, and love."

Of course, I had to translate this to Joe and Pete, and for a second I kind of stumbled over the last word. It's not often I hear anyone, especially a man, refer to an emotion as a cooking ingredient. Coming from a Spanish male, this really blew me away. But I quickly checked myself and translated his words literally. This opened the door for further discussion since we were all intrigued by his unfettered speech. Joe and Pete pressed me for more translations.

There are certain people who capture singular attention in a crowded room and this guy was one of those special charismatic characters. I couldn't keep up well enough to translate everything, but I was able to convey that Cristiano was from Barcelona and had worked as a stage designer for a well-known theatre in that city. The economic downturn had cost him his job, but it turned out to be a blessing. He described himself as a man released from prison.

"I had grown to despise the city because there was no community. Every day, I would see people walking to their jobs and they would stare down at the sidewalk, never greeting one another. Never caring what happens to their neighbor."

He spoke without bitterness, but his words were undeniably passionate. "After I left the theatre, I came to understand that I did not need much to live a happy life...just love, simple food, exercise, nature and a place to rest."

He described the albergue as a luxury, mostly for warmth and showers, because he carried a tent in his backpack and slept under the stars most nights. *The albergue as luxury? Wow, this was definitely a new perspective.*

He proudly declared, "I have very little money, but it's more than I need. I buy eggs in the morning, and then I boil them so I can eat them during the day. It's an excellent form of protein and very inexpensive."

Despite his limited income, Cristiano believed in paying forward a portion of most everything he received. "Just this morning I was given four tomatoes, and I've already shared two."

He looked down at his sauce and smiled, "God always provides."

I offered to share our dessert of rice pudding with him, but he declined graciously, pointing to his meal, "I have too much food here already, but thank you."

He seemed to detect my disappointment when I said, "I promise we didn't eat from it, I only poured it out...we didn't even touch it with our spoons."

He understood the message; it was my germ phobia speaking loud and clear. He looked straight into my eyes holding my gaze for a few moments. Then he answered, "I feel no disgust (*no tengo asco*). That is not why I declined...oh, okay, let me have some...thank you, it looks very delicious."

I could tell he was being chivalrous, but he was also using a very strong word in Spanish, *asco,* which means "strong revulsion" *or* "disgust." Is that what I have? I've always thought of it in clinical terms, as a "germ phobia." The term is sterile. The word "asco," on the other hand, is profoundly visceral. Is that why it affects me so deeply? Why I can't shake it no matter how hard I try? Is there a way to use Wise Mind with this strong emotion?

Intellect: "The chicken wings are well cooked. They are no more likely to be contaminated than anything else you've eaten in any of the restaurants on the Camino."

Emotion: "He touched the food with his hands. What if he didn't wash them before he started preparing it? What if he didn't wash the utensils?"

Wise Mind: "Joe and Pete are eating it. This man has just spent time nourishing your spirit. He's helped you learn something about why eating food prepared by others has been such a hard battle for you. There's plenty of food from the store to eat right now, so it's not necessary to eat the wings if you're not ready. But it *is* important to take the lesson and remember this moment so you can use it when the time is right."

Spanish Chicken Wings

Ingredients
2 pounds chicken wings
2 teaspoons paprika
1 teaspoon salt
$\frac{1}{4}$ teaspoons black pepper
1 tablespoon olive oil
2 tablespoons finely chopped fresh garlic
1 large finely chopped tomato

Rub the chicken wings with salt, pepper and paprika and let it marinate for 15 minutes. In a large skillet, heat olive oil over medium heat. Add the wings, working in batches if necessary, to avoid overcrowding the pan. Brown chicken wings until golden on both sides. This should take about 9 minutes. Add the chopped garlic and tomato and continue to cook for 2 minutes. Serve while hot after drizzling the sauce in the pan over the top of the wings.

Cristiano made me think about the saying, "What would Jesus do?" He's distilled his life to the most basic ingredients and love is at the core, whether it's in the form of a seasoning for food, or a humble expression of faith in a God who provides for his needs. He had lived the high life as an artist in Barcelona but felt no fulfillment. As a pilgrim, he has no prestige, but he feels at peace. Am I showing the same strength of faith in my own unpredictable life, or will I keep second-guessing God's plan for me? Would we have met this man if Pete hadn't suggested we stay at this particular albergue? I'm convinced of the answer, but I'm still not sure what to do about it.

Lesson for Today: Our fear of contact with strangers, the active decision to turn away from the unknown, masks the gifts that are waiting to be tasted.

Chapter 33: Pain and Cold and Wet and a Promise

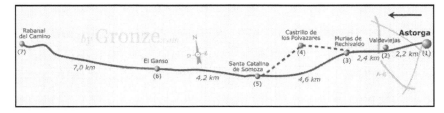

Trail Day 28, Astorga to Rabanal del Camino, 20 km

In everyone's life, at some time, our inner fire goes out. It is then burst into flame by an encounter with another human being. We should all be thankful for those people who rekindle the inner spirit.
- Albert Schweitzer

Joe: As Pete, Elaine and I stood at the café counter waiting for our morning caffeine, we met the newest addition to our small troupe. Denise is a tall, strawberry-blond, forty-six-year-old woman. She was standing next to us and heard us speaking English.

"Where are you from?" she asked.

A minute later we were all sitting together at a small table by the front window. Denise is from Wisconsin and has an outdoorsy Scottish look about her. She's been traveling alone on the Camino, starting in Saint-Jean like us. The inevitable conversation about shoes, socks and feet led to Denise expressing her need for some medical attention due to a blister.

"I need to find a pharmacy before I go any farther. My blister is starting to get infected."

Pete said, "Let me see your boots."

Denise pulled off her boots, and Pete started re-lacing them in a different pattern as we all offered some advice about the best way to heal her blister. We finished our breakfast and then the four of us headed off to find a pharmacy for some bandages.

Walking out of Astorga, our days of traveling the endless rolling farmlands in the center third of the Camino had come to an end. We started ascending the first of many forested mountains that remained between us and Santiago. We hiked 21 kilometers over mostly wet, slippery rocks the size of my fist and eventually landed in the remote mountain village of Rabanal del Camino. There's not a single level street in this village. We kept climbing and eventually found the ancient stone Refugio Gaucelmo. It's an albergue operated by the Confraternity of Saint James and is for pilgrims only. It has forty-six beds in two large rooms on the second floor. The first floor houses a kitchen and dining area as well as a warm "gathering room" with a large, open fireplace.

I walked through the small entryway and asked the man sitting behind an old wooden desk, "Do you by any chance have a private room available?"

Bill, the British hospitalero, apologetically said, "Sorry, mate, we only have two large rooms for everyone."

I reply, "We really need a private room for tonight. We'll keep looking, thanks."

Pete and Denise eased forward with their credenciales in hand, happy to get a couple beds regardless of the crowded surroundings. I stepped back outside. Elaine was sitting down on a bench beside the stone entranceway. She was in a very sorry state; the rocks, the rain, the cold and the 21-kilometer climb had taken a toll on her. She was thoroughly depleted. She could barely walk and needed some seclusion to recover, both physically and emotionally.

I said, "Don't worry, I'll find us something."

Bill stepped outside a minute later to point out the laundry room to Pete and Denise. His eyes fell on Elaine. He stopped in mid-sentence and his face changed to one of immediate concern. Bending down, he spoke to Elaine in a half whisper, "I have a room that is rarely ever used. It's unheated, but private. It even has a lock on the door."

Elaine just looked at him as his words slowly sank in. He picked up Elaine's backpack and said, "Come this way...follow me."

How long will it take me to accept the fact that people are here to help us? Not a word said, just a simple but profound observation when his eyes met Elaine's, directed us down a path of giving and of receiving.

To risk stepping out our front door everyday without a clue as to what is in store for us requires faith. The matter-of-fact part of me *expects* this day to work out, but only because of my proactive make-it-happen attitude. Bill's recognition of our need and his immediate response to meet it pushed past my logic and into my neglected spirit. It brought a lump to my throat. I hadn't realized how worried I'd been about Elaine, how focused I'd been on just forcing an outcome by saying "Don't worry, I'll find a place." My attempt at controlling the outcome blinded me to the sacredness of the Camino. The answer to our dilemma was standing right in front of me. These people are here to help and all I need to do is open up. I was prepared to have Elaine stand back up and follow me in search of what I wanted to find. But it was already there in front of me, and when it came I was unprepared for the shift in my emotions.

Elaine and I followed Bill inside and up a stone stairway to the second floor. At the top of the stairs, he turned to the right and unlocked an old wooden door with a skeleton key. We entered the small room. Bill pointed out the original 200-year-old floors that had been worn down over an inch in places. The stone walls were two feet thick and the only electricity was a bare light bulb hanging by its cord from the ceiling. "Unheated" up here in the mountains means that the room, unlike the larger dorms, was *not* located above the room on the first floor with the burning fireplace. The fireplace is kept burning throughout the night warming the rooms above it. But it didn't matter, we had warm sleeping bags and soft beds to sleep in.

Now that we were alone, I quickly unpacked both our sleeping bags and bundled Elaine up in the lower bunk until I couldn't see any part of her. I then pulled together all our laundry and turned to pull the cord hanging next to the light bulb. As the room slipped into darkness, I quietly headed out the door.

Elaine said, "Wait!"

She opened up the sleeping bags just long enough to ask, "Will you hand me the iPhone?"

In her completely exhausted and painful state, she was still going to write about her pilgrimage. I dug through my backpack and handed her the phone.

Glancing back as I closed the door behind me, she had disappeared once again under the covers.

Elaine: There have been days when I've pushed beyond what I thought was my capacity, but today was the Grand Camino. My sleeping bag is acting as an isolation and recovery chamber. We're in Rabanal del Camino, high in the mountains, in a stone building with about thirty other pilgrims. It's cold and dark and raining outside and there's no heat except for a fireplace in the common area, way too far away from here to do any good. The hospitaleros are two British men with sharp wits and great warmth. One of them, Bill, is so attuned to each arriving pilgrim that he immediately sensed there was something wrong with me and stepped forward to meet me like a parent scooping up an injured child.

I can't stop shivering, probably because my thermo-regulation center is completely on strike along with my feet, calves and knees. They've just refused to follow my will.

Why all the pain and rebellion from my body now, so far into the Camino?

Last week, when I found out about my father being ill, I struggled to make the best decision about returning home. The natural impulse for most people would be to rush home when a loved one is sick. That morning, when I turned around and walked back down the trail to reach out to our friends, they proved to be important touchstones for advice. How could I turn to people I barely know for such an important decision? I hardly believed I could do it myself. But every single one of them had trusted me with their experience of loss —and I'm talking about the loss of important loved ones – a mother, a father, a husband, a wife. They all had wisdom that derived from surviving painful life experiences. In the Spanish culture there's a saying: *Más sabe el Diablo por viejo que por diablo.* It basically means, "The Devil knows more from his age and experience than from being the Devil." In this case, I had over 250 years of collective wisdom to draw from.

When I asked each one of our friends for his or her thoughts about whether I should finish the Camino or go home, I could tell they were each pondering their responses with extreme gravity. None wanted to give a recommendation because of how important we knew the outcome would be. But when I pressed for their *thoughts* instead of their solutions, my request was met with a barrage of questions: "What do you know of his illness?" "Is it immediately life threatening?" "Have you asked your father what he would like you to do?" "What is your relationship like with your father?" "Would he feel comfortable telling you if he wanted you to come home now?" "Do you have any unfinished business, things left unsaid or undone with your dad?"

Those were just some of the questions they asked as they considered how to respond. Beyond questions, they also provided anecdotes from their own lives when they had been faced with similar decisions.

As we walked and shared, it became increasingly clear that, short of direct knowledge of what was wrong with my Pop, the family and me would be best served by finishing the Camino. My father didn't even have a diagnosis. He was feeling about the same as when I left according to both my mother and him. I have no unfinished business with him – we talked daily before I left. But could I really keep walking in Spain when my father might receive some horrible news? I resolved to wait. "Resolved" sounds like I'm sure. But I'm not. I've been racking my brain trying to figure out what I have control over with regard to my father's illness, especially from halfway across the world. Then, while attending Mass several days ago, I got my answer.

The priest started service by asking us to move to the vestibule. He told us that the Pope had declared this the year of faith and that we were all going to be baptized again in order to renew our commitment to God. He anointed us all with holy water. I knew then that I was exactly where I was supposed to be. It was right in front of me the whole time: I'm on a pilgrimage seeking a stronger faith. I've been going to church but questioning the relevancy of these ancient traditions in my modern life. That church service was one of the many little miracles I've experienced here so far, but I had a hard time connecting them to a divine source. That's when I decided to draw on a family tradition. That's when I made my *own* promesa.

My mother had made a promesa years ago; when my sister, Janet, was a baby and had a life-threatening fever. She promised God she'd wear white for a year if God would intervene to save her. My sister was saved and a tradition was born.

As the priest anointed me with holy water, I promised God to walk the rest of the Camino without any medicine for pain as a sign of faith that he could heal my father.

Now we've come full circle. I'm laying here in bed shivering from the havoc this pain is wreaking on my entire constitution. There's a rebound phenomenon that occurs when a person abruptly stops taking an anti-inflammatory, or worse, a pain medication like codeine. I'm no exception. Each day I walk without the medicine is a greater struggle. Still, I'm committed to walking the Camino with nothing except fish oil for my swelling. It's my expression of faith. I don't want to break this promesa, but my body's resisting it.

I haven't told Joe why my pain has gotten so unbearable. He doesn't know about my promesa. Maybe I should explain it to him. He seems preoccupied, though, and his words are gloomy, the saddest I've ever heard from him. I've been so worried about my own problems; I haven't been paying attention to his needs. It's so easy to take the person closest to us for granted. All this stress about my condition can't be helping him.

I strongly believe men want to please their wives and I know I've been hard to please lately. When one person promotes only his or her own interest, the relationship is starved of the oxygen it needs to survive.

One woman in a marital therapy I provided for her and her husband stands out for me as I think about this. I had asked her why she refused to have sex with her husband. She told me she didn't feel like it because she was too tired. Not because it was unpleasant. She mostly felt exhausted from the demands of raising a four-year-old. By the time her husband came home, she felt like sex was just more work. We tried exercise to get her energy up, but she didn't feel like doing that either. We tried to reduce her workload to give her more energy. Her husband took over making dinner, washing the dishes and preparing their son for bed in addition to working his fifty-hour-a-week job. But still she pushed him away. He told her he would be willing to masturbate to take the pressure off her, but she refused to even consider it as an option. Her husband began masturbating in secret, and this made her upset because it felt like a betrayal. She brought the issue up while we were alone in one of the sessions, saying, "I've had it with his selfishness!" Since she still refused sex, I asked her whether she had ever considered allowing her husband to masturbate with her lying next to him for stimulation and closeness. He was certainly willing to do this as a much better alternative to hiding for self-pleasure. Again, she rejected the idea, saying it would make her feel as if he were just "using" her. After months of trying different approaches to aid them both, I thought of something:

Dr. Foster: When your four-year-old says, "Mom, I want a peanut butter and jelly sandwich," and you're feeling exhausted, what do you say?

Patient: What do I say?

Dr. Foster: Yes, how do you respond?

Patient: Well, I guess I don't *say* anything important. I just make it.

Dr. Foster: When you're in bed for the night and your husband says, "Honey, I want to make love to you," what do you say?

Patient: I don't see what this has to do with my four-year-old. My husband's a grown man, and he knows I'm tired by the end of the day. I've told you, it's just all too much.

Dr. Foster: When your four-year-old asks for the sandwich, you're feeling tired, but you make it anyway. When your husband is starving for sex, you say it's not the same. You're right: it's not the same. There's something you're doing for your son that you're not doing for your husband. You're putting aside your fatigue long enough to take care of your son because you know he needs you. But since your husband is an adult, you don't think he needs you.

Patient: Well, I think there's a big difference between the needs of a four-year-old and the needs of a grown man.

Dr. Foster: That's also true, and yet they're both needs. Your husband is telling you about something he needs from you to feel loved, and to help him nurture his love for you. By giving of yourself even when you're tired, you're sending a powerful message about his importance and the value you place on your relationship together. You've probably heard the definition of synergy: "The whole is greater than the sum of its parts." That can also be used as a definition of marriage.

I don't think I would've pushed her to consider her husband's needs so exclusively if I hadn't witnessed his early attempts to please her and the steady demise of his love as she continued to push him away. I felt an urgency to make the point while she could still have some control over her behavior and her part in the outcome of their marriage. She was adamant she didn't want a divorce and he was becoming increasingly convinced that *she* was the source of his unhappiness.

She'd only made two peanut butter and jelly sandwiches for her husband before she discovered a newfound energy. She said, "Dr. Foster, I thought I would feel exhausted afterwards, but instead, it felt like the old days, before the baby, when I would go to the gym and come home feeling energized." She was gushing. "At first I felt tired, but by the time we finished, I was ready to get up out of bed and go outdoors.

Her husband also reported greater feelings of love for his wife. The relationship got the oxygen it needed, and they even went out to buy new running shoes together, the ones that look like feet with the individual toes. They raved about what a great tool the shoes were and how the two of them were inspired to go running like never before.

So here I am, because of my own worries I've been ignoring Joe's sadness. I'm wondering which of us is most likely to break from the Camino and head home early. *This can't be good for me! Or for Joe!*

I get up and stuff my swollen feet into my Crocs and head off for the dining area to find Joe so I can apologize for being so neglectful

I'm just in time for the first course. One of the pilgrims, Liz, had taken on the responsibility of cooking for thirty people. There are many helping hands, though, and the whole thing was done in an hour. As I looked around, I saw a mass of pilgrims all huddled together on benches by a long wooden table. They were boisterously passing the plates to one another and serving themselves heartily. I searched for Joe. He was already seated, tightly squeezed in the middle of the bench on the opposite side of the table.

"Hey, Elaine, c'mon over here!" The call came from Denise, sitting at the tail end of the bench nearest me.

I squeezed in at the very end next to her. I was half on, half off, but everyone gave an extra squeeze and I suddenly had room to sit comfortably. I then saw Liz with her arm around Joe. They were laughing and telling stories about their past adventures. She'd occasionally take his spoon to serve herself, and even eat some of the food off his plate. It was clear, she was being flirtatious. Then, suddenly, it dawned on me.

She has no idea we're married. She doesn't even know we're together.

Joe's hands had swollen during the Camino and I was the one who suggested he take off his wedding ring. *Ok, God!* I say in my inside voice, *I know you have a great sense of humor, but can you give me just a little break?*

After dinner was over and the crowd dispersed, I told Joe, "I was lying in bed writing when I realized I've been so worried about my father that I've been ignoring you."

Joe replied, "That's okay darling, I know this is hard for you. I'm a big boy. I can take care of myself."

I poke his shoulder and say, "Well, it looks like it's easier when someone is spoon feeding you like Liz did tonight."

Joe knows how to spar with me. He smiles and says, "I think she wanted me."

"I think it's the sexy way you wear your knee brace with the hiking shorts that lured her in."

Then I gave Joe a kiss and said, "Seriously, I know I'm blessed to be here with you, and I don't think I could finish this without you. I've stopped my pain medicine and it's all wearing off now."

Joe's expression changed. "I've been wondering why it's been so much worse for you lately. Why didn't you tell me?"

I thought about it, and decided, *It's now or never.*

"Because I've been taking codeine almost twice a day, and I was afraid you'd be angry with me for masking my pain. But now it doesn't matter because you're right. My body has been screaming 'you're right' with every step I take."

Joe turns away and heads for the men's bathroom saying, "I'm tired. I need to get ready for bed."

Lesson for Today: It's natural to pull away from others as a form of rest and protection when tragedy strikes, but true healing comes through the balm of compassion applied by others to the places we can't reach. A commitment to stand in place, as hand touches wound, can lead to healing.

Chapter 34: Cruz de Ferro and Fear of Letting Go

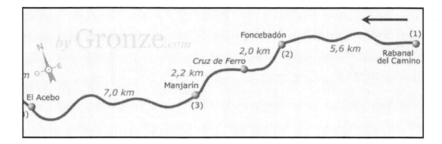

Trail Day 29, Rabanal del Camino to El Acebo, 17 km

Life is a series of natural and spontaneous changes. Don't resist them
– that only creates sorrow. Let reality be reality.
- Lao Tzu

Joe: Elaine told me last night that she'd stopped taking all of her pain medication. The immediate backlash from stopping the medicine appears to have improved, but the pain from the persistent walking hasn't. She refuses to take time off to let her feet recover because she's made a promise – a promesa – to reach Compostela for her father's health. She tells me that time is running out, but I don't really understand the urgency.

A long time ago, I'd heard some words of wisdom about women. It was from a man sitting at a bar down in Texas and I've never forgotten it. He said, "You don't gotta understand 'em, son, you just gotta love 'em." I've heard the saying several times since and for some reason it just stuck with me. So I bite my tongue and walk beside her.

Elaine's foot pain begins with a generalized ache around the 12-kilometer mark. It slowly progresses to excruciating misery by 16 kilometers. We've tried new socks, we've bought new silicon orthotic inserts, and we've even bought new shoes. Nothing gets her past 12 kilometers. I've finally decided that it's just a fact of nature: maybe feet that were raised in New York City aren't built for the kind of punishment we've been subjecting them to. Elaine thinks that since she's spent most of her life in high heels we just need to get her some "trekking heels" for the rest of the pilgrimage. She doesn't realize how close she is to the truth. Our feet adapt to our surroundings, especially when we're growing up. I grew up in the country, playing in the woods, jumping from rock to rock on the shores of Maine, running across open fields. Elaine grew up in the city, wearing high-heeled shoes and walking on flat concrete. Our feet are as much products of our environment as they are products of our genetics. When she walks, I can see her favoring the balls of her feet instead of maintaining the heel-toe-step most hikers take for granted. It's as if she's still wearing heels underneath her trail shoes.

We're on our last third of the Camino, less than 250 kilometers remaining to reach Santiago de Compostela. The farmlands and gentle rolling hills have transitioned into mountains – steep mountains. We're climbing up to the highest point on the Camino today, to an altitude of about 5000 feet. There we'll find the famous *Cruz de Ferro,* the Iron Cross. The temperature is in the high 30's and the rain is falling. The loose, round rocks slip and twist under our feet as we climb. The path has turned into a flowing stream that soaks our feet as it runs down the side of the mountain. It takes two hours of unrelenting climbing. As we approach the top of the mountain, a tall wooden pole with a solitary iron cross comes into view over the treetops.

It's a Camino tradition to carry a stone with you during your pilgrimage. The stone symbolizes something that is important to you: a person, a past event, some future goal, or maybe something that you want to discard from your life. By dropping this stone at the foot of the cross, you reinforce the intention.

It's strange how my brain can get wrapped around these rituals. I've been carrying this stone in my backpack for the last 500 kilometers. It's small, its physical weight insignificant, but when I've been slogging mile after mile along these trails and gone so far as to chop the handle off my toothbrush, I often wonder why I'm carrying the additional weight of this rock. It's because it has significance. My rock memorializes an important event in my life: my father's death on the Appalachian Trail. I want to remember him, I want to remember the miles of narrow winding trails, the mountains and forests that we traversed together. I want to remember the conversations we had while sitting in front of the campfire eating trout, caught fresh from the stream running next to us. I also want him to remember.

Because of divorce and the pain, awkwardness and avoidance that surround it, my dad wasn't a part of my childhood, not until my teenage years. I was fifteen when John stepped back into my life. I was angry, confused and distrustful. It took me a long time and a lot of growing up to start understanding. Over the years, Dad and I slowly grew close. It was never a real father and son relationship; it couldn't be. We had no idea what that was like, no foundation to build on.

John was my friend. Over the years, he showed me how to respect women and how to fix cars. He taught me how to fish and how to remain calm when surrounded by drama. He gave me confidence and helped me look at the world in a different way.

As John was falling to the ground on that spring day, alone on a mountaintop in the Smoky Mountains, did he know the role he had played in me becoming a man? Did he know the impact his life has had on me? I wish he knew the impact his death has had.

Continuing up the trail, I see the high mound of stones surrounding the Cruz de Ferro. We walk closer and I look up at the solitary cross perched high up in the sky. There's a hesitance in our group, an awkwardness as we stand there in the cold rain. Each of us has a fist buried deep in our pockets. I'm holding tightly to my rock. I step forward, approaching the mound of stones. My first thoughts were, *Thank God I'm getting rid of this extra weight.* These thoughts, what Elaine would probably label "avoidance," evaporate when my feet touch the first of tens of thousands of stones piled at the foot of the Cross.

Someone has carried each stone to this mound, each one an icon of someone's life, signifying his or her personal pilgrimage and each stone carrying a secret message. I climb up the hill of wishes, regrets, losses, loves and affirmations, the wet stones slipping and rolling under my feet. The symbolism overwhelms me. As I approach the cross I realize just how important this event really is to me. I stand on top of the mound for several minutes and say a silent prayer for John and then another one for myself. I then drop my stone at the base of the cross. It bounces several feet before settling among the multitude of stones.

I look up at the Cruz de Ferro. The raindrops are hitting my face. Pilgrims have placed small prayer flags around the edge of the mound and I can hear them flapping in the wind. I then look down, searching for my stone. I can't find it; it's gone. My stone and John's spirit have mixed with those that came before. My stone and John's spirit are now a foundation for those that will soon come. My stone and John's spirit are now a part of the oral and written history of the Camino de Santiago.

I walk down the far side of the hill, away from Elaine and the others. I don't want them to see the tears running down my cheeks, tears shed because of a small rock I just carried across northern Spain. As I wait, I watch Elaine approach the cross, then Pete and then Denise.

Each of us took our turn at the cross. We slowly gathered together on the other side of the mound and then walked away from Cruz de Ferro. In the midst of this sad, somber occasion; in the midst of the cold, falling rain and blowing clouds; something strange happened. As we stepped back onto the trail, my companions started smiling. Their hearts seemed filled with lightness. I didn't understand; I was just sad. They started talking and laughing. They were energized, as if a weight had been lifted from their shoulders. I suppose it had been; those little stones were awfully heavy. But why wasn't I feeling the relief?

As we descended the hill, we heard a group of pilgrims in front of us singing, "We're off to see the wizard..."

Elaine: Cruz de Ferro had an extraordinary impact on me, and not for the reasons I thought it would. Cruz de Ferro translates into "Iron Cross" and it's where pilgrims leave a rock or some other symbol they consider meaningful. The idea is that you carry this rock as a sacred intention. I had purchased my rock back in August when I visited my friend, Gregoria, in Brattleboro, Vermont. She was working there as a psychiatrist after retiring from the Air Force. I'd stopped in a local artisan's store and found it – the rock I would carry with me for over 3000 miles. It wrapped up all of my desires for my life and the people I love – it had the word "Hope" inscribed on it. Since my life had changed in so many ways over the last couple years, I felt that hope was one of the only things I still had to hold onto. Ben and Andrew, my two babies, had left for college, and William, my oldest, was long gone with a family of his own.

An empty nest is kind of like eating hot peppers: you start off thinking "This isn't so bad," but shortly after, it hits you with a sting that brings tears to your eyes. I'd left my job and I'd left the military. I left the only life I'd known for the past twenty-five years. I'd even left my home to move up north to support my parents who are in their eighties because they just can't take care of themselves anymore. I can't describe the degree of upheaval I've experienced in such a short period of time. I realize now I've lost a great part of my identity – as a mom, as a military officer and a doctor. On the Camino and in my new life, I'm just Elaine. Who is that? All I have now is my past and this hope of mine.

This sets the stage for the Iron Cross.

It turns out that the cross was moved so that the tour buses could have better access. It looks nothing like I had imagined. The area surrounding it is strewn with all kinds of things, from big brick-sized rocks to cards and notes, trinkets and advertisements. I watched one person in front of me go up to the cross and pick up some random rock from the ground. He held it up for a brief moment; just long enough to take a quick picture. Afterward, he just tossed it toward the cross and walked away laughing. I felt my heart and my mind racing. *This isn't what it's supposed to be like! This can't be right! How can I leave my rock of hope here in all this chaos and commercialism?* For an instant, I considered picking up another rock and substituting it for my valuable rock of symbolic hope for my children, my father, my family –my life.

Then it hit me.

Despite all the disappointment that life brings, it's our capacity to find meaning in the face of adversity that allows us to rise past the pain and into the joy. I could hold onto that rock and look for a "better" place, or just keep it in a special box or drawer back home. But that wasn't my intention for buying it in the first place. My intention was to hand it over to God on the Camino and to trust that He would know what to do with it, even before I put the words into prayer.

I decided to release that rock, and when I did, I knew I was releasing my impulse to cling to how things are "supposed" to be and my indignation when they aren't. I was releasing my desire to control the people and events that are not within my control and my belief that I must always *be* in control. I was transferring the hope in my heart directly to God and emotionally relieved for having done it.

I miss that little rock; it was a symbol of my hope in the purest sense. But I think God understands what it meant for me to surrender that stone where I left it, warts and all.

Joe: Our destination for the day was the hamlet of Acebo, about 10 kilometers from Cruz de Ferro. It was still raining and cold as we walked across the summit and down the other side of the mountain. A train of clouds was drifting up the mountain from the west, enveloping us in a thick fog. At times they opened up long enough for us to see the snow-covered peaks to the south.

"I'm sure glad we aren't over on those mountains," I said to no one in particular.

As we descended on a narrow goat trail of a path, I started noticing the raindrops changing shape.

I called to Elaine, "Look at the size of those rain drops. They're getting bigger and slower."

Over a period of minutes, we watched the rain turn into giant snowflakes. They floated down over us and melted as soon as they hit the ground, becoming part of the flowing stream that we continued hiking through for the next two hours.

With these steep declines, my toes and knees were taking a beating. In the cold, they stiffened up quickly. By the time we dropped down into El Acebo, we were cold, wet and exhausted. Looking at the village rooftops from above, I searched for one thing and one thing only: a smoking chimney. I desperately wanted to sit in front of a warm fireplace. I spotted two chimneys with good potential and kept my eyes locked on them as we entered the town.

One chimney belonged to a bakery with rooms to rent upstairs, and the other belonged to the local tavern. We headed for the tavern. We piled inside with our muddy shoes and water dripping from our clothes and backpacks. We found a small empty table in the back near the fireplace. The room was full of pilgrims, all in the same state of wet exhaustion as us. It instantly felt like home. There wasn't a single person in that crowded room that one of the four of us hadn't already met and talked to during our trek.

I immediately work my way over to the bar and order a coffee and a steaming bowl of garlic soup that is served with rich, crusty homemade bread. As I sit back down at our table, Elaine gives me a desperate stare and my soup is quickly confiscated. I roll my eyes and return to the bar for a second bowl as well as a glass of wine. As I sit back down again, Pete gives me the same look. I look right back at him and guard my bowl. He grabs my wine and laughs. The waitress comes over and Pete orders two more bowls of soup and a bottle of wine for the table. She returns quickly with our order and the four of us melt into our meals.

It was so good. I'd never had garlic soup like this before and it was just perfect for this miserable day. It reminded me of a pilgrim earlier on the Camino who advised, "Don't ever say no to soup on the Camino." Now I understood why. With renewed energy, we gathered our wits. We talked Pete and Denise into staying with us instead of moving on to the next town, and then just relaxed for a while in front of the fire.

One of the guys at the next table shouts, "I'll see your 800 miligrams of ibuprofen and raise you 1000 milligrams of fish oil and a prednisone!"

The whole room roared with laughter.

Elaine: Joe and I found a casa rural and invited Pete and Denise up for a private happy hour. We bought wine and a variety of cheeses, fruit and bread. We sat around the kitchen table drinking our wine as the conversation slowly transformed into group therapy. Pete was the first to tip us into the vat of intimacy.

"I'm trying to stay focused on building this new life in Germany with Gretchen, but it's different from my relationship with my wife. She's not as open with her feelings about me. The worst part is I'm starting to get this weird reaction, like I'm afraid of getting too close and then losing her too."

Denise drinks the last sip of her wine, pours another glass and laments, "At least you have somebody. Your wife *died*; she didn't *decide* to leave you. My husband left on purpose for a girl that's younger than our daughter...and you know what makes it worse?"

Her eyes are glistening with tears. "The worst part is that the girl he left me for is one of my students at the college."

She searches our faces for reactions. I'm trying not to play therapist, so I take my own plunge. "When I first got divorced, I felt so devastated I actually thought about killing myself. The only thing that stopped me was my kids...they were just coming out of diapers. I felt so betrayed and angry I couldn't take the pain. I kept thinking about how I never wanted that for my family."

I suddenly feel like crying myself, but instead I turn to the cutting board and slice up some more bread and cheese to soak up the wine in my stomach.

Joe has been listening intently to the conversation. He directs his words to Pete, probably to take the pressure off Denise and me. "I'm afraid of losing Elaine too, but I figure she's here now and that's all we can say for any of us."

Joe pours what's left of the second bottle of wine into our glasses. Pete offers to go across the street for more and we all nod in agreement.

Denise puts it in words: "Will you get *two* more bottles, Pete? My feet really hurt!"

We all smile; we know exactly how she feels.

As soon as Pete leaves she asks, "Why do relationships have to be so hard?"

I say, "I don't know, but I don't think they're as hard for everyone. It's usually harder for the people who worry too much about getting hurt."

Denise hears this and counters, "I could take the hurt if it was only me, but the thing I can't get over is how he left his family. My daughter idolized him. She was a real 'daddy's girl.' Now she's in college, winning awards, and he's nowhere. We used to make plans for the two of us, waiting for her to go off to college so we could be free to travel. Now I'm here alone. How could he walk away from all of it...from me?" She begins sobbing.

Denise is inconsolable. Joe reaches out and rubs her back, saying, "It's okay, we're here with you. You're recovering, your heart's broken and it needs to heal. It just takes time...sssshh, it's okay, you can cry, just let it out."

Denise continues to cry and then says, "I'm afraid. I feel like I'm always going to be alone. I tried dating online but the guys my age are only looking for girls ten, even twenty years younger. How am I supposed to compete with that?"

Joe doesn't hesitate. "Denise, you're beautiful, you're healthy, and you're in the prime of your life. Look at what you're doing. You're walking the Camino de Santiago, this huge adventure – all by yourself! Guys would die to be with someone like you."

Suddenly, Pete walks back in the door. He takes a quick look at Denise's face, wet with tears. He sees me crying too.

"Geez, I was only gone for two minutes, when did all this happen?"

We all laugh with relief. Denise is the first to reply. "That's what happens when you just leave the room, Pete."

She smiles and wipes away her tears. Now it's Pete's turn. He's like a kid with a secret he can't wait to tell. "I got a text from Gretchen. She says she misses me." He smiles furtively. "I told her I'm ready to come back. I think you're right, Joe. She can't replace my wife, but she's already a part of me. We're both alive now and we love each other. That's all that matters."

Denise turns to Pete, "Why didn't I meet you first?"

She's trying to lighten the mood and we follow her lead. I serve the snacks I'd been preparing and ask Denise, "Do you want some cheese with that whine?"

It feels like family. We finish off the night by walking to Mass together. I say a special prayer for Denise, that she'll find peace on her walk to Compostela.

Lesson for Today: Staying locked into an image of how things are supposed to be can blind us to the grace of what is.

Chapter 35: The Divorce Diet

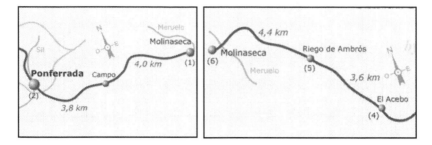

Day 30, El Acebo to Ponferrada, 16 km

The lust for comfort, that stealthy thing that enters the house a guest, and then becomes a host and then a master.
- Khalil Gibran

Joe: Pete, Denise, Elaine and I hoisted our packs onto our shoulders in preparation for the day. As we headed out the door, another pilgrim appeared. He was dressed in brightly colored Lycra tights and carried a pack shaped like a saddlebag. He was one of the many peregrinos who were doing the Camino on a bicycle. Raoul was a twenty-year-old Brazilian who had decided to bike around the world. He'd started in Rio de Janeiro, biked all the way up through North America and was now taking on Europe. He was young, good looking, in excellent shape and sported a broad, relaxed smile. Elaine heard his story and nudged me, whispering, "I'll bet you his parents are explorers." After we left, she couldn't stop talking about how fascinated she was by Raoul's decision to bike the world at any age, let alone twenty. I think her fear of traveling made him a hero.

The weather is cold and drizzly. As we depart the town, the mountain ranges open up before us. We can see that the snow had continued to fall throughout the night. The peaks are covered white and there are dark patches in the clouds where the snow is still coming down. We hope that the colder air stays south of us and the drizzle doesn't turn into the snow we'd experienced yesterday.

Our path is a mix of winding mountain roads and narrow rocky paths that descend from the peaks. The western side of the mountain is greener, more lush and wetter than the eastern slopes.

Elaine: Denise and I had some time alone on the trek into Ponferrada. It was an informal walking therapy. She described how she had married at twenty-one and raised a beautiful daughter with a man who loved her. They both worked hard to establish her husband's practice as a plastic surgeon in San Francisco, a place where people refuse to grow old. Where sixty is the new thirty, and gray is the new platinum. She described her soon-to-be ex-husband as intelligent and prominent in their community. Her daughter attends an Ivy League school and seems destined for a life of distinction. Denise was joyriding the American dream for her 5th straight decade, up until a set of steel spikes punctured the tires: her husband had fallen in love with a young student at the college where Denise taught as a professor.

Sam wanted no part of marital therapy and had already filed for divorce. At the time, the whole thing came as a shock. "This isn't supposed to happen. He promised to stay forever, it's in the marriage vows, 'till death do us part!'" Denise was stunned by her husband's resolve. No matter what she did, no matter how she pleaded or how she pushed for counter-offers, he refused to budge. It was as if he had already worked it all out in his mind and was just showing her the divorce papers as an afterthought. "He was so cold. I never saw him like that before." She couldn't stop the rush of memories and raw emotions once she started. "He said he loved me but wasn't 'in love' with me any more. What the hell is that supposed to mean? Isn't love just love? How did he stop loving me? I can't imagine not loving him anymore."

It's hard to listen to the kind of anguish Denise is feeling without trying to do some kind of therapy, even if it's on a mountain in the middle of nowhere. It didn't really matter whether we were sitting in my office or in a sleepy town in Spain. The pain was the same. "Denise, if I could share only one piece of advice with you at a time like this, when you think you'll never get over this indescribable pain, it's this: your husband is giving you what you need, not what you want."

I could tell this made absolutely no sense to her. Her face showed what she was too polite to say in words: "*What the heck does that mean?*" I expected this reaction because I get it every time I use it in divorce therapy. Every person who resists the breakup of their marriage will tell you what they need is to stay married, and therein lies the paradox. The truth is, they *want* to stay married. They want the familiar comfort of being in a steady and secure marriage with the person they love. But many of these same individuals had stopped asking themselves what they *needed* years ago. Denise was a great example. After the initial shock of hearing the needs versus wants explanation, she warmed up to the idea. It gave me the courage to ask a very personal question: "What have you been missing in your life with your husband?"

Her answer came in fits and starts, but it could all be distilled down to the one answer that brought tears to her eyes: "I gave up my dream to be a writer in order to support his practice." The light was starting to go on in her eyes. She was picking up on the distinction between "need" versus "want." She said, "Sam told me 'art doesn't pay' and he had some pretty huge medical school loans. So, of course, the practice had to take priority. I took a little part time job at the college so I could have more time to work as his office manager. I got an education in accounting, but I didn't need that. I needed – no: I *need* self expression."

Since she'd started the Camino, Denise had been writing poetry every day, "Even if its just a couple of minutes during a rest break, or right after something moves me like a bird singing 'hello' just for me." She described how the pain and poetry were breaking through a wall that had separated her from her creativity. The one time she beamed with pride aside from talking about her daughter's accomplishments was when she described her sister Kate's review of her poetry: "She calls them masterpieces."

"Now we're talking!" I encouraged as I realized she understood the concept of getting what she needed. Denise could feel it too. She quickly offered more information. "Even my daughter said, 'Mom, you're like a new person. You seem happy for the first time in a long time.' I didn't get it at the time because I couldn't imagine myself happy without my husband, but I think I know what she means." Denise couldn't stop. She had latched on, and refused to let go. "I even lost fifty pounds and my doctor said this was great because I was pre-hypertensive and he was afraid I would have to start medicine if my blood pressure kept rising."

I quickly chimed in. "We call it the 'divorce diet' because it's so common for people to lose their appetite when they first separate."

It was impossible to miss the glimmer in Denise's eyes when she added, "Even this trip here...this Camino, is something I dreamed about for years, but there was always a reason why I couldn't leave. It was never the right time for his practice. Now I'm here and I can't believe I'm almost done!"

It was easy to see how much the Camino had boosted Denise's confidence. The path had also become devotional for her. "My husband was never a spiritual man, and I gave up practicing my faith when we got married because he convinced me it was a waste of time. Now that I'm alone, I attend Mass every opportunity I get, and the more I speak to God, the more I realize I'm never really alone."

And it wasn't just the spiritual company. Denise had a sizable following as she documented her daily adventures on her blog. "It feels so good to have people reading and spurring me on...I can tell they are really getting into it. It's almost like they are traveling here beside me."

By the time we reached the Templar Castle in Ponferrada, it was clear that Denise was already immersed in the bitter-sweetness of her experience. She wasn't so outraged by the idea that she was deriving some benefit from her breakup. She could see the *needs* she'd been denying herself. No doubt, she still wanted her husband back, but she could see, far off in the distance – past Compostela, that there was a woman waiting for her attention. A woman she had neglected for years and was just starting to get reacquainted with. It was the woman her husband had discarded, ignorant of the wealth he was losing, like some long-lost piece of art discovered at a yard sale, invaluable but carelessly abandoned.

Joe: Later in the afternoon, we reached Ponferrada where we separated from Pete. He was behind schedule and needed to catch a bus to make up for lost time. The lost time was due to Denise and him deciding to stick with us with our limited range. We really enjoyed their company and it was sad to see them go.

Elaine: I couldn't say goodbye to Pete without feeling sad. What could I say in words that would do justice to the footprint he's had on this journey, every day, whether he was physically here with us or not? I want to explain to him what he's done for me personally, but I don't know how to say it without sounding like some crazed groupie. I push past the anxiety and make a start. "Pete, you're not like anyone I've ever met. You look at the world and you see splendor. You live in Grace because you believe in miracles."

I hold his gaze so I can say, "You're a miracle for me Pete, and I'll never forget you."

Pete's eyes well up and he hugs me with a strength that squeezes the air out of my lungs.

"This isn't goodbye, Elaine. He hesitates for a moment, "I'll be seeing you guys in Massachusetts when I get back. You can't get away from me that easy."

Joe and I agree we'd love to see him back in New England. I say a silent prayer that we may keep him past the Camino.

Lesson for Today: It's valiant to place others ahead of us in the name of love; it takes a conscious act of will to offer an equal measure of kindness to ourselves.

Chapter 36: Looking Down on Villafranca

Trail Day 31, Ponferrada to Villafranca del Bierzo, 22 km

> *If man is to survive, he will have learned to take a delight in the essential differences between men and between cultures. He will learn that differences in ideas and attitudes are a delight, part of life's exciting variety, not something to fear.*
> *- Gene Roddenberry.*

Joe: The three of us spent the night in a comfortable but sterile highway hotel on the outskirts of Ponferrada. After breakfast, we headed back up into the mountains. We were approaching the province of Castilla y León. I'd been noticing a change in the people as we walked through the small villages along the way. There's a sullenness about them that we hadn't seen before. Maybe it's just their attitude toward outsiders, but it was strange to see. Up until now, we'd been greeted by the local residents with smiles and "Buen Camino's," by people freely giving us directions and local information without even being asked. Now it was as if we didn't even exist; we were invisible as we walked through the center of these villages.

We ended our day in the large village of Villafranca del Bierzo, which is nestled into the base of a mountain with a wide clear river flowing through its center. We found a nice albergue and after a shower, we all arranged for laundry service. Elaine and I headed to the local church for evening Mass. It was a Sunday so there was a full congregation in attendance. As we worked our way through the crowd to find a seat, I had that same feeling of separateness. The two of us found a seat in an empty pew that could have held at least six. As the several pews in front of us filled to capacity, ours remained our own. Did I mention we'd taken showers?

As most people have probably experienced, there's a point in every Christian service where you turn and greet your neighbor with a "peace be with you" or some version of that. The Catholics tend to be a little more reserved than us Lutherans. We'd been known to take five minutes going up and down the aisles making the attempt to shake hands with every possible person we can reach. Still, the Catholics at least shake hands with those in the pew in front of and behind their own.

During this service, the time came to greet each other. As we had a wide isle behind us, there was no one to turn to in that direction, so we waited for someone in the row in front of us to turn around. It never happened; we were completely ignored. This was the first time I'd ever seen this. Is it me? Am I just being overly sensitive? My observations were confirmed at the end of the service. At every Mass we'd attended during this pilgrimage, there had always been some special pilgrim message from the priest, some words of encouragement and faith to guide us along the way. There were none. Not here, not now, not in Villafranca.

Elaine: Joe typically finds opportunity in most adversity but I guess it makes sense he would draw the line on rude behavior in church. I got the impression the townspeople have chosen to avoid the Camino tourism and to remain a close, if also closed, community. The location of the town itself is ideal, nestled between two mountain passes. It houses four churches (spanning five centuries), a 16th century castle, two palaces, and there's even a luxurious Parador Hotel here. Ironically, it's also home to a monastery that bears the moniker of St. Francis de Assisi, who notably stood for compassion and shelter for all God's creatures.

Denise came down to the dining room and asked to join us for dinner. As we ate, she shared one of the poems she was uploading to her blog that day. She wrote several a day but only posted one online. The rest she emailed to her sister. "I don't want people to think I'm spending all my time out here writing. But actually, the poems are just flowing, and they don't take much time to write at all."

"Denise, this is so moving. You've got to share your writing with a wider audience," I urged.

But she responded with worry. "I want to, but I'm feeling too raw to submit them and have some publisher say they're crap. I don't think my ego could take it, not now."

I asked if I could keep it, and as soon as she assented, I pulled out my iPhone, pressed the camera function, snapped a picture and allowed it to take its rightful place among my cherished Camino memories.

Left

Midway through Love's melody –
ah, with unsung loveliness remaining in the air –
you chose to empty our closet,
vacate the chair of your shirts,
remove your essence, and vanish like the jinn.
You broke the oak cask, overturned
Love's flagon, let its simple goodness
run like blood onto the ground.
No sound echoes like that of an empty room,
and no neon bears so bright a glare
as those spaces from which
your lovely measure has erased itself.
I feel the wings of unspent Love
flutter above in ever ascending
arcs and loops like swallows
returning to abandoned nests –
the familiar rest of your arms is denied.
No one will know how I cried.

After reading this poem, I immediately think of the quote by Kahlil Gibran: "Your joy is your sorrow unmasked." The way she described her sadness in the poem and then the relief and even pride she felt after writing it was clear to see.

I told her, "Denise, writing these poems probably beats anything you could do in therapy because you're delivering your own healing through self-discovery. It doesn't matter if anybody publishes them; they are your thoughts, your emotions, and they have value simply because they are authentic and they're yours."

I added, "But that said, I think it's better than many of the ones I've seen published. You should submit them. It's like Wayne Gretzky said: 'You miss 100 percent of the shots you don't take.'"

She smiled diffidently saying, "Maybe someday, but not now."

I responded with a story. I'm not sure why I told it; it was almost a compulsion.

"Before I retired I started a mantra that I would say to myself throughout the day, every day. Mantras are a great way to break a mental habit. There's something about repeating a phrase over and over in your head that sets new tracks over the old grooves carved into your synapses. For me, the old grooves were pretty deep. They centered on never having enough and I believed them to the point I was paralyzed from moving on even though my work was silently tormenting me. So I created a new mantra. It goes: '*There is abundance.*'"

"A mantra has to be simple so the unconscious mind can easily absorb it, and I believe it helps even more if it implies the direct opposite of your fear. I could have made a mantra saying 'There is enough,' but I made mine push way beyond that. The word '*abundance*' means there is even more than you need, and the word 'is' says it's right here, right now. Saying the phrase 'there is abundance' over and over, every day for the six months before I left my job allowed me to take the plunge to leave and to step into this unknown world I'm in right now. I had never done anything like it before and so far, I've experienced abundance in so many ways it would take a book to list them. I know it all seems like too much now, but maybe you could think of a mantra to help you with that fear of rejection."

Denise was listening. "Let's see what I can come up with."

Lesson for Today: There is ever more abundance.

Chapter 37: Depleted and Defeeted

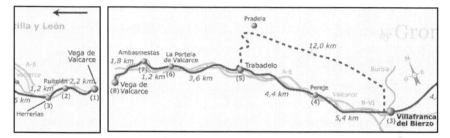

Trail Day 32, Villafranca to Herrerías, 20 km

In the time of darkest defeat, victory may be nearest.
-William McKinley

Joe: Departing Villafranca, we experienced the steepest ascent of any trail on our journey. It began as an unmarked, narrow driveway next to some apartments. I stared up at the steep incline for several minutes while repeatedly looking down at the guidebook in my hands. An Australian couple walked up and stared along with us.

Elaine said, "This just doesn't look right; it looks like someone's driveway."

"I know, and it goes straight up. But there appears to be no other choice if we want to take the original path"

The couple standing next to us introduced themselves. "Hi, we're Ray and Diane from Australia."

We introduced ourselves and talked about the options.

Ray said to Diane, "Let's take the alternate route going down the highway; it'll be less taxing for Matilda."

Matilda was their three-wheeled backpack dolly they pulled behind them.

Elaine and I had been sticking to the original Camino so we bit the bullet, said goodbye, and headed up the steep incline.

We had to concentrate on each individual step as we ascended. The driveway turned into a steep, narrow track that would be dangerous to attempt in rain or snow. The trail is on the edge of a cliff that gave us a spectacular view of the town, the river and the surrounding mountains.

Elaine said, "I bet Patty would love to have us with her for this one!"

We stopped at one point and saw Ray and Diane down below. They were standing at an intersection in the town, obviously in some type of discussion. They happened to glance way up at the cliffs above them and we waved down. It took them a few moments to realize it was us, and then they waved back. An hour later, Elaine and I were resting in a chestnut grove on the side of the mountain. We were eating a mid-morning snack when Ray and Diane came walking past. They'd decided to give the mountain a try after all.

The steep ascents and descents were hard for everyone on the trail. At one point, I heard a woman call to her companion about the spectacular view at one of the summits.

He replied back, "For throwing oneself over," as he haggardly looked over the edge of the peak we'd just climbed.

Descending down the last mountain and into Trabadelo, we entered a lush river valley that looked no different from what we might find in the Berkshire Mountains. The fast-flowing river was crystal clear, no more than ten feet deep in the deepest pools and had numerous waterfalls. It was also loaded with trout. As the trail meandered between the river and the roadway, I daydreamed about dinner.

We'd chosen to do the Camino in the fall for several reasons. Most importantly, the tourist season was over and kids were back in school. It's also the slowest time for me at work, and the weather is much more pleasant. An added benefit that we hadn't counted on was harvest time. There was so much abundance; a wide variety of ripe fruits and nuts were there for the picking.

You could easily do this pilgrimage without buying a single ounce of food. First there are the blackberries. For some reason, blackberries love to grow on the sides of trails. I stopped often to snack. Next, there are the almond trees. They're everywhere on the first half of the Camino. I just used my trekking poles to bang the branches and down came a shower of ripe almonds. Using a couple of rocks, I'd break the outer shell and eat to my heart's delight. Then there are the vineyards; here you have to be a little more selective. This is a farmer's livelihood and he doesn't want to be losing his harvest to several thousand pilgrims descending on his vines like locust. But there are numerous grape vines that have escaped the vineyard and are growing wild along the trail or as fences in the villages. My philosophy is: if I can reach it without my feet leaving the trail, then it's fair game. In the vineyards where the grapes have already been harvested, there are ripe bunches of grapes hidden under the leaves that were overlooked by the pickers. I didn't overlook them. Next are the apple trees. Once again, a quick whack with the trekking pole and lunch showers down over our heads. Lastly, there are the chestnut trees we've been walking under for the past week. Not just in groves: they grow wild all through the mountains. I'd say that for the last week there has not been a single time that we were out of sight of a chestnut tree. The only problem with chestnuts is that they are bitter if not roasted, but then that's what burning fireplaces are for.

We followed the winding river for 10 kilometers and started approaching the mountain village of Herrerías.

Elaine: After walking up and down the mountains, I'm physically drained. I'm sitting on the side of the road in a small village resting while Joe gets money from the ATM across the street. He comes running back from the machine so I assume he's done. I start shifting to stand up.

Joe quickly gestures me to stop, shouting out, "What's the date that president Kennedy was shot?"

"What do you want to know that for?" I ask confused about what that has to do with the ATM.

"It's the date I use for my PIN."

I know the date very well. "It's 22 November, 1963."

Before I finish, Joe is already bolting back across the street.

How could a person forget a PIN they use every three days out here, especially a person like Joe? He's the sharpest man I've ever met. He makes the medical school students I met at Bethesda seem intellectually deficient. One day we were out sailing and a friend of his that worked with him on classified military projects said, "Joe's scary smart. None of us at the lab in L.A. could even understand his projects. They gave him his own room and he mostly worked alone because no one could help him."

"So what's happening to him?" I wonder. What if it's not because of exhaustion? What if he's so tired of walking with me at my snail's pace he can't even think straight? After all, he's keeping up with the physical demands just fine; it's the psychological piece that's the problem. I've never seen him withdraw from me like this. Now with all this talk of divorce from Denise, it's really scaring me. Maybe he's still upset about the codeine. He hasn't said more than a few quick sentences since I told him about it. What if he thinks I'm some unreliable drug addict who's out of control and not to be trusted? I can feel the muscles in my shoulders spasm, and when I shift to rub them, they feel rock hard. I'm worried I'm going to end up divorced all over again.

Joe is back and his words break my catastrophic thoughts: "I lost my card."

After a third attempt to enter his PIN, the machine did what it's supposed to – it swallowed his card.

We walked about three more kilometers. I was carefully counting down to our final destination because my feet and brain were giving out. First they said, *Stop!* But I kept walking. Then I heard, *Don't you listen? You've got to stop now!* I just keep walking, ignoring them and counting, then praying, "Hail Mary, full of Grace…" Next they join forces, and the pain mounts, stabbing my brain with a thousand ice picks for every step. I keep walking anyway. "Glory be to the Father and to the Son…" Then it hits me like a body slam, and I can't take another step. I drop down by the side of a tree right next to a farmer's fence and just let the tears roll down my face.

I don't care who sees me. I don't even try to swallow my desperation. According to Joe's calculations, we only have two more kilometers to go. In my old life, two kilometers was nothing. So why can't I do it now? Why has my own body turned against me? *What's wrong with me?* The voice that tells me I'm not good enough, the one I wrestle with and successfully beat down most days, has taken complete charge of me. I'm crying as a sign of full capitulation to it. *Yes. You're right! I'm weak. I can't even walk two freaking kilometers even if it means getting to a place where we can finally rest for the night. Game over. I lose. Big surprise!*

Joe is silent. He knows what it takes for me to just sit there and cry openly, not caring who sees me.

I look into his eyes and say, "I hate myself."

Joe just looks at me with a pained expression. He will sit there silently beside me until morning if that's how long I need to get back up again. Just seeing that willingness to stand, or in this case, to sit by me without criticizing or telling me how I should do it, helps me to realize it doesn't matter if I can't move. I have someone who believes in me whether I collapse here or whether I skip the rest of the way – it's all the same to him. It's still me, and that's enough.

I met Joe at a time in my life when I had given up on relationships. I was divorced and decided, "I guess I just don't get the whole marriage thing." My other theory was that I just sucked at relationships. Either way, I had decided I would no longer put myself or anyone else through the torture of being in a relationship with me. I went through a period of accepting men only as friends. Just friends. Nothing deep or committed, no sex.

After about a year, I began to get lonely. I decided to cautiously date to relieve the skin hunger I was still teaching about in my divorce recovery classes but had avoided accepting myself. I went on Match.com and established an account and a meaningful profile. By "meaningful," I'm referring to the ZERO responses I got. Ok, I'm exaggerating. I got three. I think it was really because I didn't include a picture. It's well known that guys are very visual, so I blame the lack of visual aids, not my profile. Cutting to the chase, one of those responses was Joe. We wrote to each other for a month and a half before we finally met. But we both knew even within that short time that at the very least we would always be friends.

I'm still sitting here immobilized, but the tears have stopped. I absorb the blow to my ego for another minute and then I get up.

"I'm ready to go again,"

We start walking. I privately commit to stopping for as long and as often as I need in order to make it to the town of Herrerías. I talk to my punisher, that part of me that likes to ridicule my weaknesses, taunting me about how this game is over. I tell it, *If you want to believe I can't do this, I'm not going to try to talk you out of it. In fact, I don't care what you do, so you can either stay here or strap on for the ride, because I'm not giving up.* You can't beat somebody who doesn't stop trying.

Hail Mary, full of grace.
Our Lord is with thee.
Blessed art thou among women,
and blessed is the fruit of thy womb,
Jesus.
Holy Mary, Mother of God,
pray for us sinners,
now and at the hour of our death.
Amen.

Joe: The steepness of the mountains this morning took a toll on us. I hadn't noticed it until I attempted to get some money from a lone cash machine placed in the little village behind us. A four-digit number I've used for over thirty years had disappeared from my memory. After several unsuccessful attempts, my debit card had disappeared as well. Our pace slowed as we walked along the edge of the winding mountain road. A mile back we'd watched a small deer dart across the road in front of a car and climb up a cliff on the other side. It failed. Halfway up, it lost it's footing, and fell back down onto the hard pavement. The car stopped just in time. The deer stood back up slowly and then it hobbled back up the cliff. Life goes on. There's risk, there's pain, there's a journey for each of us.

Elaine keeps going when all she wants to do is stop. I don't push her. I look down at the guidebook, I tell her what we can expect and how far we are from the next town, and we walk on. The pain is a stark contrast to the beauty before us; steep mountains, lush vegetation, winding crystal clear brooks and ancient villages. Elaine can hardly walk another step and I start worrying if she'll be able to make it at all. She finally surrenders and collapses on the side of the road. I feel helpless and just sit next to her as she cries. My mind eventually shuts down and I just surrender to my surroundings. I could have sat there in the shade until morning.

There's a fast flowing creek just meters below our aching feet. As Elaine's tears dry, I start wondering how the cold water would feel on my bare feet. I look up from the creek and notice three farmers, two men and a woman, in a green pasture on the other side of the creek. There was a large bull tangled in a barbed wire fence while the rest of the herd was grazing nearby. The three slowly approached the bull. Even from this distance of maybe a hundred meters, I could see they were relaxed despite the danger. One of the men walked up and calmly took hold of the bull's horns. The woman got down on her knees and started untangling the wire wrapped around his front leg, as the other man guarded the back legs from kicking forward. It wasn't easy; the bull was alarmed and in pain, and there was a lot of tugging and pulling going on. It took some time to get him clear of the fence. Once freed, the bull casually strolled back to his herd as if nothing had happened. The three farmers walked shoulder-to-shoulder back to their pickup truck, talking and gesturing. They climbed in and drove away.

I wouldn't have experienced this moment if it weren't for Elaine's need to take a break from the harshness of the trail. I wouldn't have experienced the Camino at all if it weren't for her. I wish I could be like that farmer for Elaine, able to untangle the pain that's stopping her now.

Elaine: Joe's brain fog had caused him to miscalculate. We were less than a kilometer from the next town! We discovered this when we happened upon one of the most enchanting inns I've seen on the entire Camino. You might say, "A tenement would've looked wonderful by then," and that's true. But this was no flophouse; it was an established, stately lodge with ducks paddling in the stream below in full view of the panoramic windows of its very own restaurant. We'd arrived at Herrerías, pronounced, here-we-are-us!"

Joe: Finding a place overlooking the river, we checked in for the night. Our room was on the top floor. It had slanted walls, an open-beamed ceiling and small windows at foot level. We were in the attic of a converted farmhouse. Also, we noticed a positive attitude from the people. We were getting closer to the Province of Galicia. Tomorrow, we'll be climbing another mountain and entering this fiercely independent province with its deep Celtic roots.

The sun sank below the mountaintops and the warmth of the day dissipated. We came downstairs and sat down for a wonderful dinner, including local trout from the river just tens of meters from our table. Cold mountain breezes started flowing down from the mountains as we ate. The cold air felt good after the hot day on the trail. An hour later, fully satiated, we climbed the stairs and collapsed onto our bed. There was an old, cast iron radiator by the window that groaned as the hot steam warmed our room. It was music to my ears as I nestled into our soft bed. We slept for ten hours.

Lesson for Today: The thousand mile journey ends after several rest stops.

Chapter 38: Commerce in Its Finest Form

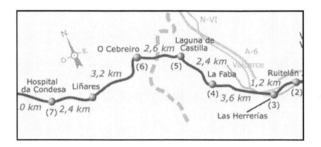

Trail Day 33, Las Herrerías to Hospital da Condesa, 14 km

Just living is not enough. One must have sunshine, freedom, and a
little flower.
- Hans Christian Anderson

Joe: We were continuously surprised by the appearance of little hamlets as we climbed up through the mountains and turned a corner in the trail. A dozen or so stone farmhouses would appear out of nowhere with cattle, tractors, barnyards, dogs, sheep, and chickens. As we walked through one village, a small, thin, elderly woman in her eighties or nineties came out of her house. She held a steaming plate of fresh crepes and a mason jar of sugar with holes punched in the cap. Elaine was tentative as the woman approached us, but I lit up with a smile. I knew where this was going. I reached into my pocket and pulled out a euro, which I handed to her. She sprinkled sugar over the fresh crepe sitting on top of the stack and I rolled it up. Elaine was a bit alarmed as I devoured the thin, sweet cake handed to me by a stranger in a strange land.

Elaine said, "Aren't you worried about where that came from?"

I smiled and said, "Elaine, she looks about a hundred years old; look how healthy she is. She's even out here feeding the pilgrims and making a little cash for her effort. I'll eat whatever she wants to make me."

The lady and I both walked away with big smiles on our faces. Suddenly, Elaine stopped dead in her tracks and said, "Hold on."

She ran back and straight over to the woman waiting for the next pilgrim and asked for one of her own. Out came the euro and we were soon heading down the trail again. Now we both had smiles on our faces.

"What was that all about? Aren't you worried where that came from?" I teased.

Elaine just munched. In between swallows she said, "Oh, it's no big deal, just something I told myself I would do. That's all."

Elaine: Today I walked and prayed my novena again. I used it to honor God, and He accepted by dulling the pain in my feet. If I'm not careful, the ritual will put me into a trance. I start by purposely coordinating my words with each step: "Our-step Father-step who-step art-step in-step heaven-step…" but by the time I've finished this and gotten through my ninth Hail Mary, the words are so familiar and the lines so repetitive, I find myself in that place you go to when you're driving to work and get there without remembering anything along the way.

I do remember passing an elderly woman in her late eighties who offered us crepes. At first, I had used my normal response: "No, Gracias." I didn't see crepes; I pictured an unsanitary mess that was just made on a stove with chickens or mice meandering over it with no regard to hygiene. But then I saw the sublime look on Joe's face as he and the woman grinned affectionately at one another. Her face had deep lines, but when she smiled, her visage looked like a young girl. She reminded me of my mother and how she cooks everything with love. "Wait! Love…cooking." I thought of Cristiano, the pilgrim we had met back in Astorga. How he used love as a cooking ingredient. I recognized the feeling I was having with the crepes: it was the "asco" again. That's what was stopping me. This was it, the time I had given myself permission to wait for. I had to take a chance; there was too much riding on this. Joe feels the love and he devours it. I feel disgust and it devours me. I had to walk back to get that crepe, to stop myself from missing out on the blessings in life simply because I'm so distracted by unlikely dangers. I think somehow that woman knew I had battled with something because when I asked her for one, she sprinkled it with extra sugar.

Lesson for Today: Anxiety is like a telescope that captures light from distant stars that may have already died. Use it at your own risk to observe things that are within easy reach.

Chapter 39: A Way of Life

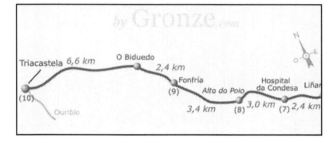

Trail Day 34, Hospital da Condesa to Triacastela, 15 km

Keep close to Nature's heart...and break clear away, once in a while and climb a mountain or spend a week in the woods. Wash your spirit clean.
-John Muir

Joe: We walked down rock-walled paths running through wooded, rolling hills. The paths transect small farmyards where I could easily tap the rear door of a farmhouse with my right trekking pole and the barn behind it with my left pole. For a second, I wondered how the owners feel about several thousand pilgrims passing their kitchen windows every year, but then I remembered; pilgrims have been passing these windows for over a hundred generations. The families within know of no other way of life and I imagine that the pilgrims' absence would be of much greater concern.

Reaching Triacastela, we found a three-story albergue and spent several minutes tracking down the hospitalero to check in. They had coin-operated washing machines and our first order of business was laundry. As our clothes tumbled and churned, we settled into the common area to relax. The large, soft couches were a welcome relief and I plopped myself down. Elaine spotted a coin-operated foot and calf massager (we had seen many of these devices along the Way). She dropped in some coins and inserted her bare feet.

I chided her once more, "Aren't you worried about germs?"

She ignored me. I'm thinking how anxieties can be quite selective at times as I watch her melt into a state of pure bliss. It's the simple things in life...

Elaine: I couldn't stand the tension of waiting any longer. My parents had told me to wait until today to see what the doctor would say. They had been waiting for some more definitive news. My father's procedure was scheduled for early this morning. I was told they should hear the findings before noon. I waited ten hours to make the phone call, ten minutes for it to go through because of the poor Wi-Fi, ten seconds to hear the news, and ten nanoseconds to fly into the clouds when I heard it. "The doctor said it's not cancer. It was some kind of a physical obstruction, like a bone or a piece of plastic. They removed it and now he's feeling great."

There are only a few times in my adult life when I've wept openly, and almost all of them have happened on this Camino! I thanked my mother and father for encouraging me to keep walking. I silently thanked Patty and Len, and Barb and Stan for keeping me on track. Joe watched my reaction on the phone and he looked relieved. We hugged and kissed each other like we'd both won the 100-million dollar lottery.

Then Joe says, "Let's celebrate with a special dinner, darling, you deserve it."

I feel my chest bursting with an energy that rises straight out of the same sorrow I'd been carrying for the last 160 miles.

I say, "I'll go anywhere you want, but first I have to go to church. I have to say 'thank you.'"

Going to eat now would be like accepting a gift and then walking off without showing gratitude. Joe and I dress quickly in order to make it in time for the 7:00 Mass. We hurriedly get directions to the church and make a wild run for it, just making it by 7:05. There's only one problem. There's no service tonight. The church is completely empty.

I'm feeling stunned, and turn to leave with a surge of disappointment. How could this be? I'm suddenly lost and not sure where I'm going as I head out the door. I look behind me for Joe but he's not there. Where is he? I go back inside and see that he's walked to the very front pew and is kneeling with his head bowed down. His eyes are closed and his lips are moving silently. I wonder why he's the one praying in a Catholic church when he's not even Catholic. It doesn't matter. I hastily join him and say my own prayer. Then we both sit. We're lost in our own private homage. It's clear that God still has more to teach me, and he is using our relationship to do it. There's no burning bush here, no grandeur, just a simple act. A display of unflinching love that pushed straight past a closed door and a sign that says "no Mass today." But more than that, it was a move toward freedom that broke barriers I had set in my own mind. I had many things to be grateful for today.

As we headed to the center of town for dinner, we met Denise. She was excited to see us and practically sprinted in our direction.

"Joe, Elaine, you're never going believe this! Remember the poem I showed you?"

"Of course I do. It was so moving."

"Oh, you're so nice for saying that. But I think it's true about using a mantra because I've been saying, 'I'm amazing.' every day. I didn't really believe it, but like you said, I wanted to lay down a new groove in my brain. So as it happens I still didn't have the nerve to send my poems out for review, but my sister who thinks I *am* amazing did, and now I'm going to be published!"

"No!" I say with fake disbelief.

"Yes! I know, it's so hard to believe…it's amazing!"

My face hurts from smiling so broadly. Joe is shooting a volley of compliments, "Outstanding!" "I knew you could do anything you set your mind to, Denise." And "Where will it be published?"

I say, "Let's all talk about that over dinner. Our treat."

The Crossing

Every man comes to the way
and the crossing he did not choose,
and gladly would he trade it
to walk just one more day
in another's shoes; no matter how it goes,
today, let me walk this road by your side
and my arms lend yours strength.
though the bitter sorrow's truth is here
with no safe place to hide your tears,
yet above and below, faith, hope,
and love abide along its quiet length.

Lesson for Today: God speaks in a soft voice I can hear better when I resolve to listen and stop putting words in His mouth.

Chapter 40: A Journey Needs a Destination

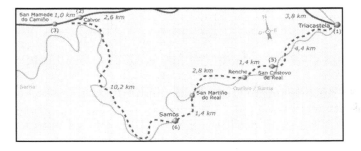

Trail Day 35, Triacastela to Aguiada, 26 km

Adversity is like a strong wind. It tears away from us all but the things that cannot be torn, so that we see ourselves as we really are.
- Arthur Golden

Joe: It's early evening and I'm sitting in front of a roaring fire trying to coax some warmth back into my bones. There are seven other pilgrims recovering on the couches and chairs around me. An old red clay pitcher of Rioja wine is sitting on the coffee table between us; it's promptly refilled by our hospitalero every time it empties. We've just walked 26 kilometers, much more than we'd planned. The last 8 kilometers of which were through pouring rain, lightning and high winds while hiking through a dense forest.

We'd made our first deviation from the path of the original Camino. There was an alternative route available to us this morning when leaving Triacastela. It was 8 kilometers longer, but took us through the town of Samos with one of the oldest and largest monasteries in Europe, originally built in the 10th century. This route also bypassed another one of the steep mountains. We'd climbed plenty of mountains during this journey and decided that looking up at the mountain as we walked around it had certain advantages as well. We were also much more relaxed. Hearing the good news about Elaine's dad last night had taken a lot of pressure off. We felt we could take our time and enjoy the scenery now.

At the last minute, we'd made the decision to deviate from our route. We were just exiting the town when we saw Ray and Diane, the Australian couple we'd met the other day. They were taking the alternate route to the left as we were making our right turn toward the mountain. As we were walking away from them, Elaine and I looked up at the top of the mountain. We had an amazingly quick conversation, and I yelled back to Ray and Diane, "Wait for us!"

Our route followed another meandering river and the lushness only increased as we moved farther west. Starting out on the side of a multi-lane highway, I was at first uncomfortable with the proximity and harshness of the traffic. But the trail soon left the highway and we found ourselves in the midst of a temperate rain forest. There was water dripping off the leaves, several waterfalls, ferns, flowers, and mushrooms everywhere.

The chestnut trees were huge and made up part of the walls of the trail we walked down. The farmer's fields on each side of us were above our heads. The Camino had eroded down into the earth from the millions of pilgrims making their way to Compostella. It was like walking through a tropical tunnel deep inside a green, wooded forest.

In this region, the geology is slate and it's used for everything: walls, roads, roofs, fences, even fence posts. The paths are lined with stacked slate walls to keep the adjoining farmland from eroding into the path. Every now and then, just to be different, the slate is laid vertically on edge and creates interesting patterns in the walls. The chestnut trees are easily ten feet wide and have completely covered the path with a new crop of freshly fallen chestnuts. After plenty of twists, turns, climbs and descents, our trail eventually led to the secluded town of Samos. The river Oribio runs right through the center and a monastery sits on its banks.

We sat in a café with Ray and Diane and two women from San Diego, Joyce and Andrea, who we'd met a couple of days before at an albergue. They were new to the Camino. They still had that fresh energy about them. We picked on them about how the Camino hadn't humbled them yet. They agreed and knew the humbling was coming. They were already starting to feel the wear and tear, especially since they were lost for an hour yesterday.

Departing Samos, we headed back into the forest to complete our day's journey. Our group quickly separated as we traveled at different rates and we were soon alone once again in the trees and pastures of the hills. On this part of the Camino, the trail markings were few and it was easy to get disoriented along the winding paths. We somehow managed to stay on track, but not before a fierce storm rolled in from the west.

Elaine: Joe's been mostly quiet, and I've conspired with him, avoiding deep conversations because I've been so worried about my father. Today we sat under a tree in a forest setting straight out of a fairytale. The woods were green and mossy with narrow paths I had imagined Hansel and Gretel tramping through when I was a child reading *Grimm's Fairy Tales*. The path turned out to be much longer than either of us had expected and we decided to sit down and rest even though we could hear a storm heading toward us. I used the break from walking to ask Joe, "Is there anything wrong?"

"No, I've just been tired, that's all," he replied.

"It's hard to believe you're *this* tired," I persisted. "It feels like something more than simple fatigue." Then I asked, "Are you still angry with me for not telling you about the codeine?"

"I was angry, but I think your rebound from stopping was enough to get me over it."

Now I was confused and asked impatiently, "So what is it, then? Why are you being so distant?"

I could tell Joe was wrestling with his answer, but then he gave up the struggle and locked in. He didn't even try to hold back. "I'll tell you why! It's because none of this even fucking matters!"

I felt shocked at his uncharacteristic cursing, but this wasn't a time to play Miss Manners. I remained silent and just listened. He continued with a fierce energy, "Your father's not going to die today. Big deal! He's still going to die, just like my dad died yesterday, and the way I'm going to die tomorrow. And the saddest part of the whole mess is that nothing I, or they, or you do will matter a hundred years from now. Hell, I don't even make a difference right now!"

It was hard for me to believe Joe could say, let alone think anything like this. He makes such a huge difference every day. But it doesn't matter what I see him do; it's what *he* sees. I think about his persistent struggle with the meaning of life. I've had the same thoughts, but now I realized that Joe has worried about this his *whole* life. I think everyone has it at some point: the fear that we'll be forgotten as soon as we're buried. Or, in my case, that people will forget me before I'm buried and not even attend the funeral. I wonder what it must be like to have this fear your entire life.

I want to make Joe feel better, but it's got to be with facts, not feelings. "What do you consider 'making a difference?'" I ask.

"I don't know," he says impatiently. "Something meaningful, something that changes peoples lives, something that improves us more than just some stupid piece of technology that will be obsolete in a few years."

"So you're talking about something with a big bang...like curing polio or stopping climate change?"

He looks at me and frowns as if I'm making light of his distress. I press on, "Joe, it's natural to want to do the big impact stuff, to change the world. I think most people would be lying if they said they wouldn't want to do the very same thing. But I think it's that limited idea of success that makes us pay teachers next to nothing, and ask a stay-at-home mom when she thinks she'll start working."

"Success! What does success have to do with it? You just don't get it, do you? I don't give a damn about success. I don't care if I die a poor man. It's not about others knowing I made a difference, it's about *me* knowing I made a difference!"

These words first confuse me because I was only thinking about how others would remember him...or me. As Joe's words sink in, it starts making sense. When I'm on my deathbed, it won't matter if others know I made a difference. The peace would come because *I knew*...then I would be able to find peace.

My words come more naturally and gentler now. "I know the difference you make will live after you, and you know how I know that?"

He's still hesitant, avoiding eye contact, but at least he asks, "How?"

"Because you've already helped the next generation. Ben looks up to you and considers you his dad. Heck, I wasn't supposed to tell you this, but the birthday present you got from him, replaced *his* twenty-first birthday gift. I'm talking *twenty-first birthday*! He was looking at one of the best gifts he could still get out of me – and he knew it! I said 'Ben, whatever you want, it's yours 'cause you're only twenty-one once in your life. What do you want?' And he still said, 'I want you to use whatever you would've spent on me to buy Joe a really nice birthday present from me.'"

I could see Joe's eyes watering as he listened. I didn't stop. "Then there's Andrew. When you heard he was failing college, you could've given up on him. You could've told him to go into the military like a lot of parents, like I was ready to do. Instead, you listened to why he was failing and got him to a new school, and now he's getting all A's. You think he's not going to remember *that* for the rest of his life? Or that it might not affect how he treats his own children, and how they treat their children?"

"What about William? He's almost an electrical engineer now and it's mostly because you supported his dreams and shared your career experiences with him. And none of them are even your biological children!"

"Danielle, your own daughter, would give her life for you, and she's saving animals who would die if she couldn't go to school and pursue her veterinary career. You've been helping her every step of the way."

"How about Makenna? She's learning exactly how a father holds on and keeps the bond with his child even after a divorce. She's learning that directly from you."

"You've taught divorce recovery classes with me and spent hours after class helping the ones that might have gone home and committed suicide because they thought nobody cared. You think they don't have families who are affected by your actions? Helping individuals has a ripple effect, and you're the master of it."

I wanted to tell Joe what a great impact he's had on me, but that list is too long, and I was sure it wouldn't fit into the "hundred years from now" rule, so I finished off with the first image that captures his impact in my mind: "You're like the little kid on the beach that's throwing the sand dollars back into the ocean. You may not get all of them, but you're making a difference in so many individual lives that your love will most definitely live on forever through them."

We sit in silence for about a minute, then I say, "But I think that's all beside the point. I'm not convinced that's what's really bothering you."

"What? Now you are going to *tell* me what's bothering me?"

"I have no idea what's wrong, but I do know you're not stupid. Maybe I need to remind you more often, but you *know* you make a difference."

I let Joe think about that for a few more moments, and then I ask him the real question, "What are you really looking for?"

Joe: I had drifted off in thought and Elaine's last words caught me off guard. They somehow found some chink in my armor that I didn't know existed and they pierced through. What *am* I looking for?

Suddenly, I'm completely aware of my surroundings. The colors, the smells, the sounds – they are all different from just moments before. I'm not observing them anymore; I'm part of them. There's no distinction between me and everything around me. Even Elaine's somehow different as she looks at me, waiting. I feel completely exposed, vulnerable and scared. Am I having a panic attack? I don't have panic attacks!

This place is just like where my Dad died. I'm on the same trail. My heart is starting to beat faster. I can hear the throbbing in my ears, and my chest is pounding. *What's happening?* Is this how Dad's heart felt moments before he fell to the ground? Did he wonder about what the next world might hold for him? Did he think about my mom, or the rest of us in this world without him? Or, did he feel exactly what I'm feeling now? A complete awareness of the only moment we have, the present.

Did Dad feel the cool mountain air passing through his lungs for the very last time? Did he see the leaves in the trees filtering the sunlight as he was falling? Did he smell the rich dark soil underneath his fallen mortality? Did he leave the world as he entered, like a newborn child, unaware of the past or the future; only aware of the moment?

Elaine and I are sitting on a moss-covered rock wall in the middle of a lush, green forest completely isolated from the rest of the world. Our backpacks are lying next to us in the leaves on the ground and our trekking poles are leaning against a huge ancient chestnut tree. I can hear thunder echoing off the distant mountains. The wind is starting to pick up, swaying the branches above me. I can smell the dust-scented rain in the air. There's an inchworm dangling from a thread over the path just a couple meters in front of me. I come back to Elaine's last words asking what I'm looking for.

I have no idea what I'm looking for.

I've always been on the journey. The next adventure has been just around the corner. Since I can remember, I've been driven to explore, to search, but it's never been enough. There's always been an emptiness when the journey was over.

I start understanding why. A journey can never end if there's no destination. A journey without a destination is not a journey at all; it's just wandering. It's me lost in the forest and it doesn't matter one bit which direction I go; I'll still be lost if there's no destination. Sure, I might be strong, independent, self-reliant, and I could probably survive in this forest forever. But without a destination, without a purpose, without a direction, I'll still be lost.

And what's wrong with that? I ask myself in an effort to hold on to my armor, to protect myself from exposure.

The answer is simple, though: I'll never, ever be at peace.

Life without a purpose is worthless. This whole cliché I've been carrying around with me for decades, "It's the journey, not the destination," is bullshit! It's the journey *and* the destination. We need both to find peace in this world.

My heart rate starts to slow down and I finally say something. "Elaine...I've been lecturing you and Patty about anxiety and risk-taking and I just realized I don't know what the hell I'm talking about."

I can tell from her expression she wasn't expecting a response like that.

"You've opened your hearts. You've made yourselves completely vulnerable to the pilgrims around you, complete strangers. You're in pain! You're suffering physically, to the point that I can't even stand to watch it!"

"What are you getting out of all of this? What did you find when you walked back down that trail to our friends and apologized for blocking them out? What drove you to poke your head out from under the sleeping bag in a freezing cold stone room in the mountains and ask for your iPhone? What did all of you find at Cruz de Ferro the other day that made you walk away smiling?"

Elaine looks confused; she doesn't know where this is going. "What do you mean, 'What did I find?'"

"I'll tell you what you found. You found joy! You found happiness! In the midst of all that suffering, that pain, that exhaustion, that dread of your dad dying...you found peace."

Elaine nods slowly.

My anger and panic subside and my voice softens to sadness. "Elaine, I'm too good at this. I'm not suffering. Sure, I get tired and sore and my feet hurt sometimes, but it doesn't faze me. I'm used to this. I'm fresh the next morning, I could walk twice the distance we walk each day. This pilgrimage is just a walk in the park for me, I..."

"Joe, *you're* not getting it!"

I look back at her. "No kidding! I know I'm not getting it!"

She says softly: "No,...you don't understand"

I just look at her confused, waiting.

She very gently says, "Joe, you're suffering so much more than the rest of us."

I stare at Elaine as the words sink in. Why did she have to say that? And why so gently?

My eyes start burning, then tears start running down my cheeks. I'm crying.

I realize with the same clarity as my perception of the forest around me that Elaine is right. She has stripped away the rest of my armor with only a few carefully chosen words.

I continue to cry while Elaine sits quietly next to me.

My whole attitude about taking risks, about adventure and exploration is for one reason only: it's to protect me from the destination.

My risk-taking pales in comparison to people like Patty and Elaine. They take risks every day. They're in an internal battle with their anxieties, fighting just to walk out the front door, to cross that bridge to a place they know holds their future. And when they do it, they go to places I can't even imagine.

I protect myself behind a mask of knowledge and experience and ambition. I pursue the next adventure because the alternative is completely unacceptable. The destination scares the hell out of me. The destination is where we sit around the fire and share our stories, our inner thoughts and fears. Where we peel away the layers and expose what lies within.

Elaine and I sit quietly just listening to the wind blow through the trees. A crack of lightning suddenly splits the air and we both jump. Moments later, the sky opens up with a deluge of rain and howling wind. The huge chestnut tree protects us from the rain long enough for us to put on our rain gear, but the thorny nuts are falling all around us. We're anxious to get out into the open before our heads are pierced like pincushions.

The Atlantic Ocean is not that far from us and this is the time of year when storm fronts come into the mountains with cold rain, winds and lightning. It's painfully clear to us that we'd be walking a lot farther than we'd planned. The little villages where we thought we might find shelter have disappeared along this stretch of the forest, so we're committed to walking through the storm if we want to find shelter for the night.

We walked in the wind and the rain for two more hours. Even with good rain gear, we were completely soaked when we reached the first village since leaving Samos. The storm had just started to die down when we spotted an elderly woman at a small, bleak farmhouse. She'd come outside to pick up the fallen chestnuts. Elaine walked down the driveway to ask if we were going in the right direction. She pointed down the road, saying there was an albergue close by.

Ten minutes later we were walking through a small village and down the side of a busy road. I heard someone yell to us, "Joe, Elaine! Over here!"

It was Ray. He'd been waiting outside in front of a small unassuming albergue that we would've easily walked right past. He knew we'd eventually come walking by. He also knew we'd be exhausted and might miss it. He bestowed a gift on us and I wasn't shocked, taken aback, or even surprised. I accepted it with gratitude and love.

Today was the most beautiful and the most challenging day of my Camino, maybe of my life. My depression had been deepening for weeks and I was wondering why the good news about Elaine's dad, the beauty of this part of the Camino or the Cruz de Ferro hadn't helped.

Elaine got me to open up about my feelings this afternoon. It was hard. I felt like one of her male patients who could only describe one emotion, anger. But then she gently asked me a simple question. She said some simple words and my depression and my anger were washed away with the tears and the rain and the wind.

It feels so good to be sitting by this blazing fire with Elaine next to me, surrounded by new friends. I'm talking freely, openly, and without fear about losing my Dad. I didn't even realize this was my destination.

Lesson for Today: A single epitaph may be witnessed by no one or make headlines across the world. But a single life can only be carried forth by the individuals personally moved by it.

Chapter 41: A Claw-Footed Bathtub

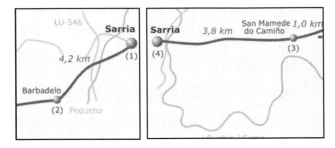

Trail Day 36, Aguiada to Rente, 8 km

This was it. The beginning of the blasted end.
- Amelie Fisher

Joe: This has happened several times before. We push ourselves too hard one day then pay the price the next. Yesterday's long, 26-kilometer trek through the torrential mountain storms took a toll on us. I was as mentally exhausted as Elaine was physically. Just a few hours into our daily routine, we passed a stone farmhouse with a "habataciones" sign out front. Elaine didn't want to stop, but I insisted. She was in too much pain and I was longing for some R&R. Walking in the front door, we wandered through the empty rooms until we met Elisa, a young woman working in the kitchen at the back of the house.

Before we started the Camino, a lifetime ago, the idea of just walking into someone's home and wandering around would've been foreign. Not now. People are more comfortable with each other, trusting of each other here. Elisa looked up from the butcher-block counter where she'd been preparing a family lunch of fresh vegetables and grilled ham.

"Buenos dias!" she said, wiping her hands on the country apron tied around her waist. She asked if we would like a room.

We explained that we were quite tired and needed to stop early. Elisa understood and took us upstairs.

We'd become accustomed to the authentic buildings along the Camino: the thick open timbers, gray slate or red tile roofs, high rock walls and adobe. It has somewhat tempered our awe of such beautiful homes, but this farmhouse was exceptional. Where we'd seen foot-thick walls before, this home had two-foot thick walls. Where we'd had tiled floors before, this home had elaborate stone hallways and thick, solid wood floors in the bedrooms. It was a fully functional farmhouse, but of such quality that you could easily imagine you were walking through a castle.

We settled into our typical routine. After partially unpacking our packs, I headed for the shower while Elaine headed for the bed.

"Elaine! You need to come see this!" I called back to her.

There's no shower. It's a huge, old fashioned, cast-iron and porcelain claw-footed bathtub sitting on the flagstone floor. As she entered the bathroom, I looked up at her with a smile. I was sitting on the edge of the tub, putting a stopper in the drain and turning on the hot water tap.

"Want to join me?" I asked, raising my eyebrows.

She smiled back at me and went back to bed.

Elaine: We spent a good part of the day just lazing in a casa rural in a town that barely shows up on the map, but it's so close to Santiago I can smell the incense! I'm now officially starting to count down the miles in the form of "days to go." I would've kept walking too, but Joe insists that we need to take our time and enjoy the little bit that's left, which is roughly 70 miles. Even if we only walk 12 miles a day, we'll be there in less than a week. Other than the rest I got today, there was one savory experience. I consider it a personal *coup de grace*. This casa rural is pretty much an ancient farmhouse dressed as a hotel. When I went to the kitchen, there were quite a few things that caught my attention, or perhaps I should say my "asco." But here's the thing: I was able to see past the germs on the apron the woman was using to clean her hands. I was able to think about the meat instead of the well-worn butcher block. When we were served dinner, I felt no disgust at all. I ate everything, and would've had seconds except they ran out. How's that for anxiety management, baby?

Lesson for Today: There are some things in life that cannot be conveyed through words, only experienced.

Chapter 42: The Trust of the Spaniards

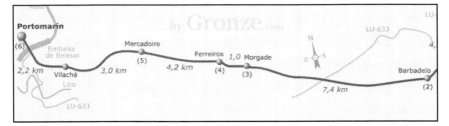

Trail Day 37, Rente to Portomarín, 18 km

The best way to find out if you can trust somebody is to trust them.
- Ernest Hemingway

Joe: We broke out of the trees near the end of our daily trek and came upon an amazing sight: the longest, highest bridge of our entire journey. It crossed the Rio Mino into Portomarín. In the 1960s, the Miño River was dammed to create the Belesar reservoir, putting the old village of Portomarín underwater. The most historic buildings of the town were moved brick by brick and reconstructed in the new town on the hillside across the river from us, including its castle-style main church, the Church of San Juan of Portomarín. Due to several years of drought, the lake had apparently returned to its original state. We could see the remains of ancient buildings, the waterfront and the original bridge below us on the narrow banks of the river.

Crossing the bridge, we walked up a long stone set of stairs that took us into the center of town. My mood had improved considerably. Elaine was happy that today's walk was over. I wanted to find a laundry where I could wash every single piece of clothing we had.

Somewhere along the trail I'd been bitten a number of times by what I suspected were bedbugs, or as they say in Spain, "chinches de la cama." I didn't know for sure, because I had never directly laid eyes on them. Lately though, I'd only been bitten when I had used my sleeping bag, so I suspected I was carrying the chinches, the fleas, or whatever vermin it was, with me. Regardless, the only way to get rid of them is heat, cold or pesticides. Assuming I'd have difficulty finding anyone with a freezer that would let me drop my mud and manure-covered clothing into, I started planning for the heat and pesticide technique.

After enjoying a snack at a street-side café, we found a hardware store. I asked for a spray can of their version of Raid and a large garbage bag. We then walked down one of the side streets in search of a pensión that had laundry machines. We found one above a café and checked in.

Our room was up on the third floor overlooking a small, central courtyard. I unloaded everything from both of our packs onto the tiled bedroom floor and I separated it all into two piles: washing machine and garbage bag. The backpacks, books, electronics, utensils, anything that couldn't go through a washer and dryer, I dropped into the garbage bag. I dragged the bag into the shower stall along with the can of Raid. I slid the little red straw nozzle into the top of the bag and pressed. Soon, the acrid, oily smell of the pesticide worked its way out of the bag, filling the shower stall with a dense cloud. I retreated quickly, closing the bathroom door behind me.

"Darling, you might want to avoid the bathroom for a while."

I don't think she heard me. Elaine had stripped naked and crawled under the sheets. She looked sound asleep. I stripped down myself and slipped on my rain pants. I picked up all of our remaining belongings and headed out the door.

The old industrial washer and dryer were outside in the small courtyard. I could barely contain all of the clothing and sleeping bags in my arms as I walked down the stairs and across the patio, leaving a trail of socks and underwear behind me. Shirtless and barefoot, the cold wind penetrated to my bones. I stuffed the sleeping bags and every thread of clothing we had into the oversized washer. I set all the knobs for "hot" and slipped in some coins. I then headed back to our room for a quick nap.

An hour later I was awake and feeling much better. Walking back down to the laundry machine, I found that the washer had finished its cycle. I loaded everything into the clothes dryer. Again,

I set the temperature for maximum heat and dropped in the coins. As I started to walk away, I noticed a large ceramic tile sitting in the corner of the courtyard. I had an idea.

Most of the dryers we'd used in the albergues didn't get very hot, taking a long time to heat up and dry our clothes. These machines looked pretty old and I really needed the full heat to ensure the bed bugs were killed. For an added measure, I slipped behind the dryer and partially covered the hot exhaust vent with the ceramic tile. This would ensure the dryer reached its maximum temperature setting. I wasn't worried about having too much heat, because all dryers have an over-temp safety switch that prevents them from overheating.

I dashed back to our room on the third floor and crawled into bed with Elaine. She'd had enough sleep for one afternoon. My cold skin woke her up immediately. Thirty minutes had passed when I noticed that the Raid smell in our room seemed to be getting stronger. I got up and opened the bathroom door. No, it actually smelled better in there. I glanced toward the bedroom window that was overlooking the courtyard. There was a heavy haze hanging in the air outside. I had an immediate, primal reaction in the pit of my stomach before my brain could even process what was happening. A flood of adrenalin reached my heart as I bolted toward the window.

Down in the courtyard, I see the dryer engulfed in a thick, dark cloud of smoke. I see the bartender run into the courtyard and reach behind the machine to unplug it. The blood drains from my extremities, my knees feel weak...I've just sabotaged our pilgrimage.

Elaine is still lying in bed. She has no idea what's going on. Then she sees my face as I turn away from the window.

"What's happening?"

"It's over."

A confused expression comes over her face. She climbs out of bed and limps over to the window. The bartender is just opening the door of the dryer and a piece of sleeping bag and some charred goose down slide over the edge, floating down to the stone floor. He shakes his head and walks away. There's nothing he can do.

Elaine is shocked. "Is that our stuff?" she yells. "Did all our clothing just get destroyed?" Who's the person who did our wash?" she demands.

"I did, I think…"

"Damn it, Joe! I can see giving up all the other crap to lighten our backpack but there's no way in hell I'm giving up my clothing!"

"How could something like this happen!"

I then tell her about the ceramic tile.

Elaine sits back down on the bed, stunned. I stand at the window watching the smoke drift out of the dryer. I know she's going to scream at me and I just wait. But nothing comes. I turn my head toward her. She's sitting there, staring up at my back.

She asks with alarm in her voice, "Oh my God, Joe! What did you do?"

"What do you mean? I just told you what I did."

She says, "No. What did you do to your back?"

"My back? What do you mean, my back?

She stands up to look closer, "Your back. It's covered with red welts."

"Oh, it's the bed bugs. I think I'm allergic to them."

"Geez, Joe, I didn't know it was so bad, I thought it was just your ankles."

"They nailed me good last night. That's why all the fuss this afternoon with the washing and drying and pesticide. They're driving me crazy."

Elaine goes into the bathroom to get some medicine out of our first-aid kit. We both sit on the bed naked. She rubs some lotion on my back while we silently contemplate how to recover from this.

I finally break the silence, "I should probably go down to talk to the bartender."

Elaine says curtly, "I'm definitely not going anywhere."

"Except maybe a toga party." I slip it in to lighten the mood.

She doesn't smile. She just says, "Are you going to tell him about the floor tile?"

"I guess I have to…this is a pilgrimage…and that looks like a pretty expensive dryer down there, even if it's a hundred years old."

Then I add with a serious face, "Do you think the 'plenary indulgence' will cover this?"

Elaine thinks for a second, then smiles, giggles, then starts laughing. She can't stop. It gets me started as well. Tears start running down her cheeks. Every time I give her a pathetic look, we both start laughing again. Then just as suddenly, we stop. Our sad expressions return. The inner thought comes back: *We're stuck in a hotel room in a strange city in a foreign country with no clothes.*

I can't help it; another arcane thought slips back into my head and I have to say it out loud. I deadpan it: "I read somewhere that the Camino strips you of all your encumbrances."

Elaine isn't smiling anymore, "Really? Did it say that it would strip you naked too?" The statement is a little too real, not that arcane after all.

I slip on my rain pants, the only piece of clothing between the two of us, and head out the door.

I walk back into the courtyard. There's a blue haze hanging about a foot off the ground. I walk over to the dryer and look in to see if there might be anything salvageable. Not a chance; the synthetic materials have melted all over anything that might have miraculously survived. I walk away thinking, *At least I killed the buggers.*

I walk out onto the cold city street and into the café where customers have started to gather for an early dinner. I ignore their stares and walk up to the far end of the bar, away from the patrons. The young bartender meets me there.

He speaks good English and asks me sullenly, "Was that all your clothes?" He already knows the answer as he looks at my bare chest and feet.

"Si, every stitch…"

He interrupts, "Don't worry, I'll find you some clothes"

I continue, "…including my wife's," holding my hand out, indicating her 5'2" frame.

He's alarmed by my words. "You are not alone?"

I shake my head. Elaine didn't go into the café when I went in at lunchtime to ask about lodging and Wenceslao was too busy with his lunchtime customers to show us to our room.

"Señor, I'm so sorry this happened. We must fix this immediately. I'm so very sorry!"

For a young man, Wenceslao is quite wise. He knows there's an important distinction between men and women when it comes to clothes. He now looks visibly worried as he picks up the phone to make a call. I can't put it off any longer. I hold up my hand.

"Before you make any calls, I have to tell you something."

After explaining what really happened, he actually laughs before making the phone call. Five minutes later, Wenceslao's mom comes walking into the café. She introduces herself. "Hola, soy Lydia." As I stand there half naked, I realize just how naked I really am without Elaine to translate for me. Wenceslao quickly starts communicating with his mom, occasionally asking me questions about Elaine's size.

Lydia asks through Wenceslao, "Does she have any clothing at all?"

I shake my head. "No."

Lydia looks concerned but pats me on my bare back, saying, "Tranquilo Señor, nosotros te ayudaremos."

I look over to Wenceslao and he says with a smile, "Don't' worry, we'll take care of you and your wife."

I then ask Wenceslao to tell her how sorry I am about the dryer and that I will gladly pay for the repairs. She replies that it's not a problem; it was old and she's wanted to replace it for some time but her husband wouldn't spend the money. "He's going to have to spend it now," she says with a smile. She then makes some other comment that Wenceslao refuses to translate for me. I think it has something to do with a mule, but I don't know if it's directed at me, or her husband.

I walk back to our room and my naked wife. I explain to Elaine what transpired downstairs and she takes it pretty well considering the state she's in. With nothing much else to do, I head for the shower. I pull out the garbage bag, and even though I know it's futile, I look inside to see if there's any clothing left behind. It's a stupid gesture, but I have to look. I reach in and pull out our hiking shoes.

"At least I didn't burn up our shoes!" I yell back to Elaine in the other room. I then turn on the water and take a long, long hot shower.

While the steaming hot water is pouring over my head, I realize we're not only being stripped of our old attitudes and our old ways of looking at the world; we're now being stripped of our possessions. That is what we asked for when we stepped out onto this path. We wanted to experience a different way of living, and that is what we're receiving. As Elaine has said several times during this journey, "We just need to let go of how we believe these changes are going to happen."

An hour and a half later I'm sitting on the floor with a towel wrapped around my waist, cleaning the Raid off of our gear. I wipe down the utensils and anything else I thought we'd have close contact with, which is about everything, and repack them into the front pouches of our backpacks. There's a knock on the door. I get up while Elaine sits up on the bed with a sheet wrapped around her. I open the door and it's Lydia. I stand back and she walks right past me as if she walks by naked strangers every day. She's carrying two large canvas bags, the kind used for grocery shopping. They are stuffed with clothes. Despite her modesty, Elaine jumps up with the sheet trailing behind her, excited at the prospects. Elaine and Lydia quickly introduce themselves and become instant friends. They dump the bags onto the bed and we start sorting through the clothing. They talk back and forth in Spanish as I grab the first pair of pants I see and a T-shirt and head for the bathroom.

Elaine translates. "Lydia has collected all the clothing that's been left behind at the albergues by the pilgrims attempting to lighten their loads. There are a number of albergues in Portomarin. As soon as she called and told them about our mishap, there was an overwhelming response. Each one of the hospitaleros carried a variety of clothing over to the café. They also brought toiletries, a pair of hiking boots, and look, someone even brought us some fresh sandwiches."

As I stand in the bathroom pulling on someone else's pants, I can't help but wonder how fast this story is traveling throughout the small city. I imagine there's laughter right this minute in about every bar in town. I hope this doesn't get back to the other pilgrims. My earlier feelings of hopelessness and defeat with this whole affair have gone away now that I have a pair of real pants on.

I was amazed at the variety of the clothing laying on the bed, and not just discards, but good quality hiking apparel. It didn't all fit us perfectly and our color coordination was certainly lacking, but compared to the helplessness and exposure we'd been feeling that afternoon, it was a Godsend.

I said innocently enough, "Elaine, I feel like a child at Christmas."

She smiled and nodded her head. Then paused.

She looked up at me, her voice solemn. "Joe, it's actually *our very own nativity*." Tears start rolling down her cheeks. It takes me a few moments to realize what she's saying. Nativity means, "birth." My tears start to flow as well. We'd been stripped of all our material possessions; we were as naked as newborns. The word of our mishap had gone out and within an hour there were people coming to our assistance, complete strangers, bearing gifts like the Magi.

"Why is this trip making me such a blubbering fool?" I ask no one in particular.

Lydia looks up from the clothes and sees my tears. She doesn't understand what's going on, so Elaine explains. Lydia stands up with a big smile and heads for the door. Before walking out she turns around and says, "El Camino le ofrece a todos."

Elaine smiles in return and says, "Gracias, muchas gracias."

After she leaves, I ask Elaine, "What did she say?"

Elaine smiled, "The Camino provides for all."

Lesson for Today: Losing things we take for granted but can't live without helps us appreciate the importance of charity, both that which we give *and* receive.

Chapter 43: 100 Kilometers Left

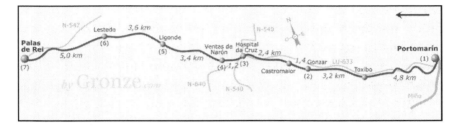

Trail Day 38, Portomarín to Palas de Rei, 25 km

To be fully seen by somebody, and be loved anyhow – this is a human offering that can border on miraculous.
- Elizabeth Gilbert

Joe: We were well rested and anxious to get moving; the Camino was calling and so were the coffee and croissants. Our new clothing will take some getting used to, but pilgrims are not necessarily a stylish lot to begin with so I suspect the only people that will take notice are Elaine and me.

Walking out through the courtyard and onto the street, we turned toward the café entrance prepared to pay our bill and have a bit of breakfast before setting out. It's just a few minutes past 6 a.m. The interior lights were out and the door was locked. The sign on the door said it doesn't open until 8 a.m.

"Shouldn't they have asked us to pay last night?"

I shrugged. "These people are so trusting. I didn't even ask how much they charged for the room last night. I guess I'll go leave some money on the bedside table."

I walked back up to the room and unlocked the door. I'm trying to learn my lesson: it's better to leave too little than insult their generosity with too much, but I just couldn't do it. I put 50 euros on the bedside stand for a room that cost less than half that and walked out. I rationalized that I could have left enough to pay for a dryer. I walked back downstairs and dropped the key in a bowl sitting on an old wooden credenza by the front door. I added a note thanking them for their generosity along with my address and email in case they changed their mind about the dryer.

We stepped out onto the cold, dark streets. There was a drizzle of rain coming down, making everything shine by the occasional streetlight. "I hope the next town is pretty close – I'm hungry!" Elaine nodded in agreement and we headed out.

Leaving Portomarín, the wind and the rain increased. It was mostly an uphill trek along paved roads with the occasional little village to stop at for coffee and tapas. The cold had seeped into my bones. Every time Elaine stopped to rest her feet, I quickly cooled down to the point of shivering.

"I can't keep stopping like this," I complained.

I knew she was suffering much more than I was.

Later, I said, "I'm sorry. I guess this weather has me in a bad mood."

The day wore on without any improvement in the weather. In fact, the westerly wind was getting stronger and colder. I slipped on some gloves and a thick-furred Russian hat I'd found in the pile of donated clothes.

"There must be another weather front coming through, tomorrow's going to be even colder. But at least the rain will be gone."

Later in the afternoon we turned a bend in the road and came upon a restaurant with a number of cabins out back. We walked in the front door and found a bar filled with pilgrims, mostly Americans. It was strange after being on the road for so long in complete solitude, with only an occasional pilgrim here and there.

We walked across the warm threshold and that's when I noticed that Elaine was limping.

"How are your feet feeling?" I asked.

"Oh, they're okay, my hip's just a little stiff."

I was too withdrawn to interact with anyone, but it felt good just to be around people who spoke English. We squeezed into a small table in the corner and just watched and listened to the familiar words.

Contrary to what we actually experienced on the trail, this part of the Camino had become much busier. We were all too spread out to notice it when walking, but the bars, the albergues, the town centers were becoming more crowded. The requirement for a pilgrim to receive their Compostela in Santiago is that they walk the final 100 kilometers. We passed that mark today. For those people that have neither the time nor capability to take on the traditional 800-kilometer trek, this will have to do. I felt a bit sorry for them. Suffering is part of the journey. I wondered if there's a connection between the 100-km mark and the number of Americans we've been seeing.

Lesson for Today: When surrounded by trust, our desire to do good grows as it feeds on the milk of human kindness.

Chapter 44: Exhale and Let Events Unfold

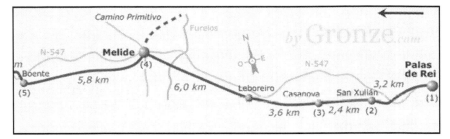

Trail Day 39, Palas de Rei to Boente, 21 km

> *Because things are the way they are, things will not stay the way*
> *they are.*
> *- Bertolt Brecht*

Elaine: We all have to make compromises in our relationships. I get that concept, no problem. But there are some times when there can be no compromise and today's that day. I woke up like most people. My intention was to rise out of bed like every other day. Only this time, my pelvis refused to cooperate. It sent a searing pain through my entire body that jolted me, saying, "Back off! Now!" I had no choice but to obey.

Joe saw me wince and said, "Really? Is it that bad?"

All I could say was, "Wow!" still frozen in place.

I was afraid to move again so I just stood there at the edge of the bed, like a frame on a video that suddenly stops: half on the bed, half off. I made a second attempt to finish the movement, but this time I didn't even make it onto one leg before dropping back down in full surrender.

Joe says, "That's it! We're done! I'm not going to watch you cause some kind of permanent injury to yourself when all I wanted out of this trip was some fun and adventure."

"What?" is all I can think to say in stunned disbelief.

I'm stuck on the bed and can't speak. I feel like a squirrel in the middle of the road that sees a car coming but can't move out of the way.

"I'm serious. It's turning into a disaster. We had the fire the other day and now you're completely incapacitated and you still want to push it? For what? So we can say we walked – no, crawled – into Compostela? Big deal! We've come so much farther than either of us expected. Let's just be happy with what we've accomplished and take a cab into Santiago."

I hear his words, but they don't sink in. They can't sink in! I have my promesa, and that is a vow to God. It's not some crummy declaration made on a whim. It's a serious commitment not to be broken even if I have to crawl into Compostela. But instead of saying all of that to Joe in a reasonable manner, all I say is: "I made a promesa and I'm keeping it!"

As I say this, I move to get up. I turn carelessly and just as quickly fall back to the bed from the shock of bone on nerve.

"You see that! You can't even get up! I don't buy all that crap about the promesa. You've walked without medicine. Damn it, you've been in pain for a whole month already and it's only getting worse. God sees what you've done, and he's already rewarded you. Look how great your father's doing now. It's a sign. You did what you set out to do. It's done!"

I finally figure out how to get out of bed by twisting and using momentum to get past the initial stabbing jolt.

"I'm not breaking my promise, Joe, no matter how you try to package it."

Then he makes it final. "Well, you'll just have to walk without me then, because I'm not going. You may be willing to suffer for this empty cause, but I don't have to watch."

By this time I've put my socks on and reach for my pants saying, "You do what you have to do and I'll do what I have to do. I've got to walk my own Camino and that means I'm going with you or without you. It's not up for debate."

I finish getting dressed in the bathroom to avoid showing the struggle I'm going through just to put my pants on.

Joe: I'm upset. Elaine shouldn't be doing this to herself and it's all my fault. It was my idea to do the Camino, and I knew how determined she'd be to finish this no matter what. While Elaine is in the bathroom getting dressed, I dump her backpack onto the bed and stuff anything that weighs more than a few ounces into my backpack. I grab the medical kit, the toiletries, and the snacks. I stick them in the side pouches and zip them up. I stuff all her clothes deep down into the center. At least we're a little bit lighter due to the fire. We no longer have our sleeping bags, but we'll have to be especially careful. They were our insurance in case we got stranded for the night in the cold.

I spot Elaine's shoes sitting on the floor and a sneaky thought creeps into my head: "What if I throw them away?"

I run through the possibilities.

Act innocent? "No! I haven't seen your damn shoes, where's the last place you saw them?"

Maybe the caveman approach: "Yeah! I took 'em and you can't have 'em!"

The problem is I know Elaine all too well. She'd pick up her backpack and head out in her stocking feet. It's below freezing out there, I know this caveman would cave and give her the shoes back. I finished packing most of her stuff into my pack, leaving just enough light stuff in hers so that it doesn't look completely empty. I then leave the room and wait out in the lobby so she won't fell free to argue with me in the privacy of our own room.

Elaine: I step back into the bedroom. Joe is gone. I slip on my shoes and grab my backpack. It's amazingly light. Next I reach for my trekking poles to stabilize me. Today they'll have to be an extra pair of legs helping me to stay vertical through the shock waves that erupt each time I offend my right flank.

Joe: Elaine walks down the hallway and into the lobby where I'm standing. She gives me an angry look while glancing at my backpack but she says nothing. She's won the big argument, so she lets the backpack issue go for now.

We walk out of our cabin and onto the road. The puddles from last night had turned to ice. We pass the side of the restaurant and stop to talk to an elderly couple from the U.S. standing next to several suitcases. They told us they were doing the Camino. We glanced down at the suitcases and looked back at them with a questioning expression. The husband explained that at their age, the pilgrimage involved short strolls and long taxi rides. Because of the temperature this morning, they'd decided to forego the short stroll.

A passenger van pulls up with plenty of room for four. The couple starts rolling their suitcases toward it.

"Elaine, please, enough is enough," I plead.

She looks longingly at the van for a just a second and then limps down the road.

I wish the elderly couple a "Buen Camino."

I turn away from them and yell down the road to Elaine who's heading south, "Hey! It's this direction!" as I head west toward Santiago.

Our day is like any other day: put one foot in front of the other and endure whatever hardship comes our way. Today, it's the bitter cold and Elaine's hip. She's certainly going to build up some arm muscles judging by how much weight she's to putting on them to propel her forward. This is the first time since we started that something has caused her more grief than her aching feet. In spite of the limping, the cold kept us both moving briskly just to combat hypothermia.

We sit down at a café for an afternoon break and ask the owner, "Do you know of any rooms available in town?"

He shakes his head. "No, I'm the only one who has rooms and they are all booked."

We're not disappointed. It just is. I'm starting to have faith; I know the Camino will provide for us. With the cold wind blowing outside, we're in no hurry to leave the warmth of the café; even the threat of "no lodging" can't get us out the door in search of a bed.

A half hour later, while I worked on my second café con leche, the owner received a phone call. I could see from Elaine's eyes that the conversation, in Spanish, was getting interesting. I, of course, was clueless as to what was transpiring. He hung up and had a quick, animated conversation with Elaine. She turned to me with a smile. "He has a room for us. A group with a reservation just called to cancel."

Canceling a room on the Camino is a rare but very thoughtful thing for pilgrims to do. There are no credit cards or deposits required to reserve a room. You just call, leave your name, and your room is reserved until about 7:00. After that time, it's opened up to anyone in need. People rarely call to cancel. It was now 3:30 and we were about five minutes away from walking out to search for lodging in the next town.

Lesson for Today: We must all walk our own Camino, even when it's side by side.

Chapter 45: My Husband - Oh Brother!

Trail Day 40, Boente to Rúa, 26 km

Your friend is your needs answered.
- Kahlil Gibran

Elaine: A pilgrimage is an extremely personal endeavor with as many purposes as there are pilgrims. I've seen many couples and close friends walking together on this path. Often they don't even realize how much they're taking care of one another. The other night we slept in an albergue with Ray and Diane, the Australian couple. I found myself spying as Ray meticulously checked his wife's feet for blisters while gently reminding her to take magnesium to help her muscles endure the long walk. He also hauls her backpack and his on a little three-wheeled dolly they affectionately named "Mathilda."

The Camino is not just for married couples. We met two women from California, both forty-two, who had been best friends for thirty years. They left their significant others at home in order to walk the Camino together. One had supported the other through a battle with cancer and the two were celebrating their hard-won victory together, doing something they considered physically and spiritually healing. It was easy to see their bond was already sealed, and that the Camino was just an expression of their gratitude for one another.

They laughed about each other's eccentricities, like the fact that one was a "germ freak" and spent hours cringing in the albergue beds because she, ironically, was frequently assigned a bed near the same pilgrim with a bad cough who they had code named "Mr. Dengue." When they told the story, it reminded me how God has a great sense of humor, even with His "no coincidences" rule. The two women purposely divided their labor. "I make sure we get up and out on time," said one. "And I'm the navigator," quickly interjected the other. They were both beaming about the way they took care of each other when they shared this vital information.

The married couple we'd spent so much time with, Patty and Len, were a heartwarming example of teamwork. When Patty first started the Camino, she suffered from a debilitating fear of heights, but later, hand-in-hand with Len, she was able and willing to cross bridges at dizzying heights. Even the most die-hard relationship cynic would feel inspired watching Len, who no matter what he was doing at the time, would stop all activity when approaching a bridge and purposefully find Patty to start the crossing together. "Remember, it's just one step at a time," he would say as he took her hand and coached her through her various shades of panic. Patty truly wished to overcome her fear of heights and she allowed her husband, and later me, to push her boundaries. By the way, Len was no "enabler." As soon as Patty became proficient at crossing some specific type of bridge, he would only walk near her at the next one, extending his hand only for heights she had not yet conquered. Now that's true love – and free therapy!

I've witnessed various acts of compassion and support on the Camino, but none has been greater than the ones I've personally experienced with Joe for the past two weeks. He's done the one thing most of us only dream about (or pay for) on the Camino. Because of the problems with my feet, and now my hip, he's carried the lion's share of my backpack. Each morning we go through the same ritual: he takes everything out of my backpack, and I protest. Then starts the bargaining about what he and I will carry. This morning I had the hardest time locating my backpack. *How can you lose a whole backpack,* you ask? Well, you probably guessed it...Joe had packed my entire *mochila* inside of his!

It's an unwritten rule that pilgrims should carry only 10% of their body weight in their backpacks. Joe is carrying over 20%. He's taken the extra load since I stopped taking pain medicine as part of my promesa. I've suffered from heel spurs, tendonitis and now a swollen ball and socket. But I won't stop walking. I want to carry my backpack at full weight, but Joe insists on some compromise. "You promised to finish it without medicine for your father, but you didn't say anything about what would be in your backpack," he says as he hoists about forty pounds of weight onto his shoulders.

I feel like a heel for not forcing him to give up the backpack, even if it's empty. Sometimes, especially when Joe says, "I don't even notice a difference in weight!" I think about that old song, "He Ain't Heavy, He's My Brother." It's then that I realize my husband is my brother, acting as unselfishly as I believe Jesus would if faced with similar circumstances. What a wonderful discovery in the face of this recent adversity – to find out we're more than partners: we're family! My anxiety about divorce has breathed its last gasp. I hope.

Joe: Many years ago, a pastor once asked me during a marriage counseling session if I thought that marriage was a 50 - 50 partnership. I said with confidence, "It certainly is." He went on to explain to me that it wasn't, that it was a 100% - 100% partnership. I understood intellectually what he was trying to say and I guess I agreed with his rationale. That wasn't good enough, though. It took me a long time and three marriages to finally learn it in my heart and to live by it. Elaine and I are a team: we're partners, but we're also human beings with faults, strengths and weaknesses. We're all sinners.

Watching Elaine suffer day in and day out was very difficult for me. I complained about the promesa, I complained about her pushing too hard, and I complained about not taking a day off. I've also bandaged her feet and massaged her feet. I've tried to be motivational: "Just one more kilometer, darling, and we'll have a bed to lay in." It's all just part of a loving relationship.

For anyone wanting to give the Camino a try, it's important to realize that it really is a personal experience. It's something that should probably be done solo if at all possible. It's not a vacation, it's not a race or competition. It's going to bring out lots of hidden stuff, both good and bad, as the miles pass under your feet. If you're going to do the Camino as a couple, be prepared to experience a serious relationship-building exercise. It's going to be a hardship on you physically and emotionally. You are walking long miles through often-rugged terrain, up and down mountains in all kinds of weather. You don't always know when you're going to find your next meal or where you're going to lay your head for the night. Most of us don't know the language or the culture.

Then there's siesta time: just as we're finishing our day's walk and looking for food and rest it seems like everything is closed. All of this brings out the best and worst in us. I guess that's why we do it. It's a huge learning exercise that pushes our individual limits. Walking it as a couple, the Camino amplifies those things that you do well together and it amplifies those things you do wrong. And then you work on them.

We're only 20 kilometers outside of Santiago de Compostela, in the small town of Rua, on the outskirts of O Pedrouzo. I can't believe it. We're one day away from walking into the cathedral in Santiago. I'm sitting by a fire in a beautiful albergue. We've just finished a nice dinner and I've wrapped Elaine up in a couple of blankets as she tries to recuperate from the 28-kilometer day. It was below freezing as we started out this morning, but it warmed up to perfect walking conditions for our last big push. The variety of pilgrims around us has expanded to include the short-timers who have started at the minimum required distance of 100 kilometers, but surprisingly the actual total numbers seems to have decreased compared to the crowds of just the other day. I don't know if it's because it's getting late in the season or if people have just dropped out from injuries or exhaustion…maybe they're taking cabs. Either way, we see fewer pilgrims now and we have the trail to ourselves.

Lesson for Today: In relationships, just as in trekking, stumbling does not break the journey: the inability to recover does.

Chapter 46: Santiago and the Cathedral

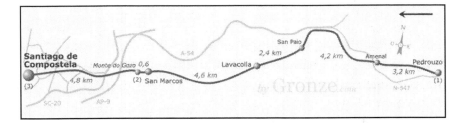

Trail Day 41, Rúa to Santiago, 21 km

Heaven is under our feet as well as over our heads.
- Henry David Thoreau

Elaine: It seemed only fitting that the day we walked to Compostela was the most challenging for me because of the foot and hip pain threatening to take me down with every unplanned step. Often it did. I would reach my limit and say to Joe, "Can we sit down again, I need to retie my shoes." Or put on another pair of socks...or apply more Vicks...anything that would stop the pain for just a few moments. It was like being stuck in traffic in New York during rush hour: you move forward half a block then stop for twenty minutes, all the time thinking, "I could get there faster if I walked." But this time, it was just the opposite. I knew I could get there faster in a car, on a bike or even on a skateboard – anything with wheels. The Camino gives you a greater appreciation for the phrase "It's the next best thing since the invention of the wheel."

Completing the pilgrimage today will mean the fulfillment of the promise I made two weeks ago to sacrifice anything necessary to complete the pilgrimage. That was a lifetime ago. Setting foot on the ground in Santiago will realize the promise the pilgrimage made to me: the absolution of my sins. It was a fair bargain because I had given all I had and then scraped even deeper past my physical being straight through to my spirit in order to make it this far. It's only fitting that my spirit will be the vessel to benefit from St. James' plenary indulgence.

Joe: It's surprising to be so close to such a big city and still be surrounded by nature: hills, forests, small pastures and farm houses. For the last few days, we've been walking through broad stands of eucalyptus trees. The aroma of the manured farmland has been pleasantly replaced with the scent of the trees. I hadn't realized how huge eucalyptus trees grow. Some are over six feet in diameter and shoot up absolutely straight as an arrow for over 150 feet.

Elaine usually hits the trail with lots of energy, but ever since Portomarín it's been slow going right from the start. On top of her foot and hip pain, she's now just completely worn out. Up and down hills, through narrow tunnels of stonewalls and overhanging vegetation, over country roads and along the side of major highways, we wended our way toward the city. There was a heavy rain shower along the way that drenched our clothes before we had a chance to put on our rain gear.

We entered the city limits of Santiago but there still remained another 5 kilometers to reach the cathedral in the ancient, central part of the city. Our pace was slowing by the minute as the pain and exhaustion sucked our energy, but I think it was also something else. Maybe sorrow. Each step brought us closer to the end, the end of a short but very significant chapter in our lives.

It will be the end of beautiful mountain vistas; fast-flowing, crystal clear streams; the wide variety of crops, farms and livestock; and the endless array of Spaniards going about their daily lives. It's also the end of walking around a corner and meeting up with Camino friends, of sitting at roadside cafés drinking strong coffee and eating fresh chocolate croissants. It's the end of sitting around communal dinner tables and sharing large pots of stew, loaves of bread and bottles of free-flowing wine. It also means the end to the daily pain and exhaustion.

As we walked through the city, we stowed our trekking poles in our backpacks and held each other's hands. I wanted to share this day as closely as our backpacks, equipment and pain would let us. The path to Compostela was difficult to follow in the maze of intersections, traffic circles and the constant parade of cars, trucks, busses and pedestrians. When we eventually reached the ancient part of the city, our slow, plodding pace ended. Any exhaustion, dismay or sorrow we were feeling disappeared as our goal became more real and we drew closer to the finale. We had our destination and we were going for it despite the confusion of which way to go at every intersection. Nothing was going to get in the way.

There was one more lesson in store for me before completing our pilgrimage. It was a final gesture from the Camino. My take-charge, make-it-happen ego had taken over once again and I was practically dragging Elaine along even though I hadn't any idea which direction to go. I'd felt I'd learned to accept the gifts that the Camino had offered, but there was one more reminder, just in case I forgot.

Elaine and I entered the old city center, searching for any sign of which way to go in the mass of people and mid-day traffic. Then, out of the midst of the crowd came a smiling bearded face. He walked up to us and with a warm embrace said, "Welcome to Santiago!" It was Jim, the retired Army Scout we'd met at Westover at the start of our adventure.

Jim had decided that at the end of his pilgrimage he was going to live in Santiago for six months. He was just walking back to his small apartment and would've disappeared around a corner in a matter of seconds if he hadn't caught sight of us approaching through the crowd.

We'd been in contact with him through emails during our journey so we knew he had reached Santiago in a short 28 days, but he had no idea we would see him again. Jim held out his hand and said, "Follow me." He led us down the meandering narrow streets to Compostela. Our scout had already cleared the way ahead.

We were so happy to see him. The miles, the fatigue or even our acceptance that these things just happen, did not soften the surprise over this last lesson from Saint James.

As we approached the central square with Saint James Cathedral on the left, Jim tried to explain the layout, the entrances, the location of the pilgrim's office and the times for Mass. We were completely overwhelmed and the helping words flowed right through us. The joy and sorrow of ending our journey, the beautiful cathedral standing before us, the exhaustion and weariness and the layers of pain mixed with just as many layers of relief, all welled up in us as we stood there quietly in the midday sun.

We stood and looked at the long flight of stairs leading up to the Cathedral, our last sacred steps on the Camino. Should we start the climb? Are we ready? Can we even make the climb? What are we supposed to do first?

I looked at Elaine. She had an expression on her face that I couldn't identify. All of her emotions were completely exposed; joy, fear, sadness, relief. She just stood there, looking up at the spires in the bright blue sky.

I looked down at our clothes. They were wet and dirty, our shoes covered in mud. I remembered something Elaine had told me a while ago. There's a luxury Parador Hotel somewhere on this huge central square. Looking around for several seconds, I spotted a uniformed man unloading luggage from the back of a large car on the far side of the plaza. I spoke so softly I'm surprised Elaine even heard me. "Darling, there's the Parador over there." She pulled her eyes from the Cathedral and looked over at the historic building. "Would you mind if we checked in and cleaned up a bit? It's too late for the noon Pilgrims' Mass anyway. Why don't we complete our pilgrimage in the morning after we're clean and rested?"

My words brought Elaine back to the present. She looked at me with love in her eyes. I'd found an angel and somehow she'd decided she was going to spend the rest of her days on Earth with me.

She hesitated for a second and then smiled at me. "Let's be pilgrims for one more night."

"I think Saint James will understand," I said.

"Plus, tomorrow's All Saint's Day, it'll be perfect," Elaine replied.

I arranged with Jim to meet for dinner and then took Elaine by the hand as we headed for the doors of the Parador.

I went up to the desk and asked if there were any rooms available. Elaine walked over to one of the overstuffed lounge chairs in the elaborate sitting room and sank down into its folds. I booked a room for two nights and walked back to Elaine.

"Joe, it's like we just walked through purgatory and now we've reached heaven!"

Lesson for Today: The battle for lead between faith and reason can be settled by accepting the guiding hand of an experienced navigator.

Chapter 47: All Saints Day

Trail Day 42, Santiago de Compostela

If you would not be forgotten as soon as you are dead, either write
something worth reading or do things worth writing.
- Benjamin Franklin

Elaine: Arriving in Santiago was a strange experience; it certainly wasn't what I would've predicted. Yes, there was the indescribable sense of relief over the realization that my days of walking way past the point of agony were over. No longer would I have to call a "stop action" every twenty minutes to throw myself onto a bench, a rock or even the skin-pricking thistles infesting the ground because I couldn't take one more step. I will be honest and admit that if it weren't for my promesa, I don't think I would have put myself through that kind of persistent physical torture. Also, my guilt over the effect it had on Joe, walking at half his normal pace with twice the weight on his back, would've had me crying "No mas!" way before kilometer 800. But here I am in Santiago, knowing it's done and any future walking is completely my call.

Or is it?

Are you crazy? Don't tell me you are thinking of doing this again?

My answer is: "I would rather stick two hot pokers in my eyes than do this again!"

But the real surprise is that the walk into my new life is only beginning. We made it to Compostela on 31 October, the eve of All Saint's day.

Things like this have been happening throughout this journey, and it's why my response to arriving in Santiago has been so inspired. I thanked God for getting us here safely and for my father's health, and I was grateful, but I just didn't feel the sense of satisfying finality I'd expected. I couldn't put my finger on it until I thought about why it was so important to arrive here in the first place. I understand that this is where St. James is buried and where millions of pilgrims have completed their pilgrimage for centuries. But I think it's fair to ask, "If this is such a personal, spiritual experience, why not end it in a church of my own choosing?" Why not stop my Camino in the town of Rabinal? I found a church so simple and austere there; I imagined it was exactly the kind of church Jesus would have built.

The answer is because a pilgrimage is not about pleasure, it's about sacrifice. It's a voluntary demonstration of faith. As one priest on the Camino put it, "No Christian is required to complete a pilgrimage as a sign of faith." Therefore, a pilgrim is one who *chooses* to sacrifice. It's based on free will.

Not everyone who walks to Santiago considers himself a pilgrim. I know I didn't when I started. It took a harrowing circumstance to draft me. But once I let go of my fear by surrendering to the faith I had lost many years ago, I was transformed. Through all the flexing and extending of my feet and will, I joined the ranks of the pilgrims who came before me, and those who will come after.

When Jim walked out of the crowd yesterday and took us by the hand, leading us to the cathedral, it felt like God was saying, "Why did you doubt I would deliver you here? I can perform any miracle if you'll only surrender and accept that I am."

Most of the people we admire in history don't start off by saying, "I'm going to change the world." People like Mother Teresa and Gandhi, believed in something greater than their individual existence. Even Albert Einstein, who some called an atheist, understood that a power exists beyond our limited intelligence to understand, and that we may better realize it by promoting higher ideals.

A person who is religiously enlightened appears to me to be one who has, to the best of his ability, liberated himself from the fetters of his selfish desires and is preoccupied with thoughts, feelings and aspirations to which he clings because of their super-personal value."
-Albert Einstein

I realize today that this pilgrimage is really just the beginning of my life as a mature Believer: knowing that my actions are based on the teachings of Christ, not in the service of my own immediate desires. This pilgrimage has brought me closer to the Spirit in a way I have never experienced before, even after twelve years of Catholic school!

In the past, I was so busy looking for the things I didn't like or agree with in the churches I attended that I lost the power of community through shared ideals and committed faith. I listened with judgment to the priest or people who attended church. I actively screened for the comments I found disagreeable. It was so easy to believe that the Church community just wasn't a good fit for me. It gave me the perfect excuse to turn away from other believers because I was "still looking" for the right place, the right people.

This Camino has brought home a profound realization that we're all imperfect beings and that includes me. It's not because of my inadequacy. It is just inherent to our nature as humans.

I'll never find the perfect church or the perfect congregation. I'll never be a perfect believer. But the difference for me now, post-Camino, is that this awareness brings me closer to God and to other people instead of keeping a force field of separateness around me. I don't take offense if a priest says something I disagree with. I don't condemn the pilgrim who just told me, "I asked for the religious Compostela because it's prettier." It's not my place to sit in judgment of any other person. I'm too imperfect myself.

So you see, this pilgrimage is far from over. The grueling days of walking 28 kilometers are mercifully done. But, my willingness to serve and my understanding of the value of service is just coming into focus with newfound clarity. Today, during the Pilgrim's Mass in Santiago, I cried when I received the Eucharist. I welcomed God into my body and spirit as a healing force for my pain and my anxiety. I could have never anticipated the miracles I've experienced during this walk to Santiago. I'm still holding on to its gifts with faith and gratitude. There are many more miles of service and sacrifice ahead of me, but my soul is renewed because I know there is a divine force that connects me to every person, in every corner of this world.

Before you mistakenly assume I've adopted an overly-zealous life of religious asceticism, I want to say that I've also discovered a small slice of heaven right here in Santiago. Joe booked us into the

Parador Hotel, and after forty-plus days of walking, this was the equivalent of Dorothy reaching the Land of Oz. For those who haven't watched the movie thirty times like I have, there's a scene in which she and the other characters (Scarecrow, Tin Man and the Cowardly Lion) are given a major primping session before they can be presented to the "great and powerful Oz." Even Lion gets his mane curled! In our pilgrim's version, the Parador has a tub that Joe's 6' 2" frame can actually recline in and it even comes with real toiletries and bath towels. Today our breakfast has transformed from the daily café con leche y tostada to lox, caviar, pastries, champagne, real fruit – you name it. We have *heat* in the room! A bidet in the bathroom! I sometimes feel guilty for pulling out all the stops, but then I restart the hot water in the tub and sink into the muscle-soaking goodness. God made me capable of feeling great pain, but also great joy. I really like the joy.

Joe: We had a wonderful dinner with Jim, it seemed like all three of us talked at once about our individual experiences and our plans now that we've finished. We then walked along the narrow streets luxuriating in the sights, sounds and smells of the city. We ended our night with a nightcap at the Parador before sinking into the soft mattress of our huge canopied bed.

This morning, clean and rested, we walked over to the pilgrim's office to present our credenciales and receive our Compostela. We were early, the only ones in the small reception area. We took our time reveling in the moment as we logged our pilgrimage into the record books. A representative of the Church handed us our Compostela and it was official. We now had documented proof of receiving a plenary indulgence, a pardon from the Pope himself. But I was skeptical.

My plenary indulgence is not a reward for a good deed, nor is it a piece of paper, a Compostela, with an official seal that's handed to me at the end of my journey. My plenary indulgence was brought to life as a small spark, born in a village in southern France sitting at the foot of the Pyrenees. That spark slowly grew into a flame and finally a roaring fire. It was being fed by my sorrow, my guilt, and my sins. The light from that fire began exposing me to others as well as to myself, allowing all to see inside. I'd initially recoiled from the exposure like a turtle withdrawing into its shell. Then, I slowly adjusted to the light, but not enough. It was too soon, too fast.

I obtained my plenary indulgence through the openness of our fellow pilgrims, through the unending gifts from complete strangers and through my belief in a higher power that we, as mortal beings, can't even begin to fathom. Luckily, I don't have to understand how or why it works: I just have to believe in it to heal.

The Camino handed me these gifts every day: a simple meal, a smiling face, a warm bed at night, and so many new friendships. From the moment I met Pete in the most unlikely of circumstances to our last day, when Jim stepped out of the crowd to guide us to Santiago. A guiding hand led us to the Camino and a guiding hand led us to its completion. The Camino takes care of all of us who are on a path toward forgiveness and acceptance.

I began this journey with an unquenchable thirst for the next big adventure and a heavy feeling of guilt surrounding my father's death. My guilt and my thirst for adventure has been quenched for the time being. They've been replaced with self-forgiveness and the realization that my physical journeys are not nearly as adventurous as those inner journeys I must take. The Camino has seen to that. I mourn the loss of John and of my guilt; they had both been constant companions on this journey. But their loss doesn't lessen me. Instead, I'm slowly learning to celebrate the life of my father. I suppose this is where my real journey begins.

Epilogue

Joe: I must warn any reader who's inspired to pursue his or her own Camino: it will change you. And don't think it will be a thoroughly pleasant experience. Change, important change, is always painful. Elaine and I returned to what we thought would be our normal lives. We talked a lot about what we learned along The Way. How we would change our daily routines and habits.

Then reality set in. My body and my mind had been conditioned for a life on the trail, a life where our daily concerns were simple and uncluttered: water, food, companionship, an inspiring sunset, a welcoming church and a soft bed.

In our "normal" lives, these daily concerns have all but disappeared: they are automatic and I think little of them. Instead, I worry about bills, how our kids are doing in school, or what I need to accomplish at work. I've changed. I'm no longer content in this cluttered normal life.

Throughout the journey I often described the Camino in terms of its geography, presenting the mountains, farmland, and long dusty roads as obstacles that had to be overcome. I also described the Camino as some type of external, altruistic power that led us down a spiritual path, delivering people and events to us that carried important messages. The Camino is neither.

I'm a born engineer and explorer. I'm one of the lucky few that knew his profession long before stepping out into the world. I love to sort and characterize my environment, to organize the world into categories that can be described and dissected in order to find understanding. It's the Aristotelian way, the Western way, its empiricism, the basis of modern scientific method.

I was the observer.

The real Camino is no more an external physical object than the air we breathe or the food we eat. I've eaten of its fruit and drunk of its wine. The Camino nourished me. It lives inside of me;

it lives inside each of its pilgrims. The Camino is composed of wonder and of searching. It's made of wisdom and trust, faith and love, ethereal ideas that defy the scientific method. My physical journey along The Way pealed away a lifetime of observing, of standing on the outside peering in. I started the journey as an observer, but I was slowly transformed. I became part of the Camino and the Camino became a part of me. Without me, without its pilgrims, the Camino is but a dirt, stone and paved path that connects two points on the surface of a small planet.

After our return home, my depression returned. I experienced withdrawal; I was moody, short tempered and disorganized. This had happened before, after returning from an extended trip. With each journey's end, I became a little more uncomfortable with my normal life. There was a big difference this time; I now understood why. The journeys are what sustain me.

I'm in a quandary; how can I expect Elaine to live such a transitory life? We are more than just married; we are connected. I'm not sure I have the strength to tear the flesh that has bound us together.

My travels have always helped me to understand how the world fits together, but it's now apparent; it's time to understand how I fit into the world. My next journey must include a more personal destination. But I'm not sure how to take the first step.

Must I return to the Camino for the answer?

Elaine: The Camino de Santiago started out for me as a trekking trip, a way to reboot after twenty-five years as a military psychologist. I knew that there was a whole world to get acquainted with, a world of fascinating cultures and strange customs I had learned about mostly through books. The Way of St. James seemed like the best approach to treat my anxiety and build my physical endurance. How ironic. I had to leave the military to get into shape, mentally and physically. The ultimate paradox was discovering I could leave the military and still live a life of service.

Before the Camino, I spent many years losing ground through failed relationships and mounting hopelessness. The Camino added 800 kilometers of new ground beneath my feet. It provided messages from strangers that became my therapy. It gave me the capacity to understand for the first time and first-hand what it felt like to struggle with unrelenting physical pain. I learned greater patience with truly important things like allowing my family to be who they are instead of trying to mold them into my pre-formed image of the people I thought they should be. The Camino was my road to accepting pain as a door to joy. I learned to stay with discomfort instead of avoiding the unpleasant.

The field of medicine likes to label and categorize. Once we have the diagnosis, then the treatment is evident. If the problem persists, then either the diagnosis is incorrect or the treatment is inadequate. Those are the only two choices. Walking the Camino taught me about a third, or better yet, a first option – believing in the existence of things we can't see or measure. This allows us to remain open to the world that exists outside of our immediate vision. I learned how faith and commitment could heal the body and, even more importantly, the soul. I started with a basic faith, old and dusty from neglect and years of doubt. The Camino would not stand for this. Like a parent who won't give up on a missing child, it refused to accept my apathy. To this day, I can only marvel at how quickly my father recovered once I focused on the force I knew could heal him, regardless of his prognosis and the miles of distance between us. After I surrendered and cut through every ounce of skepticism in me, everything changed. It was as if all God wanted from me was some demonstration that I was willing to surrender and believe in His power in my life. It was through my renewed respect and trust that I witnessed true wonders, and not just with my father's recovery. I'm no longer obsessed with death. I have too much life in me to let it define my actions. To focus on death is to miss out on life and to mistrust God's divine plan.

I hope this book inspires anyone who believes his or her life could be better or more meaningful. Try something radically different; exhale and aim for inspiration. There are few things in this life that can catapult you straight into joy like the sensory and spiritual awakenings inherent to walking this beautiful, historical and metaphysical landscape.

Since the Camino, I've often thought about the importance of staying in the moment. I've inwardly debated why traveling or taking time for experiences makes any difference in the long run. After all, as long as you enjoy this moment, does it matter whether previous moments were spent at work, in conflict or at play?

My answer is, "Yes, it does matter." This moment, right now, is the product of all the moments that came before it. If they were stress-filled, then it's likely you'll feel unsettled in each new moment. The war between the frazzled mind and the self that longs for tranquility plays out endlessly until we build a bridge using this moment as a building block that connects the past with the future so that they become seamless and sacred. Along the way to Santiago, I exercised my faith and my body. But it did more than build muscle mass and quell anxiety; the Camino was the place I found God. I moved forward under His light and I gained peace.

About the Authors

ELAINE ORABONA FOSTER is one of the first 10 prescribing psychologists in the US. She holds a Diplomate in Clinical Psychology and is a Fellow of the American Psychological Association (APA). Elaine received a B.A. in psychology from New York University and a Ph.D. from Nova University. She completed a Fellowship at the Uniformed Services University of the Health Sciences (USUHS) in Psychopharmacology. She's worked extensively with soldiers afflicted with Posttraumatic Stress Disorder and Traumatic Brain Injury. Elaine has taught classes and symposia on women's issues, anxiety, depression, and cultural factors in medicine throughout the US, Canada and Europe. She has contributed to several books including: *The Psychologist's Desk Reference, Pharmacotherapy for Psychologists: Prescribing and Collaborative Roles, and Trauma Psychology* [2 volumes]: *Issues in Violence, Disaster, Health, and Illness.*

In her spare time, Elaine enjoys pushing through the limits of her own anxiety by traveling to places far off and unknown.

JOE FOSTER has had a passion for travel his entire life, it's led to his now famous saying, "Getting lost is just an excuse to explore." He's an engineer and a scientist but most of all he's an experienced adventurer. He's hiked, sailed and flown all over the world, searching for unique, off-the-beaten-track places. Joe's a certified Divemaster, an FAA-licensed Pilot, and a USCG-licensed Boat Captain. Whether it's sailing an open sea or climbing a mountain, he's always exploring his physical and emotional limits. He's helped to train new scuba divers, teaching them how to combat the anxieties that sap their emotional strength and endurance. As a flight test engineer, he's had to test new aircraft technologies during high speed flight, in low altitude, mountainous terrain. He's also had to face his own fears and anxieties while solo sailing long distances, battling extreme weather conditions, critical gear failures and fatigue.

For relaxation, Joe loves to camp under an open sky, sitting by the fire with his wife and enjoying the beauty of nature.

Made in the USA
San Bernardino, CA
21 November 2016